Trevor Lynch's

Classics of Right-Wing Cinema

by

Trevor Lynch

Edited by Greg Johnson

Counter-Currents Publishing Ltd.
San Francisco
2022

Copyright © 2022 by Greg Johnson
All rights reserved

Cover design by
Kevin I. Slaughter

Published in the United States by
COUNTER-CURRENTS PUBLISHING LTD.
P.O. Box 22638
San Francisco, CA 94122
USA
http://www.counter-currents.com/

Hardcover ISBN: 978-1-64264-186-8
Paperback ISBN: 978-1-64264-187-5
E-book ISBN: 978-1-64264-188-2

Contents

Preface ❖ iii

1. *Africa Addio* ❖ 1
2. *American History X* ❖ 5
3. *Black Narcissus* ❖ 12
4. *The Bostonians* ❖ 16
5. *The Bridge on the River Kwai* ❖ 22
6. *A Clockwork Orange* ❖ 27
7. *Conan the Barbarian* ❖ 31
8. *Dirty Harry* ❖ 36
9. The *Dirty Harry* Sequels ❖ 41
10. *Doctor Zhivago* ❖ 47
11. *Dune*: The First Trailer ❖ 54
12. *Dune*, Part I ❖ 61
13. *The Elephant Man* ❖ 69
14. *Fanny & Alexander* ❖ 78
15. *House of Gucci* ❖ 86
16. *The Incredibles & The Incredibles 2* ❖ 88
17. *The Last Emperor* ❖ 93
18. *Lawrence of Arabia* ❖ 99
19. *The Life & Death of Colonel Blimp* ❖ 111
20. *The Man Who Shot Liberty Valance* ❖ 118
21. *The Matrix Resurrections* ❖ 126
22. *Milk* ❖ 131
23. *Mishima: The Last Debate* ❖ 136
24. *No Time to Die*: The Trailers ❖ 140

25. *No Time to Die* ❖ 145

26. *Red River* ❖ 147

27. *The Red Shoes* ❖ 154

28. *The Sailor Who Fell from Grace with the Sea* ❖ 160

29. *The Searchers* ❖ 164

30. *Taxi Driver* ❖ 172

31. *Tenet* ❖ 179

32. *Twin Peaks* ❖ 182

33. *Twin Peaks: Fire Walk with Me* ❖ 189

34. *Withnail & I* ❖ 194

BONUS:
35. Louis Theroux Meets Nick Fuentes ❖ 201

Index ❖ 205

About the Author ❖ 214

Preface

This is my fifth Trevor Lynch volume. I discuss thirty-five movies, two television series, and one episode from a series. It took me eighteen years to write my first three Trevor Lynch books but only a little more than a year to write this one and the one before it. That's because I have been writing a lot more on film and television since 2019, when I started writing two pieces a month for *The Unz Review*, where everything in this volume except the last "bonus" chapter was first published.

The title of this book refers to a series of essays and reviews that I wrote throughout 2021 on such movies as *Taxi Driver*, *Dirty Harry*, *American History X*, *The Man Who Shot Liberty Valance*, *The Searchers*, *Conan the Barbarian*, *The Bostonians*, *The Incredibles* and *The Incredibles 2*, *Doctor Zhivago*, *The Last Emperor*, and *Red River*. To be a Classic of Right-Wing Cinema, a movie need not have an explicitly Right-wing director or message. Indeed, very few movies fit that description. Instead, a movie simply needs to have a message that resonates with the Right. Thus all the films I discuss have anti-liberal, anti-communist, anti-feminist, pro-masculine, pro-family, and generally anti-egalitarian messages, whether or not that was the director's intention. Most of the other films in this volume fit this description as well, even if they were not included in the series, for instance *Africa Addio*, *Black Narcissus*, *The Bridge on the River Kwai*, *Dune*, Part 1, *Lawrence of Arabia*, *Twin Peaks*, *Twin Peaks: Fire Walk with Me*, and *Withnail & I*.

I want to thank Ron Unz for exposing my work to a wider audience and making this book possible. I also wish to thank Kevin Slaughter for his work on the cover; Jef Costello, John Morgan, James O'Meara, and Alex Graham for help with the proofs and index; the commentators at *The Unz Review*; and, of course, the whole *Counter-Currents* community. This book is dedicated to Colin "Millennial Woes" Robertson, who introduced me to *Withnail & I*.

Greg Johnson
February 15, 2022

AFRICA ADDIO

Africa Addio (*Goodbye Africa*) (1966), co-directed, co-edited, and co-authored by Gualtiero Jacopetti and Franco Prosperi of *Mondo Cane* fame, is a must-see documentary for enlightening people about the reality of race. Filmed between 1963 and 1965 in Kenya, Tanganyika, Zanzibar, Rwanda, Angola, the Belgian Congo, and South Africa, *Africa Addio* chronicles the exit of the British and Belgian colonial powers from Africa, as well as the attempts of Portuguese and South African whites to hold on.

Many of you will find this movie simply unbelievable, for reasons of style and content. *Africa Addio* is so superbly filmed and edited that it does not seem like a documentary. Riz Ortolani's lush Morricone-like music, as well as the magic of Italian dubbing, reinforce this impression. But as far as I can tell, only one sequence was created entirely by the filmmakers: a graveyard with headstones for white farms in the Kenya highlands.

As for the content: the colonial worlds created by whites as well as the results of the African takeovers seem equally surreal.

In the Kenyan highlands, British farmers recreated English country life, complete with fox hunts (although the quarry is an African runner carrying part of a frozen fox). The headquarters of a British wildlife rescue operation looks like a set from a Bond movie or *The Thunderbirds*. The beach in Capetown, with its high-rise hotels and beautiful blondes surfing and sunning, looks like California or Australia. Surely it must all have been staged. But no. White people actually did this.

The sequences in post-colonial Africa seem so surreal, terrifying, and deeply unflattering to blacks that that movie has been denounced as racist propaganda. It definitely leads to racist conclusions. But all of it appears to be real. Still, one wonders: If blacks really are that bad, why did whites ever settle there? Why did whites give blacks power over them? And why, in the name of all that is holy, are we allowing these people to colonize us today? But again, it is all real.

The first thirty minutes focus mostly on Kenya. We see the trial of Mau Mau terrorists and their accomplices, who slaughtered white families and mutilated their cattle. They also tortured and killed baboons, for no fathomable reason. They are sentenced to life in prison. A few years later, Jomo Kenyatta pardoned the Mau Mau. The white farmers of the Kenya highlands are forced to sell. We see their houses and European treasures being auctioned off by Indian merchants. Then we see their yards and gardens being bulldozed, their trees dynamited, to create subsistence gardens for hundreds of blacks, who fill the European houses to overflowing, covering everything in filth and smoke, and slowly dismantling the houses to burn in their fireplaces—since it is easier than fetching wood, and it does not occur to them that at some point, the house will become uninhabitable. In a stunning sequence, we see Boer farmers from South Africa who settled in Kenya returning home with their herds the way they came: in covered wagons.

In colonial Kenya, blacks could look at white women but not touch. In free Kenya, blonde British nannies become status symbols for the black elites, and an old blonde whore does a strip tease for a roomful of sweaty blacks. At the end, she offers "Bwana" the privilege of popping off her pasties. Unreal? No.

Africa Addio is filled with unflattering contrasts between blacks and whites. The white colonists are remarkably good-looking in Kenya, Angola, the Congo, and South Africa. The Africans, many filmed in extreme closeups, are often hideously ugly, with alarmingly discolored eyes and teeth. The filmmakers could be accused of seeking out exceptionally attractive whites and ugly Africans, but there are a lot of goofy and plain-looking whites as well. There are scenes of European order and grace: soldiers on parade—a ceremony in a church where the former colonial flags are being entrusted to the clergy—contrasted with noisy crowds of Africans swarming and rioting. We cut from disciplined and well-dressed British soldiers to clownish, shambling African troops and policemen. Post-colonial Africa began as a farce, a grotesque parody of European civilization.

Then it descended into tragedy. Throughout the continent, African rebel groups, usually backed by the USSR or Communist China, used terrorism to eject whites. Then, once the whites were gone, they went on to massacre their tribal enemies.

In Zanzibar and Tanganyika, the enemy was "Arabs," meaning fellow Africans who had converted to Islam under the rule of Arab slave traders along the East African Coast. In 1964, the newly independent government of Zanzibar was overthrown by a communist-backed revolution, and up to 20,000 Arabs were massacred. The filmmakers hired a plane in Tanganyika to document what was happening. They were fired upon when they tried to land but over two days managed to film from the air burned out villages, columns of Arabs being marched to their deaths, as well as mass graves and random heaps of corpses. One day, we see pitiful refugees fleeing to the beaches; the next day the beach is littered with countless corpses. It seems that genocide is part of every communist revolutionary playbook. That would include the playbooks of the communists that Donald Trump allowed to run amok in America in 2020.

The filmmakers were on the ground during the Arab massacres in Tanganyika. At one point, they were pulled from their car by soldiers and put against a wall. They were about to be shot when someone looked at their passports and said: "Wait, these aren't whites. They're Italians." The birth of a meme?

We also visit Rwanda, where we see the aftermath of a genocide of Hutus against Watusis. I guess there were many. We see Watusi survivors and their cattle streaming into exile in Uganda, as well as rivers choked with the corpses of those who were not so lucky. It is slick and cinematic, but the blood and bodies are real.

In the Belgian Congo, we see European troops and mercenaries repelling rebels who seized Stanleyville. The aftermath is sickening. The rebels had raped, killed, and tortured white nuns, nurses, and schoolchildren. They had also tortured, killed, and sometimes eaten 12,000 fellow Africans. We see European families who had narrowly escaped rape, torture, and death. Later, the filmmakers fly over a mission school where the rebels were holding nuns and children. A few days later, the mission has been burned to the ground. The grounds are littered with the corpses of nuns. Fortunately, the rebels were rather easy to defeat. They believed that magic made them immune to bullets. We see close up that this is not so as we witness the summary execution of two rebels. The filmmakers were actually accused of staging these murders, as if the Africans needed any incentive given the carnage we have seen already.

Two sequences deal with the mass slaughter of wildlife after whites pulled out and could no longer protect them. They are totally sickening. There are two kinds of hunters: whites and blacks. The white hunters are seen mowing down fleeing zebras by towing a rope between two jeeps. Another has a helicopter drive an elephant toward him before shooting it down. I have no patience for people who kill big game, even on sustainable game reserves, even if they are white. No, *especially* if they are white.

But the most sickening spectacle is of thousands of blacks cordoning off huge areas and killing everything that moves by chucking spears at them. The attempts of white conservationists to save the victims of the slaughter are touching but mostly futile. Again, you will wonder, "Can this be real?" But the blood is real. The fetal hippos and elephants ripped from their mothers' wombs are real.

The final sequence is set in South Africa, Africa's "sanctuary for whites." It begins with a huge crowd of uniformed black children running toward a low set camera. The narrator declares that five blacks are born for every white in South Africa. It is a very effective way of communicating the demographic problem. Here comes the future!

We then visit the mines of Pretoria, where armies of blacks mine gold and diamonds. Although ordinary whites tried to build a nation in South Africa, it was always a colony, an economic zone in which a tiny oligarchy imported cheap nonwhite labor to heap up gold and diamonds. The lure of cheap labor plus high black fertility doomed South Africans to demographic eclipse and political impotence. The film ends with the Cape penguin colony, marooned far from their home in Antarctica. The analogy with whites is obvious. We never belonged there.

I highly recommend *Africa Addio*. This strange and sobering masterpiece is not just a record of the past but a glimpse of the future, for Africa is everywhere now.

The Unz Review, August 19, 2020

AMERICAN HISTORY X

Director Tony Kaye's anti-skinhead morality tale *American History X* (1998) is proof that propaganda is far from an exact science. Just as Stanley Kubrick's *Full Metal Jacket* caused a surge in Marine recruitment, *American History X* actually increases audience sympathies with neo-Nazi skinheads, despite its best efforts to present them as hateful hypocrites and losers.

American History X stars Edward Norton as Derek Vinyard, a young skinhead in Venice Beach, California. It is a riveting and compelling performance, Norton's finest work. I saw *American History X* after I saw *Fight Club,* where Norton's character is so unimposing and unassertive that he projects Brad Pitt's Tyler Durden as an alter ego. Thus I was surprised that in *American History X,* Norton plays a character every bit as swaggering, self-confident, and violent as Tyler Durden. They seem like two different men, not the same actor playing two different roles.

Derek Vinyard is the eldest of the four children of a fireman who was murdered by blacks while putting out a fire in their neighborhood. Derek was outraged and became involved with a local neo-Nazi mastermind, Cameron Alexander (Stacy Keach) who is supposed to remind us of Tom Metzger. Derek is highly intelligent and articulate. He is also a natural leader. With Cameron's help, he builds up a serious and well-organized skinhead gang.

Three incidents stand out. First, Derek challenges some Crips to a basketball contest for control of a local public court and wins. The game is one of the best-shot sequences in the film. Second, Derek makes a rousing, well-argued speech against race replacement immigration then leads his gang to trash a Korean-owned grocery store that employs illegal aliens. Third, when Derek's widowed mother Doris (Beverly D'Angelo) begins dating Murray (Elliot Gould), a Jewish teacher at Derek's high school, the dinner table conversation becomes explosive. Derek refers to Murray as a "Kabbala-reading motherfucker" and flashes a huge swastika tattoo which he says means "not welcome."

One does not need to endorse Derek's Nazi ideology, rhetorical excesses, and physical violence to admire his sincerity and conviction, or to see the merits of his arguments. As for his opponents, they have nothing to offer but hurt looks, breaths sharply drawn in disapproval, and mumbling about racism and social inequalities.

Since the purpose of this film is to warn us against Derek's ideas, one wonders what director Kaye and screenwriter David McKenna were thinking. They could have presented Derek as a vulgar, hateful loser like his fat friend Seth, whom Murray could easily best in a battle of wits. Instead, they chose to make Derek highly intelligent and articulate. This was a gutsy move, which goes against all media stereotypes about skinheads. However, if they are going to present Derek as fearsomely intelligent, then they need to match him with a more capable opponent, and they don't. This means that Derek Vinyard can win any fair debate, which matters to some movie watchers.

Derek's opponent and ultimate salvation is supposed to be Bob Sweeney, a black teacher played by *Deep Space Nine*'s Avery Brooks. Sweeney is said to be a brilliant guy. He has two Ph.D.s. (Why is he teaching in a high school then?) He claims to see "holes" in Derek's racialist worldview, which he dismisses as "bullshit." But it rings hollow from the start. Brooks has made a career reading lines in his resonant, well-modulated black man's voice. But he doesn't come off as particularly intelligent. Derek's father Dennis dismisses Sweeney's pontificating as "nigger bullshit," impressive only to the witless and gullible. (Dennis is clearly an intelligent man who offers excellent critiques of affirmative action and political correctness.) When Sweeney actually argues against Derek, it turns out that dad was right. Sweeney's arguments are terrible. Again, one has to ask what the filmmakers were thinking.

The most well-realized black character in the movie is Lamont (Guy Torry), an amiable buffoon. The rest of the black characters are vacant, mindless thugs. This too proves problematic for the film's anti-racist message, for it supports Kipling's characterization of non-whites as "half-devil, half-child."

American History X is primarily the story of how Derek

Vinyard *stops* being a skinhead. He starts when his father is murdered, then he falls in with the wrong crowd. He stops when he gets thrown in prison. When three Crips try to steal Derek's car, he ends up killing two of them and is sentenced to three-and-a-half years for manslaughter.

While in prison, Derek immediately allies with the Aryan Brotherhood gang. This makes sense for two reasons. First, Derek is a neo-Nazi too. Second, even if he weren't, it would be smart to join them, because whites who go it alone in prison are picked off by non-whites, who form gangs.

But cracks begin to appear in Derek's racial collectivism. While working in the prison laundry, Derek bonds with a goofy black guy, Lamont, over their common interests in basketball and pussy. Derek also falls out with the Aryan Brotherhood because for some reason he objects to them selling drugs to non-whites.

One of the most memed moments in *American History X* is when Derek declares that "Pot is for niggers." Derek regards non-whites as soulless subhumans. So why not sell drugs to them? Or, at the very least, why make trouble with your allies over it?

But Derek is a bit abrasive and autistic about "principles." The Aryans tire of Derek's preaching, so one day, their leader forcibly sodomizes him in the shower. This is a pretty much complete inversion of the truth. Prison rape is largely a black thing. White neo-Nazis are probably the least likely perpetrators of this particular crime.

Being raped somehow causes Derek to change his whole worldview, which is dumb and out of character. Derek keeps getting himself into trouble because he is a stickler for principles. But nothing that has happened challenges his basic principles. Lamont proves only that every group has likable outliers, apparently even in prison. And yes, we aren't so different after all when we focus on the least common denominators, like food, sex, and games. As for the Aryans: they are not supposed to sell drugs and rape one another. But is it realistic to expect sterling characters in prison? Besides, when people betray their principles, couldn't that be because the people are bad, not the principles?

Derek is taken to the prison infirmary. He needs some stitches. There he is visited by Sweeney, who makes a little speech:

> There was a moment when I used to blame everything and everyone for all the pain and suffering and vile things that happened to me, that I saw happen to my people. I used to blame everybody. Blame white people. Blame society. Blame God. I didn't get no answers because I was asking the wrong questions. You have to ask the right questions.

When Derek asks Sweeney what the right questions are, the answer is: "Has anything you've done made your life better?" To which Derek tears up, because no, he has suffered quite a lot for his ideas. Derek then begs Sweeney to help get him out of prison. He has a parole hearing coming up soon.

Sweeney's arguments are terrible.

First of all, it is merely a shaming tactic to liken complaints about white dispossession to blacks blaming the white man for their own failings. It might appeal to an older generation of "pull yourself up by your bootstraps" conservatives, but Derek would see through it. What matters is the question of truth. White dispossession is real. The solution is not to "try harder" in a rigged system but to change the system. Blacks who still fail in a system of objective black privilege can't blame the system for that. They can only blame themselves.

Second, when Sweeney chooses to focus on his individual life rather than questions of social justice, this is not moving from the "wrong questions" to the "right questions." It is just a subjective change of focus. But focusing on your own life doesn't make social problems disappear. It simply distracts you from noticing them. Individualism is just escapism. It is a form of cowardice.

The system deals with white dissidents by piling on personal problems: doxing, defamation, deplatforming, censorship, legal persecution, etc. That's on top of the wearisome drama endemic to the movement itself. When enough negative consequences accumulate, many people simply give up. They have not, however, achieved some sort of enlightenment. Their convictions have not been disproven. They have simply been broken by the system. Derek is a broken man.

Sweeney speaks for Derek, and he is paroled. Somehow, he manages to survive on his own for the final months of his sentence. The conditions that drive men into racial prison gangs have suddenly been suspended. The movie explains this miracle with a ridiculous *deus ex machina*: the spindly black buffoon Lamont somehow has enough credibility with the various prison gangs to "protect" Derek. I guess they were afraid he would rumple their sheets. I'm pretty sure Derek's dad would call this some species of bullshit.

American History X is also the story of Derek's younger brother Danny (Edward Furlong). Danny idolizes Derek. While Derek is in prison, Danny joins Cameron's skinhead gang. Danny gets in trouble when he writes a paper on *Mein Kampf* for the civil rights portion of Murray's class on American history. Sweeney, who is now the principal, tells Danny that he is in a new class, called American History X. His assignment is to write a paper on Derek, who has just gotten out of jail. Danny's paper, related as a voice-over, is the narrative framework of the movie.

Once Derek is paroled, he does not want to get back into the gang. Instead he wants to get Danny out of it. This is irrational. Derek killed two Crips. They will seek revenge. He has a better chance if he has the gang behind him. If he really wants to extract Danny and break with the gang, then he needs to be diplomatic about it. Otherwise, he will simply multiply his enemies. His best option is just to say that associating with them violates the conditions of his parole, which would probably be true. Derek bungles his exit rather badly. He ends up punching Cameron and having a gun drawn on him. Now both the skinheads and the Crips are gunning for him.

The next morning, Derek has a meeting with his parole officer, and Danny has to turn in his paper. But it turns out that the same system that broke Derek now has a use for him. The Crips have attacked Cameron and Seth. Sweeney—who is clearly acting outside the purview of a high school principal—and a cop approach Derek for help. Derek is now a police informant.

When Danny shows up at the High School, we hear a voice-over of the end of his paper: "my conclusion is: hate is baggage.

Life's too short to be pissed off all the time. It's just not worth it." Then he quotes Abraham Lincoln's pious folderol about overcoming enmity — this time between the North and the South — by the better angels of our nature tugging on the mystic chords of memory. The emptiness of these high-minded sentiments was, of course, soon demonstrated by America's bloodiest war. As if to underscore this very point, the voiceover follows Danny's bloody murder in a school bathroom by a Crip.

Again, I am not sure what the filmmakers were thinking, but this conclusion does not support their anti-"hate" agenda.

Yes, hate is arguably "baggage." Being angry all the time is definitely no fun. If we were but atoms floating in a social-historical void, we would surely benefit from simply shrugging off hate and anger. But that's not the world we live in.

You may decide one morning not to have any enemies. But your enemies may still have it in for you. In fact, they might think your change of heart is a weakness to be exploited. Danny and Derek did not choose to be in a race war. The race war was imposed on them. Derek decided to fight, which is necessary if one wants to have a chance of winning. The system broke Derek, but it didn't stop the race war. Nor could it protect him or his brother once he broke with the gang.

Derek bears some responsibility for his brother's death: not for exposing him to "hate" but for pulling him out of the gang. As a member of the gang, Danny enjoyed some protection, because the Crips knew that attacking him would lead to retaliation. But once Derek and Danny were out of the gang, they became targets of opportunity.

Lincoln's hope that "memory" could overcome enmity presupposed that the North and the South had deep commonalities and old friendships that had simply been forgotten in the struggle over slavery. Memory will not heal the divisions between blacks and whites in America, because there was no common community before slavery. There is enmity all the way down. Memory only polarizes race relations in America, which in turn polarizes whites against each other.

After Danny's murder, the film ends with Lincoln's high-flown rhetoric over a sunset at the beach. In short, a typical liberal retreat from racial reality into sentiment. An anticlimax. Dare we wonder what happens next? The most logical ending for this story would be a repentant Derek shaving his head to rejoin the struggle. But that's clearly not the intended message.

American History X is beautifully filmed. Kaye himself often operated the camera. It has an excellent orchestral score by Anne Dudley. Some scenes drag, and the use of slow motion is about as annoying as teeth scraping against concrete. But this might not be due to Kaye, who turned in a 95-minute final cut. Norton and the studio insisted on a longer edit, which added back in 24 minutes. Kaye's reaction to this was highly neurotic, to say the least, and he was branded unemployable, even though the film went on to enjoy commercial and critical success.

Why does *American History X* fail so splendidly as propaganda?

We can discard the idea that Tony Kaye is secretly sympathetic to Nazi skinheads. He is what Derek would call a "Kabbala-reading motherfucker." He would arrive on set in a chauffeured Lincoln with the license plate "JEWISH" and had matzos delivered to the set at Passover.

The most likely hypothesis is that the filmmakers were just smug. They thought that Derek's views are self-evidently evil and that their own views are self-evidently good. Thus they felt that both sets of ideas simply needed to be stated aloud, with no real argument, and the audience would see things their way.

But people outside the Leftist bubbles of academia and the media don't react like that. Intelligent normies see the logic of Derek's positions. They can separate the truths Derek utters about white dispossession and liberal coddling of black criminals from the violent skinhead trappings. They also see the truth of what Derek's father says. Finally, they can recognize the vacuousness of the film's liberal message. Thus *American History X* qualifies as a classic of Right-wing cinema, despite the best efforts of the filmmakers.

The Unz Review, February 22, 2021

BLACK NARCISSUS

Michael Powell (1905–1990) is one of the tragic geniuses of film: a genius because he is one of the most visually dazzling directors in the history of cinema, tragic because he too often he wasted his talents on inferior scripts, most of them provided by his longtime collaborator, Emeric Pressburger, a Hungarian-Jewish refugee to whom Powell often gave co-director credit.

Powell worked his way up from a studio gofer to a leading director. Many of his journeyman efforts are lost. His career as a mature director begins in 1937 with *The Edge of the World*. With the exception of *The Edge of the World* and *I Know Where I'm Going* (1945), Powell spent his first ten years churning out anti-German, pro-cosmopolitan war propaganda, visually and technically dazzling but often quite silly: *The Spy in Black* (1939), *Contraband* (1940), *49th Parallel* (1941), *One of Our Aircraft Is Missing* (1942), *The Life and Death of Colonel Blimp* (1943), *A Canterbury Tale* (1944), and *A Matter of Life and Death* (1946). Powell also directed a number of short propaganda films for the British government with titles like *The Lion Has Wings* (1939), *An Airman's Letter to His Mother* (1941), and *The Volunteer* (1943).

Powell's genius only flourished fully after the war, in such apolitical works as *Black Narcissus* (1947) and *The Red Shoes* (1948), which is one of my favorite films. Aside from *The Tales of Hoffmann* (1951), an adaptation of Jacques Offenbach's opera of the same name, most of Powell's films in the 1950s were mediocre. Then he produced one last masterpiece, *Peeping Tom* (1960), the story of a serial killer that was so shocking and distasteful that it pretty much destroyed his career.

Black Narcissus is based on the 1939 novel of the same name by (Margaret) Rumer Godden about a small group of Anglican nuns who set up a convent and school in Mopu, a princely state in the Himalayas. The local potentate, General Toda Rai, gives the sisters an abandoned palace, a former harem decorated with erotic art, perched on the edge of a dizzying precipice with a magnificent view of the Himalayas. Near them is a Hindu holy man, who turns out to be the former owner of the palace. Below them is a bewilderingly complex, violent, and superstitious society. Their only guide is Mr. Dean, an Englishman who manages a tea plantation for the General.

Black Narcissus seems, in part, to be about what can be called "the spirit of place," understood in terms of landscape, culture, and even human structures. The nuns are all European women, and even though they have already spent some time in India, they seemed to have been relatively cloistered, whereas in Mopu, they are on their own, founding a new convent. Beyond that, the atmosphere in Mopu is particularly potent, bringing each member of the order to a crisis.

Sister Briony, known for her strength, becomes sick due to the high altitude. Sister Philippa, who was brought to tend the vegetable gardens, is overwhelmed by the beauty of the place and plants flowers instead. Sister Honey's soft-heartedness leads her to give medicine to a fatally ill baby, against the advice of Mr. Dean, who knows that the locals will blame the sisters for the child's death, which will endanger their mission and perhaps their lives.

The most dramatic crises, however, are those of Sister Clodagh, the young Sister Superior, and Sister Ruth, who is both highly neurotic and affected by the high altitude. Both Clodagh and Ruth are prideful women, which pits them against one another from the start. Beyond that, both women are stirred by the palace's erotic history and décor, as well as the presence of a highly attractive bachelor, Mr. Dean, into an increasingly conscious sexual rivalry. Dean too, for his part, is clearly attracted to Sister Clodagh, although at first they both seem to hate each other. Dean is also dismissive of the Sisters' Christian faith and mission. Toss in a budding romance between the General's son, who is being tutored by the Sisters, and a nubile vixen of the lowest caste who lives at the convent, and you have a simmering cauldron of sexual tension that soon boils over, with disastrous results.

The story's combination of aestheticism, eroticism, and riveting dramatic conflicts inspired some of Powell's best work. From start to finish, *Black Narcissus* is visually ravishing, with tension and suspense mounting until the viewer feels, like Sister Ruth, that he is losing his mind. As the story unfolds, the production becomes increasingly stylized, from the stark simplicity and Vermeer-like light of the scenes before the nuns depart for Mopu, to the voluptuous colors and décor of the palace, to pure German Expressionist horror at the end. The music by Brian Easdale, who also composed the score for *The Red Shoes*, is some of his finest work. The cast is excellent, with outstanding performances by Deborah Kerr as Sister Clodagh, David Farrar as Mr. Dean, and Kathleen Byron as Sister Ruth.

Black Narcissus was filmed in Technicolor entirely on soundstages, except for some scenes in a London botanical garden, because of Powell's desire to meticulously control light, color, and atmosphere. Some of the matte paintings look fake, but you are more forgiving when you realize that practically everything else you took for real is fake as well.

Black Narcissus was released in 1947, when the British Empire was pulling out of India. In that context, a story about British nuns going mad because they are "out of place" in India was taken as anti-colonialist, anti-imperialist propaganda. That may well have been Pressburger's intent. As an ethnonationalist, I don't have any problem with an anti-imperialist message. But I doubt it occurred to Powell, or to the original novelist, that *Black Narcissus* was about much more than sex.

The Legion of Decency in the US regarded *Black Narcissus* as anti-Christian and demanded a flashback to Sister Clodagh's life before becoming a nun be removed. Clodagh came from a wealthy Anglo-Irish family. From childhood, she thought she would marry her sweetheart Con. When she discovered that he planned to go to America and leave her behind, she decided to take her destruction into her own hands and become a nun. She engineered an honorable defeat for herself.

I don't see anything anti-Christian about acknowledging the fact that some people join religious orders out of disappointment with the world. Nor does it strike me as anti-Christian to acknowledge that celibacy often leaves a lot to be desired.

The deeper message of *Black Narcissus* is not about sex but about race. Mr. Dean did not lack opportunities for sex in Mopu.

Nor were Sister Clodagh and Sister Ruth shut away entirely from men before coming to Mopu. They were constantly surrounded by the natives, after all. What upset the plans of all three was not the presence of a member of the opposite sex, but of a member of the opposite sex *of the same race*.

Each time I watch *Black Narcissus*, I prize it more highly. I have avoided spoilers, because I want you to watch it too. But be sure to seek out Michael Powell's *Black Narcissus*, because there is now a pretender to the title. In 2020, a three-part British miniseries of *Black Narcissus* was run on BBC One and FX.

Frankly, I dreaded watching it, wondering how it would be spoiled by political correctness. Fortunately, the production is marred in only one place. When Mother Dorothea (Diana Rigg in her last role) dispatches the nuns to Mopu, she tells Sister Clodagh to take Sister Philippa with her, to depend on for her skill as a gardener—and for her wisdom. This time, however, the wise Sister Philippa is played by a black woman.

The rest of the production is pretty much by the book and helps one appreciate Pressburger's script, which removed only inessential clutter. The cast, sets, and music are all first rate. Gemma Arterton plays Sister Clodagh, and Alessandro Nivola plays Mr. Dean, with real chemistry between them.

The only improvements are a lack of fake-looking effects and Aisling Franciosi's portrayal of Sister Ruth. In Powell's film, you know that Kathleen Byron's Sister Ruth is trouble right from the start. Franciosi's Sister Ruth seems sweet and vulnerable at first and only slowly goes mad. It is interesting to see her character develop.

Most importantly, the underlying racial dynamic and message remain unaltered. White people have explored the whole planet, running toward wealth, knowledge, and adventure—or merely running away from trouble and heartache. But no matter the forces that drive us apart, *Black Narcissus* shows that nature is stronger, that blood is thicker than water—even holy water—and that like seeks like in the end.

The Unz Review, April 30, 2021

THE BOSTONIANS

Not every Merchant-Ivory film is a visually lush period drama based on novels by prestigious writers like E. M. Forster and Henry James, but the most memorable ones are, including *The Europeans* (1979), *The Bostonians* (1984), *A Room with a View* (1985), *Maurice* (1987), and *Howards End* (1992). Another in this vein is *The Remains of the Day* (1993), based on a novel by Kazuo Ishiguro.

All these films were produced by Ismail Merchant, an Indian Muslim, and directed by his gay partner James Ivory, an American Protestant. With the exception of *Maurice*, they were adapted for the screen by Ruth Prawer Jhabvala, a German Jew married to an Indian Parsi.

Yet for all the intersectional diversity of their creators, there is something "problematic" about these films, for they feed on a deep nostalgia for the nineteenth and early twentieth centuries, characterized by overwhelming whiteness, patriarchy, sexual repression, and heteronormativity. Of course, all the characters struggle against this world in the name of an old-fashioned, white, and Eurocentric liberalism that is also problematic these days. But it is impossible to overlook that the world they are struggling against is far more attractive than the world they ended up making for us.

The archetypal Merchant-Ivory film appeals to pretty much the same people who love *Downton Abbey*: overwhelmingly white, predominantly female, disproportionately gay, and very liberal. The average Merchant-Ivory viewer loves to imagine himself or herself as rich, beautifully dressed, and at home in the most glamorous locales, all while being terribly oppressed but also enlightened and virtuous. It is a kind of porn for the NPR/BBC4 set: middle-aged, middlebrow, middle managers in our neoliberal Left-wing oligarchy. But race-conscious whites can also enjoy the nostalgia if they are willing to bracket out the propaganda.

In the case of *The Bostonians*, however, they don't have to, for through some strange twist of fate, this is one of the most anti-liberal, anti-feminist movies I have ever seen. Starring Vanessa Redgrave, Christopher Reeve, Madeleine Potter, Jessica Tandy, and Linda Hunt, *The Bostonians* is based on Henry James' 1886 novel of the same name, which is a satire of the Eastern liberal establishment circa 1875-76 set primarily in Boston but with forays to Cambridge, New York City, and Martha's Vineyard—pretty much their same haunts today.

It is a world of bossy women and low-testosterone men. All the characters are either rich or the professionals, courtiers, and charlatans who feed off the rich. Mesmerism, spiritualism, homeopathy, and feminism are the current rages in their salons.

The Bostonians focuses on a circle of wealthy suffragettes. Now that blacks have been emancipated and the South put to the sword, feminism is the next great progressive crusade. The main suffragettes are the elderly Miss Birdseye (Jessica Tandy), a gentle soul who lives in a word of high-minded fancies; Mrs. Burrage (Nancy Marchand), a fabulously rich New Yorker with a son at Harvard who hosts radical salons at her Fifth Avenue mansion; and the fifty-something spinster Olive Chancellor, a lesbian and wild-eyed fanatic who is beautifully played by Vanessa Redgrave.

The dramatic conflict of *The Bostonians* is between Olive and her distant cousin, Basil Ransom (Christopher Reeve), a Confederate veteran from Mississippi who now works as a lawyer in New York City. Basil is a writer on topics like honor, virtue, and aristocracy. He is unapologetically conservative, even reactionary. When one of his essays was rejected for being "300 hundred years out of date," he replied: "On the rights of minorities, I am 300 years out of date. But you see, I haven't come too late. I have come too soon." A man after my own heart.

Basil also rejects feminism. He thinks that "for public uses" women are entirely "inferior and second rate." Instead, he thinks that women are best suited for the private realm of family life. He also mocks the feminist complaint that women are oppressed. Basil thinks women have enormous power as it is, and their desire for equal footing in public would in fact lead to the oppression of men by women. Which raises a question: If men could see this in the 1880s, how did we end up where we are today?

Basil does have one ally, Dr. Prance, warmly portrayed by the diminutive, husky-voiced Linda Hunt. Dr. Prance takes care of the wealthy valetudinarian Miss Birdseye, along with a Mesmerist, a homeopath ("It is now recognized as the true system," chirps Miss Birdseye), and who knows what else. Even though Dr. Prance is a female professional, she rejects feminism and women's suffrage. But, as she tells Basil, the suffragists are completely uninterested in her opinion. They think it is far more significant if a man agrees with them.

Olive and Basil's main conflict is not, however, over political philosophy. Instead, they are fighting over a woman: Verena Tarrant (Madeleine Potter). Verena is the daughter of "Dr." Tarrant, a spiritualist and Mesmeric healer who never gets too transported to forget to present his bill. Both Basil and Olive meet Verena at a suffragist meeting where she is trotted out by her father and "started up" with some parlor magic to deliver an impassioned oration for women's equality. It is love at first sight for both cousins.

Olive wants to groom Verena, both as a feminist speaker and a lover. She basically buys Verena from her parents, handing her father a check for $5,000 for the privilege of overseeing her "education" for a year, after which he can expect the same amount again. In 1875, that was the equivalent of $120,000 today, in a time when the cost of living was far lower. Today, parents hand over that much to universities for the privilege of having their children seduced and ruined, ideologically and otherwise.

Verena's education consists of readings, museum outings, and Olive's wild-eyed orations about dedication and sacrifice for the liberation of humanity—in the lap of embarrassing luxury, to the fey strains of the Wagner's *Lohengrin* Prelude. Redgrave was really born for this role.

Basil tells Verena "I don't think you mean what you preach." Instead, he thinks that she simply has a "sweet nature" that makes her want to please the people around her: her father, Olive, Miss Birdseye, etc. In short, Verena is exactly the kind of woman he wants for his wife: someone who will be devoted to pleasing *him*, which of course implies motherhood and child-rearing as well.

But can't Verena "have it all"? No. Basil doesn't want a wife who is famous for preaching dangerous nonsense. He wants her to give up politics altogether and devote herself entirely to private life. He asks, "Can't I make you see how much more natural it is—not to say agreeable—to give yourself to a man, instead of to the movement of some morbid old maid?" Basil is also shrewd enough to know what Olive is after. They didn't call lesbian cohabitation "Boston marriages" for nothing, which adds a new shade of meaning to the title.

I'll leave you to discover the twists and turns of Olive and Basil's struggle over Verena for yourselves. But I should at least tell you that this movie does not follow the model of politically incorrect heroes (Archie Bunker, Tony Soprano) who "grow" over time. *The Bostonians* wouldn't be remarkable unless our chivalrous Confederate hero won out in the end, without compromise, his character and principles entirely intact.

Henry James was known for extremely subtle studies of character and psychology. The movie does them justice. The tiniest gestures are revealing and often quite funny. For instance, during one of Dr. Tarrant's mesmeric healing sessions, he breaks out of his prophetic voice twice to ask an unctuous weasel of a reporter (Wallace Shawn), "Have you got that, Mr. Pardon?" Another great moment is when Mrs. Burrage assures Olive that she is devoted to the cause of "we poor women" as they are served tea in her sumptuous Fifth Avenue mansion. (Aside from Basil and Dr. Prance, the characters spend quite a bit of time assuring one another of their good intentions.)

Olive and Basil are polar opposites in character as well as in sex and politics.

Basil is unfailingly polite and kind, despite his inegalitarian convictions. But he is always firm and frank about who he is and what he wants. He is not threatened by people who disagree with him, perhaps because he doesn't suffer from the grandiose delusion that his beliefs are ordained by the God of the Bible or the God of Progress, such that disagreement is equivalent to damnation. This is Christopher Reeve's best role. He is completely natural and credible. In everything else I have seen him in, he comes off as smug and precious, like an overpraised child.

Olive is rude and supercilious, despite her professed humanitarianism. She is dogmatic about her political views: "He's an enemy!" she whispers about Basil with the same trembling fanaticism that her Puritan ancestors said, "She's a witch!" Olive is on the side of the angels, so woe to us.

But Olive refuses to take a stand on what she wants in her relationship with Verena. Verena wants to please Olive, but Olive always throws it back to Verena, "I want you to do it because *you* want it." Note that she doesn't want Verena to *do* what Olive wants, *despite* what Verena wants. She wants Verena to *want* what Olive wants—and without the necessity of Olive telling her.

There's a strange sort of narcissism here. Olive is setting herself up as a sort of idol or oracle and demanding that her worshipper orbit her perpetually, trying to *guess* what would please her. It is utterly maddening. No wonder there's so much violence in lesbian relationships. Of course, there's a real possibility that Olive doesn't consciously know she's a lesbian. She may be the last to know.

The Eastern liberal establishment of *The Bostonians* is pretty much recognizable as today's hostile elite, using their money and connections to launch destructive ideologies into the world, confident that their wealth and power will insulate them from any blowback. But this is an indigenous white Protestant hostile elite, not the Jewish-dominated one that arose in the twentieth century. There is, however, a hint of what is to come. At Mrs. Burrage's salon, we learn that a Professor Gougenheim will soon deliver a lecture on the Talmud.

James' novel received savage reviews from the Eastern liberal establishment it lampoons. Which makes me wonder how this movie garnered positive reviews and award nominations. It is a miracle that it was ever made. It is hard to believe that Jhabvala and Ivory didn't see the humor and the horror in their depictions of characters like Olive, Miss Birdseye, Mrs. Burrage, and Dr. Tarrant. But if they did, would they have dared to make the movie at all?

It is also impossible to believe that they sympathized with the character and philosophy of Basil Ransom, yet here he is on the big screen, both admirable and undefeated. I'd like to think that this is a rare example of liberals being genuinely broadminded about their opponents and critical of themselves. But sometimes dissident ideas leak into the mainstream simply because our opponents are so smug that they can't imagine anyone actually taking them seriously.

I highly recommend *The Bostonians*. It is a nostalgic, escapist feast for the eyes that won't insult your intellect or your values.

The Unz Review, June 28, 2021

THE BRIDGE ON THE RIVER KWAI

David Lean's *The Bridge on the River Kwai* (1957) is not just a great film, it is a nearly perfect one. Even better, it was recognized as such from the start by virtually everyone. The critics lionized it and continue to include it on their "best" lists. The movie business showered it with prizes. *Bridge* won seven Oscars, including best picture and best director. Audiences made it the biggest film of 1957 and a perennial favorite ever since.

Bridge was Lean's twelfth film and his first "epic," which cast the die for the rest of his career. It was followed by *Lawrence of Arabia* (1962) and *Doctor Zhivago* (1965), also classics. Then Lean ended his career with *Ryan's Daughter* (1970) and *A Passage to India* (1984), which fail as films in part because their slighter stories were overwhelmed by Lean's epic style of treatment, which had hardened into mannerisms.

Bridge might have shared the same fate because of its source material. Lean's film adapts Pierre Boulle's best-selling 1952 novel *Le Pont de la rivière Kwaï*. (Boulle is also famous for another novel that made it to the screen as *Planet of the Apes*.) The novel is set in Japanese-occupied Thailand during the Second World War. The Japanese are building a railroad to connect Bangkok with Rangoon using forced labor, both native civilians and British prisoners of war.

The British prisoners in a particular camp are tasked with building a bridge over the river Kwai. The main conflict is between the Japanese camp Commander Saito and British Lt. Colonel Nicholson. Saito demands that officers do manual labor. This being contrary to the military code, Nicholson refuses, and he and his officers are punished. Naturally, the construction project is plagued by sabotage. Saito eventually relents because he needs the cooperation of the British officers to finish the bridge on schedule.

Nicholson then marshals his men in order to build a better bridge than the Japanese could have done. Nicholson appeals to legalism, *esprit de corps*, and British chauvinism—but they all fall short of a case for enthusiastic collaborationism. The core of the novel is the absurdity of a man who collaborates with the enemy out of a misplaced sense of duty. It is not clear if Nicholson is supposed to be an imbecile or a madman, but he's definitely something of a buffoon: a snob, a bore, a martinet, and ultimately a traitor.

Most Brits who read the novel found it to be offensive and rather tasteless: offensive, because it comes off as a crude Gallic lampoon of the British national character, especially the British military; tasteless, because approximately 13,000 prisoners of war died during the construction of the railway, plus up to 100,000 of the local civilians. It is just not something to be treated lightly.

Lean followed Boulle's plot fairly faithfully. The main departure—the destruction of the bridge at the end of the film—was approved by Boulle. Where Lean departed from Boulle is his treatment of the character of Nicholson. Lean turned Nicholson from a buffoon into a tragic hero worthy of Sophocles or Shakespeare. In Lean's eyes, Nicholson stands for genuine virtues: patriotism, loyalty, duty, and pride in one's his work, as well as obedience to law, authority, and moral principles. He wouldn't be a tragic hero unless he had genuine virtues.

Nicholson's "tragic flaw" is that he does not see that his virtues only really make sense when practiced among his own people, for their benefit. In the prison camp, however, these virtues are being exploited by a ruthless enemy who aims to destroy the empire that Nicholson so loyally fought to preserve. There's a lesson in this for white people today, since our openness to strangers, altruism, and moral idealism are being exploited by a system that is destroying us as well.

The Bridge on the River Kwai is masterful at exploring the fundamental distinction between aristocratic ethos that prizes honor above all else and the bourgeois ethos that prizes comfort, security, long life, and pleasure above all else.

G. W. F. Hegel famously claims that history begins with a battle to the death over honor, in which two men are willing to risk their lives for an idea. Prehistory is governed by the necessities of life. History is governed by ideas. If both men prize honor above life, and one is defeated, he will choose death before dishonor. But if the defeated party chooses life at the price of honor, he is revealed to be a very different kind of man who is reduced to the status of a slave, to toil for the victor.

This is exactly how Japanese Commander Saito (played by Sessue Hayakawa) sees the matter. By surrendering, the British have lost their honor and have been reduced to slaves, including the officers, thus all must work. Saito will not spare the officers from the full measure of their disgrace because of a mere legalism that forbids imprisoned officers from doing manual labor, as if they were still gentlemen. To him, the Geneva Convention is nothing compared to the Japanese warrior code of *bushido*. The Japanese military felt superior to the British because the Japanese still committed suicide to avoid the dishonor of defeat, whereas the British, being a Christian nation, rejected suicide and used legalisms to preserve their honor even in defeat.

The dispute between Saito and Nicholson—brilliantly portrayed by Alec Guinness—becomes another struggle to the death over honor. Saito puts Nicholson in a metal box in the blazing sun to break his will, but he refuses to relent and do manual labor, even if it kills him. Unfortunately for Saito, the bridge is behind schedule, the Japanese engineer is incompetent, and the prisoners are at best sullen workers, at worst prone to malingering and sabotage.

If the bridge is not completed on schedule, Saito will be expected to commit suicide, a fate that he wishes to avoid. Thus Saito uses the anniversary of the Japanese victory over Russia as the occasion for a face-saving amnesty. Nicholson and his officers will not have to labor but will organize their men to complete the bridge on time. The roles have been reversed. Nicholson has chosen death over dishonor, and Saito has flinched, choosing dishonor over death. It is Nicholson's high point. After that, his fall begins.

Nicholson's quest to build a better bridge than the Japanese also makes sense in terms of Hegel's master-slave dialectic. Nicholson has beaten Saito on an essential point of honor. But he is still a prisoner, and his men are still slaves. However, Hegel describes a pathway by which the slave can restore his self-respect and humanity. The master rules over men, including slaves. The slave, however, can make himself a master over nature, which is what Nicholson and his men do by building the bridge, and doing it better than the Japanese could. Saito is shamed by this, and even though the bridge is completed on time, he still plans to kill himself.

But in a deeper sense, the Japanese have still won, because they got their bridge, which is an important strategic asset in their war against the British. Next stop: India.

Since both Saito and Nicholson are master types, albeit at times "temporarily embarrassed" master types, the film needs a well-developed slave type as a contrast. The American studio wanted a big American star to appeal to American ticket buyers. Enter William Holden as the American Commander Shears. (In the novel, Shears is British.) The Americans also wanted a love interest to appeal to chicks. Lean groaned, because war stories are guy stories. (Lean got his way on his next film, *Lawrence of Arabia*, in which there are no speaking roles for women.)

Lean gave in to the studio but turned defeat into victory, because the character of Commander Shears is a brilliant encapsulation of the slave type: cowardly, dishonest, and cynical about honor. Shears' character is brought into sharper focus by making him an American, since America is a thoroughly bourgeois society that took pride in throwing off European aristocratic civilization, although vestiges of its ethos survived among the military and Southern planters. Making Shears a womanizer to boot perfected the character. But don't fear: Shears has a redemption arc and chooses death over dishonor in the end. There is still hope for the Yanks.

By making an American the voice of cynicism, cowardice, and dishonesty, Lean also perfects another trait of the film. Inverting Boulle's Gallic snark, Lean's *Bridge* valorizes the British character and especially the British military. Lean's politics are a bit complicated. He was conservative, patriotic, and despised communism. He was a tax exile for years because he also despised the British Labour Party.

But Lean was also drawn to such anti-colonial, anti-imperialistic figures as T. E. Lawrence and Gandhi. (Lean wanted to do a movie about Gandhi and actually met Nehru to discuss the project.) Yet in films like *Bridge* and *Lawrence of Arabia*, Lean presents the British Empire in a highly flattering light. (*A Passage to India* is anti-Imperialist, but these sentiments are primarily expressed by two repulsive liberal females, whose desire to mix with the natives creates chaos for all involved. So in the end, it subtly affirms the wisdom of the colonial regime remaining aloof from the natives.)

Like every Lean film, *The Bridge on the River Kwai* is a first-class production. The cast is excellent, with particularly distinguished performances by Alec Guinness (who won the Oscar for best actor), William Holden, and Jack Hawkins. The musical score by Malcolm Arnold is one of his best and was duly rewarded with an Oscar. The striking locations in Ceylon were captured by cinematographer Jack Hildyard, who also received an Oscar, as did editor Peter Taylor.

The script of *Bridge*, which also won the Oscar for best adaptation, is a masterpiece. Originally, the script was credited to Boulle, who didn't even speak English. Boulle's name was there in place of two blacklisted writers, Carl Foreman and Michael Wilson. But everything that makes the script deep and powerful is the work of David Lean.

I have talked about the central themes of *Bridge*, but I have left out a great deal of the story, because I want you to enjoy discovering it for yourself. But I should warn you that, although *The Bridge on the River Kwai* is a beautiful and entertaining spectacle, it is also gut-wrenchingly tragic. This makes the film's popularity all the more remarkable. It is proof that even "the masses" are not satisfied by mere entertainment. They hunger for deep feelings, even painful ones, if they are stirred by an encounter with deep truths about the human condition.

The Unz Review, June 18, 2021

A Clockwork Orange

For years now, readers have been urging me to review Stanley Kubrick's *A Clockwork Orange* (1971), which adapts Anthony Burgess' 1962 novel of the same name. I have resisted, because although *A Clockwork Orange* is often hailed as a classic, I thought it was dumb, distasteful, and highly overrated, so I didn't want to watch it again. But I had first watched it decades ago. So I thought I might see it differently if I gave it another chance. I approached it with an open mind. But I was right the first time.

A Clockwork Orange is set in Great Britain in a not-too-distant future. Alex (Malcolm McDowell) and his three buddies are violent hooligans who engage in rape, assault, robbery, and wanton destruction. The movie opens with an amphetamine-fueled crime spree. They beat up an old drunk, brawl with another gang, run people off the road while joy riding, then use a confidence trick ("There's been a terrible accident. Can I come in and use your phone?") to invade a couple's home, whereupon they beat the man, rape his wife, and trash the place. The whole sequence is deeply distasteful. Violent sociopaths like Alex and his friends should simply be killed.

Alex is high-handed and cruel to his buddies as well, using treachery and violence to assert dominance over them. This merely breeds resentment. One night they decide to rob a wealthy woman's house. The old accident trick does not work, so Alex breaks in. There is a struggle. She attacks him with a bust of Beethoven, so he kills her with a sculpture of a penis. Hearing sirens, he exits, whereupon his ex-friends clobber him with a bottle and leave him for the police.

Let that be a lesson to you.

Alex is imprisoned for murder. He seeks to ingratiate himself with the authorities by feigning Christian piety. (As a violent sociopath, he finds the Old Testament more to his liking.)

When a new Left-wing government comes into power, they want to free up space for political prisoners, so they introduce an experimental cure for Alex's violent sociopathy: the Ludovico technique, which is basically a form of Pavlovian conditioning. Alex is the test subject. He is injected with a nausea-producing drug then forced to watch films of violence, including sexual violence. Eventually, he can't even think of violence without becoming violently ill. Pronounced cured, he is released into society.

Newly paroled, Alex bumps into the bum that he assaulted, who recognizes him and wants revenge. He calls together his fellow bums to beat Alex, whose Ludovico conditioning makes it impossible for him to fight back.

Ironic, huh?

Let that be a lesson to you.

When the mob of hobos is broken up by two cops, they turn out to be two of Alex's old gang, the very ones he humiliated. Eager to exact further revenge, they beat him mercilessly and abandon him in the countryside. Alex is helpless to resist.

Ironic, huh?

Let that be a lesson to you.

Alex wanders through the countryside until he takes refuge at the home of the very couple he and his gang brutalized. Ironic, huh? The husband was crippled by the beating. The wife has died and been replaced with a gigantic muscular dork named Julian. The husband figures out who Alex is and drugs him. Then he and some of his friends, who oppose the government that introduced the Ludovico technique, try to drive Alex to commit suicide, hoping to create a scandal that will embarrass the government. Alex throws himself from a window and is severely injured but does not die.

To contain the scandal, the Justice Minister throws the cripple in prison and tries to win Alex's favor by tending to his wounds. While unconscious, he is also given brain surgery to reverse the Ludovico technique. The happy ending is that Alex returns to being a violent sociopath, but this time he will enjoy the patronage and protection of the state. Thus the tale veers from pat moralism to pure cynicism in the end. Apparently, the book's final chapter was "redemptive," but this was omitted as being contrived—as if that weren't true of the whole story.

But isn't this all redeemed by a "deep message" about human freedom? No, not really, because the moral psychology of *A Clockwork Orange* is remarkably crude.

The Ludovico technique is based on the observation that normal people have a distaste for violence and cruelty directed at the innocent. Then it simply ignores the fact that normal people don't necessarily have a distaste for violence, even cruelty, directed at *bad* people. It also reverses cause and effect, reasoning that since normal people feel distaste at violence, if they can create a mechanical association between violence and sickness, that will somehow make Alex a morally normal person, curing him of his violent sociopathy.

Of course, this whole theory completely ignores the element of empathy. Normal people feel disgust with violence and cruelty because they can empathize with the victims. Sociopaths lack empathy, and the Ludovico technique does not change that. Alex does not feel sick with empathy for victims, he just feels sick. And his physiological response makes no moral distinctions between violence meted out to the deserving and the undeserving. When he is attacked, he can't defend himself, because even violence in self-defense makes him sick.

Of course utter stupidity is no objection to most progressive social uplift schemes, so it doesn't exactly make such a "cure" for crime implausible.

Burgess's "deep" objection to the Ludovico technique is equally crude and dumb, but in a different way. The prison chaplain argues that the Ludovico technique is evil because it takes away Alex's freedom, which takes away his humanity. Alex, being a sociopath, takes pleasure in hurting innocent people. The Ludovico treatment conditions him to feel disgust at violence, which denies him the freedom to do evil, thus it is dehumanizing.

But if this is a dehumanizing assault on freedom, what are we to make of our own disgust with Alex's behavior? Is that also a dehumanizing form of unfreedom? Presumably so.

Does this mean that when Alex becomes a violent sociopath again his humanity has been restored? Presumably so.

Since Alex the sociopath can contemplate violence without

any feelings of disgust, whereas normal people cannot, does this mean that Alex is both more free and more human than normally constituted people? If so, this is a pretty good example of a *reductio ad absurdum*.

The Ludovico technique and Burgess' alternative both depend on a pat dualism between body and mind, which leaves no place for what the ancients called virtues and the moderns called moral sentiments. For the ancients, virtue is rooted in habit. For moral sentiments theorists, our ability to perceive the good is caught up in feelings like empathy and disgust. But to the Ludovico technique, virtue is indistinguishable from Pavlovian conditioning, and moral sentiments are indistinguishable from a sour stomach. From the chaplain's point of view, the freedom of the mind is so separate from the body, habit, and feeling that a sociopath's lack of virtue or moral sentiment actually make him freer and thus more human than morally healthy people.

But isn't Kubrick's treatment of this material brilliant? No, not really. Kubrick's treatment of sex and violence veers between the pornographic and cartoonish. The entire movie is crude and cynical parody, with an ugly cast, grotesque costumes, hideous sets, and dreadful over-acting. The whole production reminded me of the comics of R. Crumb, who puts his prodigious talent to work churning out pornography, grotesquerie, and world-destroying cynicism. Crumb obviously hates America. He especially hates women. Likewise, the director of *A Clockwork Orange* obviously hates everything about Great Britain. He also takes particular pleasure in the mockery and degradation of women. Handling such material with technical skill does not redeem it. Indeed, by making it seductive, Kubrick actually it makes it worse.

A Clockwork Orange is violence-porn and porn-porn combined with a middle-brow, moralistic "message" and some classical music. But these function merely as an alibi, like the interviews in *Playboy*. *A Clockwork Orange* is obscene in the literal sense of the word: it should not be watched.

The Unz Review, April 1, 2021

CONAN THE BARBARIAN

Over the years, I caught bits and pieces of John Milius' 1982 movie *Conan the Barbarian*—starring Arnold Schwarzenegger as the big lug himself—on cable TV. But I was never tempted to watch the whole film. I finally gave in when I started writing my series on Classics of Right-Wing Cinema, and friends urged me to add *Conan* to my list.

I admit that a film about Robert E. Howard's iconic hero, with visuals borrowed from Frank Frazetta, starring the future California Governator, and directed by Right-wing Jew Milius *sounds* like a formula for a classic of Right-wing cinema, teeming with paleo-masculine heroics and illiberal political realism. After all, Milius wrote the script for *Dirty Harry*, which is a genuine paleo-masculine, anti-liberal classic of Right-wing cinema. Sadly, though, *Conan the Barbarian* is nothing like *Dirty Harry*, but it is very much like its sequel, *Magnum Force*, also scripted by Milius, in which the character of Harry Callahan is systematically subverted in a decidedly anti-white and politically correct manner.

The *Conan* movie went through more than a decade of development hell before finally moving forward with Milius at the helm. Oliver Stone had apparently written a four-hour script set in a post-apocalyptic future. Milius discarded Stone's script entirely, even though Stone and Milius share the final screenwriting credit. Instead of setting *Conan* in classical antiquity, Milius sets the story in the Dark Ages, borrowing elements from the Norse and the Mongols.

Howard's Conan is a fearsome warrior, but he is also intelligent, witty, learned, and cunning. He can read and write. He is fluent in a number of languages. He can solve problems and crack codes. These traits set him apart in a world teeming with warriors, enabling him to become a king. In short, Howard's Conan is no mere barbarian. Milius' Conan is strong and cunning, but otherwise he is an oaf with very few lines. It is impossible to imagine this man becoming a king, because he really is just a barbarian.

But surely Milius used some of Howard's 21 Conan stories? No, not really. He borrowed some names and events, but the plot is his invention. This is John Milius' *Conan*, not Robert E. Howard's, which is something of a cheat if you grew up liking Howard's Conan. Ultimately, though, Milius' *Conan* has to be judged on its own merits.

The story opens with Conan as a child. His father is a blacksmith who explains the "riddle of steel" to his young son. Later, Conan's village is attacked by a marauding band. Actually, they look like a marauding *heavy metal* band: Spinal Tap, but with real axes. It is a bit much.

The band is led by Thulsa Doom, who is played by James Earl Jones. Jones, of course, was the voice of Darth Vader, so he was an iconic choice for a villain. But Jones is a black man, who is as absurdly out of place in Conan's world as the llama we glimpse later on in the movie. Thulsa Doom has the power to hypnotize people, which he uses on Conan's mother, who lowers her sword, allowing Thulsa to lop off her head.

The children of the village are marched off as slaves to toil in a mill, where eventually Conan grows up to be a giant, muscular brute played by Schwarzenegger. Then Conan is sold to another master, who makes a gladiator of him. Howard's Conan was a free man from birth and would never have acquiesced to such treatment. Of course such an origin story could be compelling if Conan overcame it, for instance by gaining his freedom through strength and character. But no, at a certain point, his master just lets a highly profitable slave go. It makes no sense and adds nothing to Conan's rather murky character and motivations.

Conan wanders a bit, finding a sword. Then he meets a witch, who seduces him. When she begins transforming into something unsavory, he simply tosses her into the fireplace and leaves. It is genuinely funny. At that point, I wondered if this film was trying to be camp, like Mike Hodges' 1980 *Flash Gordon*, which was also produced by Dino De Laurentiis.

Conan then rescues Subotai, a thief who has been imprisoned by the witch. Played by Gerry Lopez, dubbed by a Japanese actor, and named after one of Genghis Khan's generals, Subotai is our white hero's non-white sidekick. Because those are the rules of

Hollywood: no white hero can act without a non-white sidekick.

Conan wants revenge on Thusla Doom. The witch told him that Doom can be found in the city of Zamora, so Conan and Subotai set out for there. In Zamora, they meet Valeria (Sandahl Bergman), a strong, independent female thief, because the rules of Hollywood also dictate that no white hero can be depicted without a strong, independent woman who doesn't need him.

When Conan asks about Thulsa Doom's snake standard, he is told of the towers of the cult of Set: "Two or three years ago, it was just another snake cult," but now franchises are popping up in every city. At this point, I was wondering if Lorenzo Semple, Jr., of *Flash Gordon* and the *Batman* TV series fame, had a hand in the script.

The three thieves sneak into the tower of Set, where they find a member of Thulsa's heavy metal band feeding nubile females to a giant serpent. They kill the serpent, steal some treasure, and go celebrate. Conan and Valeria become an item.

Suddenly, the trio are arrested and dragged before Osric, the king of Zamora, played by the great Max von Sydow. The fact that he played Emperor Ming in *Flash Gordon* reinforced the camp interpretation. But then Von Sydow does something quite unexpected. He takes a campy script and gives a riveting and passionate performance. His daughter has joined Thulsa Doom's snake cult, and he wants to hire the thieves to bring her back.

Subotai and Valeria don't wish to risk it. When Valeria gives her case for quitting while they are ahead, again it is well-acted and touching. It is the dramatic high-point of the film, which then lapses back into camp, spectacle, and mindless action. But for a few minutes, we get a sense of the great sword and sorcery movie *Conan* could have been if Milius had just played it straight, with sincerity rather than irony.

Conan wants revenge, so he heads to Thulsa Doom's headquarters alone. Milius portrays the Doom cultists as degenerate, credulous flower children being exploited by ruthless sociopaths. Using an amusing ruse, Conan steals a priest's costume but is caught. Doom makes a rather chilling speech about the relative powers of steel and flesh. By flesh, he really means the hypnotic power of his words over the minds of his followers, which he demonstrates by enticing one to leap to her death. This contrast between words and steel is central to the whole plot, but it also dictates a fundamental change in Conan's character. Howard's Conan was a master of steel (well, bronze) *and* words. Milius' Conan is an inarticulate thug.

Doom orders Conan to be crucified on a tree, but Subotai rescues him. Then Subotai, Valeria, and another Asian sidekick, a wizard with an annoying voice named Akiro, use magic to bring Conan back from the brink of death. The wizard warns, however, that the magic will have a heavy toll. Valeria is willing to risk it. Akiro is played by an Asian, because a white hero cannot be aided by a wise white mentor, and Morgan Freeman was otherwise engaged. Those are the rules of Hollywood.

Once Conan is restored, the three thieves penetrate the temple, where Doom is presiding over a drugged-out orgy and cannibalistic feast. (These people are really disgusting.) Conan and Co. slay the guards and capture the princess. Doom, however, transforms into a serpent and slithers away. Later, as the thieves flee down the mountainside, Doom kills Valeria with an arrow. She interprets her death as the toll for bringing Conan back.

Conan and Subotai take the princess back to Akiro's camp, where they prepare for the onslaught of Doom's troops. His cult consists mostly of women and hippies, so not many men are capable of carrying steel. Using guile and brutality, Conan and friends kill off Doom's soldiers. Doom flees back to his headquarters. Having lost his steel, he will take refuge behind the flesh of his followers.

Conan follows and confronts Doom, who tries to beguile him with his hypnotic words until Conan simply chops off his head. It has all the laconic directness of Alexander cleaving the Gordian knot. Call it the *argumentum ad barbarum*. It is still the swiftest way to silence liars.

Deprived of their leader, the cultists conveniently disperse, even though they could have mobbed and killed Conan. Conan then burns down their temple and returns the princess to king Osric. The End.

There are many good elements to *Conan the Barbarian*. Schwarzenegger looks great and moves magnificently in the action sequences, which are snappily choreographed. Bergman and Von Sydow are also good. Jones is out of place, but his voice and menacing presence are used to great effect. He's a memorable monster.

The design of the sets, weapons, and costumes is frequently excellent, particularly when inspired by Frazetta. But these elements often stray into the realm of parody. For instance, Thorgrim's huge hammer is ridiculous.

Basil Poledouris' orchestral score is wonderfully old-fashioned and sometimes quite good. At its best, it brings to mind Miklós Rózsa's glittering, barbaric music for epics like *Quo Vadis*, *El Cid*, and *Ben Hur*.

I understand why people on the Right like *Conan the Barbarian*. Conan is a paleo-masculine white hero using cunning and strength to triumph in a world that is savage but also refreshingly free of liberal cant and illusions. Thulsa Doom, with his word magic and hippy cult, is a superb image of modern liberalism: honeyed words and sentimentality on the outside, devil worship, cannibalism, and perversion at the core.

But Milius' anachronistic casting of a black villain, plus giving the white hero Asian sidekicks, is pure Hollywood diversity propaganda. Beyond that, if you are going to make a Conan movie, why stray so far from the original character? Isn't it fraud to call such a radically different character by the same name?

A Conan film that takes the character and original stories seriously could be great. How great? Peter Jackson's *The Lord of the Rings* showed us the heights that sword and sorcery films can attain when artistry and technical skill join with fidelity to the author's vision and genuine love of the story.

Admittedly, Howard is no Tolkien. His stories are pulps, but they are *classic* pulps. They are loaded with anachronisms and improbabilities of their own. All of them could be deepened and tightened. But even unaltered, every one of them is better than what Milius has dished up. I prefer sincere pulp to smirking camp every time. *Conan the Barbarian* is not a terrible film, but the character and the audience deserve much better.

The Unz Review, May 18, 2021

DIRTY HARRY

Dirty Harry (1971), directed by Don Siegel and starring Clint Eastwood as San Francisco Police Inspector Harry Callahan, is a classic of Right-wing cinema. *Dirty Harry* was hugely popular with moviegoers, spawning four sequels and a whole genre of films about tough cops whose hands are tied by the system and are forced to go outside the law in order to protect the public.

Dirty Harry articulated the growing reaction to the racial unrest, hippy degeneracy, and liberal mush of the 1960s, which led to skyrocketing crime in American cities and white flight to the suburbs. Liberalism holds that society can be ruled by impersonal laws, not men. Thus any film giving a favorable view of vigilantism—in which laws break down and individuals take justice into their own hands—is anti-liberal.

Dirty Harry was seen as a reactionary film at the time. Paul Newman declined the title role because he thought it too Right-wing. Feminists protested outside the Academy Awards with a banner reading "Dirty Harry is a Rotten Pig." Thus I found it surprising that *Dirty Harry* was viewed favorably by leading critics, most of whom were liberals and Leftists. For instance, Pauline Kael recognized the film's technical merits and emotional power but decried it as "fascist," "a remarkably singleminded attack on liberal values," and "a deeply immoral movie." *Dirty Harry* ended up in many "Best" lists, including the *New York Times'* top 1000, *Empire* magazine's top 500, *Total Film's* top 100, and *TV Guide's* and *Vanity Fair's* top 50.

I can't include *Dirty Harry* in any of my best lists, but it is still a remarkably good film, with compelling lead characters, a gripping plot, and a tight script. Filmed on locations in and around San Francisco, with creepily effective music by Lalo Schifrin, *Dirty Harry* captures the beginning of the long, seedy cultural hangover of the '60s, imbuing it, if not with a glamour, at least with a gloss, bad haircuts and all. Clint Eastwood as Harry Callahan and Andy Robinson as the loathsome villain Scorpio give compelling performances.

Harry Callahan is another one of Eastwood's taciturn Aryan heroes, a physically imposing and highly capable alpha male who becomes a protector of public order. Like most of Eastwood's classics, the world of *Dirty Harry* is divided into sheep, the wolves who prey on them, and the sheepdogs who protect the flock, to borrow a scheme from *American Sniper*. However, despite their opposed roles, wolves and sheepdogs have more in common with each other than they do with sheep, and the flock starts bleating nervously when the dogs bare their fangs at the wolves.

Harry Callahan is 40ish. (Eastwood was 41 in 1971.) He is an Inspector for the San Francisco Police Department, a position of responsibility that requires intelligence. He is contemptuous of college boys, so he probably came up through the ranks. He is a widower. His wife was killed by a drunk driver. He does not appear to have children. His work is his life now. He probably also harbors a death wish, or at least an indifference to his own interests, which makes him more effective at doing his duties. Because Harry is more driven than other cops, he prefers to work alone. Partners tend to slow him down and get wounded or killed.

Callahan is not called "Dirty" Harry because he is a corrupt cop. He is Dirty Harry because people trust him to do dirty jobs. He gets "the shit end of the stick." Dirty work means actually confronting criminals. Sometimes you get dirt on your hands. Sometimes you get blood. Sometimes you have to go outside the law to enforce the law.

The clean jobs are reserved for the city government and police brass, whose biggest worries are lint and bad press. Their jobs are to demand results from their underlings then second-guess their every move. Dirty Harry is a populist hero because he is the stoic, competent white Atlas who carries the system on his shoulders but is also treated as deplorable and expendable by the elites.

Harry is also supposed to be a dirty because he is a hater: "Harry hates everybody: limeys, micks, hebes, dagos, niggers, honkies, chinks." To which Harry adds for the benefit of his new Mexican-American partner Chico Gonzalez (this movie is not exactly subtle), "Especially spics." *Dirty Harry* didn't just pioneer the loose cannon cop genre, it also established the convention of pairing these white alpha males with non-white sidekicks. (A white alpha male mentoring another white man as a guardian of society would make Don Siegel hallucinate the sound of marching jackboots.) However, if Harry hates honkies, he can't be a white racist. And if his name is Callahan, that makes him a self-hating Mick. In truth, Harry is merely a detective. He's trained to notice patterns.[1] That makes him politically incorrect.

Harry has more than just a touch of sadism, which is brought out in the movie's most quoted scene. During his lunch break, Harry foils an armed bank robbery by three blacks, killing two with his .44 Magnum and wounding the third, whom he taunts:

> I know what you're thinking: "Did he fire six shots or only five?" Well, to tell you the truth, in all this excitement, I've kinda lost track myself. But being this is a .44 Magnum, the most powerful handgun in the world, and would blow your head clean off, you've got to ask yourself one question: "Do I feel lucky?" Well, do you, punk?

When Harry repeats the same taunt almost word-for-word at the end of the movie, the effect is chilling. You glimpse a bitter, sadistic side of his character. You wonder how many times he has done this. He clearly enjoys killing scum. Hence his preference for pistols that can decapitate and rifles that can stop elephants.

The plot of *Dirty Harry* is a standard neo-*noir* police thriller. Harry's quarry is a serial killer, Scorpio (based on the Zodiac killer). Scorpio was so effectively brought to life by Andy Robinson that the actor received death threats and had to change his phone number.

Scorpio is a Dostoyevskyian criminal *Untermensch*. He's physically weak, unmasculine, and cowardly, palpably seething with resentment. He squeals like a pig, blubbers like a child, and develops a severe limp after Harry stabs then shoots him in the leg.

Scorpio is attracted to weak victims: a young woman in a

---

[1] Greg Johnson, "In Defense of Prejudice," *In Defense of Prejudice* (San Francisco: Counter-Currents, 2017).

swimming pool, a couple of homosexuals, a ten-year-old black child, a Catholic priest, a teenage girl, an old man, a bus full of schoolchildren, a little boy fishing. He prefers to kill like a coward, shooting two victims with a sniper rifle, burying another alive.

Two scenes are especially repulsive. Scorpio has kidnapped, raped, and buried a teenage girl alive. She is running out of air. Harry tracks him to his lair and doesn't wait for a warrant. He just kicks in the door. Pursuing Scorpio out onto the field of Kezar Stadium, Harry brings him down with a .44 shot to the leg, then stamps on the wound, demanding to know the girl's location while Scorpio shrieks "I have rights. I have rights." If you have any doubt about where a person falls of the F scale, just show him this scene.

Of course Scorpio is released because Harry didn't follow proper procedure. His defense was that a girl was dying, so there really wasn't time for a warrant and a genteel interrogation. But that doesn't matter to the Jewish DA and the Berkeley Law professor he consults. Scorpio had rights. Harry violated them. So all of society must be punished. When healthy people watch this scene, their blood boils.

Harry, of course, won't let this drop. He begins to shadow Scorpio in his spare time, hoping to prevent him from killing again. Scorpio is repulsive with his long hair, gimp, and fruity hippy costume, including a grotesque peace sign belt buckle. As he wanders around parks and playgrounds looking at small children, your blood will run cold.

When Scorpio realizes he is being shadowed, he doesn't confront Callahan or go to his superiors. Instead, he pays a black thug $200 to beat him to a pulp, then blames it on Callahan. This sequence is a viscerally powerful critique of modern liberal slave morality which rewards and weaponizes victimhood, creating an incentive to fabricate police brutality and hate crimes.

Dirty Harry's final act after bringing Scorpio to justice is to take his badge and throw it away. John Wayne refused the role because he thought this gesture "un-American." Eastwood did not want to do it either but came to see the logic of it.

Harry has been living in the zone of what Carl Schmitt called the "*Ernstfall*,"² the emergency situation in which the reigning liberal norms are not capable of securing justice. Faced with the choice of law or justice, Harry chooses justice. It is the first step down the path to the vigilante—or the superhero.³ The gesture, however, is wasted. Instead of evolving into something higher, Harry Callahan is sucked into the Eternal Recurrence of the movie franchise. But his viewers don't have to be.

Dirty Harry turns fifty this year. Judging from the film, San Francisco was just as degenerate half a century ago as it is today. The main difference is that there are no adults like Harry Callahan to keep it together anymore. One has to ask: How much more ruin is left in this country before it all falls apart? Is anyone up to the dirty job of putting it back together again?

The Unz Review, January 30, 2021

---

[2] Greg Johnson, "Schmitt, Sovereignty, and the Deep State," *Counter-Currents*, August 12, 2014.

[3] Greg Johnson, "Superheroes, Sovereignty, and the Deep State," *Toward a New Nationalism* (San Francisco: Counter-Currents, 2019).

THE *DIRTY HARRY* SEQUELS:
DECONSTRUCTING A HERO

Dirty Harry (1971) is a compelling neo-*noir* thriller about San Francisco Police Inspector Harry Callahan (Clint Eastwood), who is increasingly forced to choose between liberal legal norms and bringing a sadistic serial killer known as Scorpio to justice. Once Harry kills Scorpio, the movie ends with him throwing away his badge, symbolizing a momentous decision. When justice and law conflict, Harry chooses justice.

This is what makes Harry "dirty." Harry Callahan is not corrupt. He is not willing to dirty his hands with illegality for selfish and petty reasons. But he will go outside the law to secure the higher good. The various events of the movie's plot beautifully reveal elements of Harry's character, so that his final choice makes sense.

Dirty Harry belongs in the category of first-rate crime *thrillers* like *The French Connection, L.A. Confidential, To Live & Die in L.A.*,[1] and *Drive*.

Director Don Siegel frames *Dirty Harry* with sweeping Bay Area vistas. Then the camera dives into the action and draws the viewer with it. The script is tightly written and the story swift-paced. Lalo Schifrin's jazz fusion score marries perfectly with the action and heightens the emotional impact. This being a gritty crime thriller set in swinging San Francisco, there are some racy elements: violence, cussing, nudity, homosexual couples, etc. But Siegel avoids outright obscenity. It is easy to overlook the artfulness of *Dirty Harry* because the story is so captivating.

The best way to appreciate *Dirty Harry* is to compare it to its four terrible sequels: *Magnum Force* (1973), *The Enforcer* (1976), *Sudden Impact* (1983), and *The Dead Pool* (1988).

Dirty Harry was decried as "fascist" for making a hero of a vigilante cop who was also characterized as a racist, although

---

[1] Reviewed in *Return of the Son of Trevor Lynch's CENSORED Guide to the Movies*, ed. Greg Johnson (San Francisco: Counter-Currents, 2019).

the movie pulled its punches on this particular matter by making Harry an equal opportunity hater and partnering him with one Chico Gonzalez. But *Dirty Harry* was also a huge hit, especially among white men. This dictated two things. First, there would be sequels because there would be money in them. Second, the sequels would subvert everything that Leftists found "problematic" about Harry Callahan.

This would dictate that the sequels could not build on the evolution of Harry's character in the original movie, because that was the biggest problem of all. So instead, they just reduced *Dirty Harry* to a formula and repeated it four times. Each *Dirty Harry* sequel required Clint Eastwood, a big gun, some shootouts with hoodlums, some California degeneracy, a clever line he repeats from time to time, and a jazz fusion score, preferably by Lalo Schifrin.

Since Harry is racist and presumably sexist, they have to pair him with a non-white or female partner. Since *Dirty Harry* was very much a guy movie, they also tarted up the sequels with some romance.

Since the formulaic repetition of tropes without any character development gets boring fast, these movies feel hollow and meaningless. Thus the filmmakers punched them up with fistfights and car chases and made the sex and violence extra lurid. *Dirty Harry* had dashes of *Playboy*. The sequels in the sleazy seventies were pure *Hustler*.

The first sequel, *Magnum Force*, is the worst. With a script by the allegedly Right-wing Jew John Milius, *Magnum Force* is less a sequel than a hard reboot. At the end of *Dirty Harry*, Callahan looks like he is quitting the police force and going rogue. In *Magnum Force*, Callahan is back on the force as if nothing has happened. Moreover, as a large number of criminals start getting gunned down, Callahan suspects that the culprit is actually a rogue cop gone vigilante. Our new Squeaky-Clean Harry is determined to bring him to justice.

It turns out that the culprits are four good-looking white motorcycle cops played by David Soul, Robert Urich, Tim Matheson, and Kip Niven. Of course the "real" Harry Callahan would have been mentoring young men like this, not trying to arrest them. But instead Harry has a black partner, complete with 'fro, named Early. Naming a black man "Early" sounds like a racist joke to me, but surely that was not Milius' intention.

It turns out that the young vigilantes are mentored by Lt. Neil Briggs, played by Hal Holbrook, a pencil-necked prig who spends a lot of time chewing out Callahan for being trigger-happy. When Briggs finally reveals himself to Callahan, our Squeaky-Clean Harry argues (1) that vigilantism is a slippery slope that will lead to shooting people over parking tickets, (which is absurd), and (2) that the system may be broken, but it is the only one we've got, and we can't let go of it (which is Republican). At this point, Milius has completely destroyed the hero of *Dirty Harry*. And it was premeditated.

It would take a free-standing essay to detail all the ways *Magnum Force* is lame, tasteless, and subversive. But life is too short for that, so here are a few highlights.

Magnum Force was directed by Ted Post. I didn't need to visit Wikipedia to know that he made his career in television. Despite being shot on location in and around America's most scenic city, *Magnum Force* looks and feels like television: scrunched shots, dull camera work, sclerotic pacing. Not even Lalo Schifrin's excellent score—the only first-rate thing about this movie—can breathe life into Post's directing.

The acting is all TV-grade as well. The only thing that would keep this movie off TV is its extremely lurid treatment of sex and violence.

In good dramatic conflict, the outcome is determined by the characters of the antagonists. Action is revelatory of character. Events have a deeper meaning. But during the climactic battle with the vigilantes in *Magnum Force*, one of them . . . dies in an accident. This reduces heroic Harry Callahan to hapless Forrest Gump.

The allegedly clever line that Harry repeats is, "A man's got to know his limitations," which is a far cry from, "Do you feel lucky?" and completes Milius' transformation of the hero of *Dirty Harry* into a smug old fart.

Three years later, Dirty Harry returns in *The Enforcer*. A mostly white group of hippy criminals has stolen military weapons and explosives from what is apparently a private warehouse guarded by a single geezer. They style themselves the People's Revolutionary Strike Force and try to extort money from the city by planting bombs and kidnapping the mayor.

Harry is paired with a female rookie (Tyne Daly), because the mayor wants to court feminists and good press. She tries hard to be a good cop. She also tries to seduce Harry. But her lack of experience gets her killed while rescuing the mayor. Thus *The Enforcer* actually amounts to a powerful critique of affirmative action and the political flakes who push it. Too bad it isn't a better movie.

The Enforcer is directed by James Fargo, who like Ted Post captures the Bay Area's spectacular scenery, as well as lurid sex and bloody violence, with all the cinematic sweep and dynamism of an episode of *The Golden Girls*. Harry's pursuit of the criminals takes him to a whorehouse and onto the set of a porno movie. The killings are extra bloody and lurid. There are plenty of chases to a very routine jazz fusion score by Jerry Fielding.

But none of it has any higher meaning. There is no character development, just repetition of the formula: Harry mows down bad guys with his big gun, gets heat from the brass, and mutters the word "marvelous" occasionally, because that's this script's idea of wit.

Aside from Eastwood, the acting is barely serviceable for television. When Tyne Daly flirts with Harry—"Isn't Coit Tower phallic?" "Ooh what a big gun you have." "Do you use a .44 magnum for penetration?"—the acting is barely serviceable for porn.

Eastwood himself directed *Sudden Impact*, his fourth outing as Dirty Harry. *Sudden Impact* was the best of the sequels and a huge box-office smash. It has the best one-liner of all: "Go ahead, make my day." But this film is mediocre at best.

Eastwood's girlfriend Sondra Locke plays Jennifer, the victim of a gang rape who decides to hunt down and kill her assailants ten years later. She kills her first victim in San Francisco, which puts Callahan on the case. Jennifer then leaves for the fictional town of San Paulo (filmed in Santa Cruz), where the rest of her assailants live. Callahan, meanwhile, gets in some heat with the brass and is forced to take a vacation. He *just so happens* to go to San Paulo, where he gets involved with Jennifer and notices a pattern when new bodies start turning up.

Mick, the most dangerous of Jennifer's targets, turns the tables and attacks her, using her gun to kill the local police chief. Harry kills Mick and rescues Jennifer. Harry suspects that Jennifer is the real killer, but since Mick has the murder weapon on him, Harry pins the other murders on him and lets Jennifer walk away. It is a strange ending. It is not really an endorsement of vigilantism, however, because Harry doesn't actually know why Jennifer is killing these people. It is just a bizarre lapse of responsibility.

Unlike the other sequels, however, *Sudden Impact* at least had the potential to be a good movie. All it needed was a better script, better actors, and better directing. It is certainly Eastwood's weakest work as a director. Locke's character is almost as bland as her comatose sister. The villains are ridiculous, cackling caricatures. The acting is TV-grade.

The plot is filled with dumb, disconnected events with no larger meaning. For instance, as in *Magnum Force*, when some of Harry's enemies attack him, they die . . . accidentally in another Forrest Gump moment.

Since Harry is on vacation for most of the film, he can't be paired with a female or non-white partner. But *the formula* dictates a diverse sidekick, so one was contrived. As Harry practices shooting, a black man with a gun creeps up behind him. The actor is Albert Popwell, who played different criminals in the three previous Dirty Harry movies. We worry that he is about to shoot Harry, but no, the stalker is one of Harry's police colleagues, Horace King. The whole scene is pointless manipulation. Then, for no particular reason, King shows up in San Paulo to present Harry with an ugly bulldog, who also adds nothing to the story. Then King shows up back in San Paulo just in time to be killed by racists. He's a useless character who does absolutely nothing to advance the plot, but he's there because diversity demands it.

There's little to be said about the final Dirty Harry movie, *The Dead Pool*. The movie is purely by the numbers. This time the brass decide it would be good for the department's image to partner Harry with a Chinese-American cop, Quan (Evan Kim), who knows kung fu. *The Dead Pool* features the world's most ridiculous car chase, in which Harry screeches and lurches through the hills of San Francisco pursued by a *toy* car. Harry's clever line is, "You're shit out of luck," which is how I felt watching this turkey.

Eastwood was 58 in 1988 when *The Dead Pool* was released, so he decided it would be the last Dirty Harry movie. Having made more than $30 million from *Sudden Impact*, Eastwood decided to cut some of his friends in on the payday. The director of *The Dead Pool* is Eastwood's stunt double, Buddy Van Horn. The story was thought up by two goofy libertarian pill and smoothie merchants, Durk Pearson and Sandy Shaw. It's everything you'd expect from such a brain trust. Given the cynicism of this exercise, it was a clever deflection to make the putative villain an even more cynical director of slasher films, Peter Swan (Liam Neeson).

This being the Eighties, the *Hustler* magazine sleaze of the Seventies sequels is gone from *Sudden Impact* and *The Dead Pool*. Lalo Schifrin returns to write the scores, but this being the Eighties, we hear drum machines, funky basslines, and insipid melodies.

As for the message of *The Dead Pool*, there's not much left of the old Dirty Harry to deconstruct, but I do note that he is now *respectable*. He's made the cover of *San Francisco* magazine, which he indignantly trashes. You see, Harry's primary conflict with the brass is no longer about trampling on the rights of criminals but about cooperating with the press. In the course of the film, however, Harry learns that reporters are not all bad. In the end, he even saves one from a serial killer. Since the press is the ultimate enforcer of liberal norms throughout the whole series, if you are looking for an anti-establishment hero here, you're shit out of luck.

The Unz Review, February 8, 2021

DOCTOR ZHIVAGO

David Lean's epic anti-Communist romance *Doctor Zhivago* (1965) is a great and serious work of art. *Doctor Zhivago* was initially panned by the critics—probably not because it is a bad film, but because it was very bad for Communism. Nevertheless, it was immensely popular. It is still one of the highest grossing movies of all time, adjusted for inflation. It also won five Oscars—for Best Adapted Screenplay (Robert Bolt), Best Original Score (Maurice Jarre), Best Cinematography (Freddie Young), Best Art Direction, and Best Costume Design. (It was nominated for five other Oscars, but *The Sound of Music* won four of them, including Best Picture and Best Director.) Over the years, critics have also warmed to *Doctor Zhivago*, routinely including it in their "best" lists.

If *Doctor Zhivago* had been the work of almost any other director, it would have been hailed as his greatest film. But *Doctor Zhivago* was directed by David Lean, who had just completed one of the greatest films of all time, *Lawrence of Arabia* (1962). So *Doctor Zhivago* was bound to suffer somewhat from the comparison. But what's really remarkable about *Doctor Zhivago* is how little it disappoints.

The greatness of Lean's film comes into even sharper focus when you read Boris Pasternak's original novel. Pasternak was born in Imperial Russia in 1890 to a cultivated, upper-class Jewish family. His father was a painter, his mother a pianist. He achieved fame as a poet but fell out of favor with the Soviet Communist Party, found publication blocked, and ended up supporting himself as a translator, writing during his off hours "for the drawer."

Pasternak started *Doctor Zhivago* in the 1920s and finished it in 1956. It was smuggled out of the USSR by a dissident Italian Communist and published in 1957 in Italian translation. The first Russian edition of *Doctor Zhivago* was published in 1958 by the US Central Intelligence Agency, which sought to embarrass the Soviets by painting them as repressive cultural philistines who refused to publish one of those great Russian novels that few people manage to finish. Pasternak and *Zhivago* became a liberal *cause célèbre*. In 1958, Pasternak was awarded the Nobel Prize for Literature, which he refused under duress from the Soviet government. He died in 1960.

As a lover of the film, I expected to like the novel. I *wanted* to like the novel. But I found it surprisingly boring: a sprawling, flaccid story cluttered with useless and forgettable characters and digressions. Everything goes on much too long. It also seems unstructured. Good stories are unified from end to end. They have spines. But Pasternak's *Doctor Zhivago* is a spineless blob, held together with a tissue of increasingly unlikely accidents, as the main characters—in a Moscow of millions, in an empire of tens of millions—keep *bumping into one another*.

As a critique of Communism, Pasternak's novel is unfocused and superficial. We gather that Communism created chaos and unleashed ugliness and nihilism. But we don't really get a sense of why. Pasternak renders surfaces in a wordy, impressionistic blur. But when he tries to go deep, he comes out with lines like this: "Art is always, ceaselessly, occupied with two things. It constantly reflects on death and thereby constantly creates life." It sounds profound, but it is verbose, woolly-minded, and just isn't true.

Finally, the main character of Yuri Zhivago, a doctor and poet, is not particularly likeable. Thus it comes as a shock when one learns that Zhivago was Pasternak himself in thin disguise. The man must have loathed himself.

But I can't justly review Pasternak's novel, because like many readers, I tapped out before the end. On second thought, that is my review.

A great deal of the credit for turning Pasternak's mediocre novel into a great movie goes to screenwriter Robert Bolt, who also wrote the screenplay for *Lawrence of Arabia*, as well as the stage play and screen adaptation of *A Man for All Seasons*. Bolt removes needless characters and digressions, giving the story more of a spine. He also renders the horrors of Communism more crisply, giving greater insight into why they happened— and what the alternative is.

I will sketch out the film's basic plot, but I will skip over most of the details, leaving much to first-time viewers to discover. Yuri Zhivago is an orphan raised in Moscow by his wealthy godparents, the Gromekos. He is a gifted poet who has chosen medicine as a career. Just before the First World War, Yuri marries Tonya, the Gromekos' daughter, with whom he grew up. When the war begins, Yuri becomes a doctor at the front. After the Revolution, Yuri returns home to find the Gromekos living in one room of their mansion, the rest of which has been given over to seedy proletarians. Moscow is in the grip of the Red terror. Typhus and starvation are rampant.

Worse yet, Yuri is "not liked." His attitudes "have been noticed." His poetry has been deemed too "private" and "bourgeois." He does not conform to the party line, which increasingly consists of managing Communism's failures through lies, excuses, and scapegoating. Yuri's half-brother, Yevgraf, is a Bolshevik secret policeman. He knows Yuri and his family will not survive what is coming (we are now around the winter of 1919) and arranges for them to leave Moscow for the Urals, where they live in a cottage on the Gromekos' former estate.

While in the Urals, Tonya becomes pregnant with their second child, while Yuri begins an affair with Larissa ("Lara") Antipova, a young woman he met in Moscow and again at the front. Yuri is then torn away from both women by a band of Red partisans, who need a doctor and simply kidnap him. Two years later, Yuri manages to return to find the Gromekos have left Russia. He is reunited with Lara briefly but separated again. Lara, it turns out, is carrying his child. Both die some years later without ever being reunited, just two of the many millions of lives blighted and destroyed by a monstrous ideological enthusiasm.

The cast of *Doctor Zhivago* is uniformly strong. Casting an Egyptian Arab, Omar Sharif, as a Russian poet seemed odd to some. He doesn't look like Hollywood's idea of a typical Russian. (Originally, the role was offered to Peter O'Toole.) But the character of Zhivago was based on Pasternak, who didn't look typically Russian either.

The main problem bringing the character of Zhivago to the

screen is conveying that he is a poet without actually including any of his poetry. Lean solved this problem brilliantly, perhaps by borrowing a bit from Michael Powell's *The Red Shoes* where composer Julian Craster suddenly goes blank while we hear the music in his head. Lean asked Sharif to look as detached and absent-minded as possible—a pure spectator—while Maurice Jarre's brilliant music (his greatest score) communicates Yuri's flights of poetic imagination.

Julie Christie as Lara is so beautiful I don't think that the cast had to *pretend* to be in love with her, and her performance is excellent. Alec Guinness as Yevgraf, Tom Courtenay as Pasha, Geraldine Chaplin (Charlie's daughter) as Tonya Gromeko, Ralph Richardson as her father Alexander, and Siobhán McKenna as her mother Anna all turn in strong performances. Klaus Kinski has a memorable bit part as an anarchist turned into a slave laborer. But the most compelling performance is Rod Steiger as V. I. Komarovksy. He has many of the film's best lines. I wouldn't exactly call him a villain, although he's far from pure. Let's just say that he's very much alive.

Even though *Doctor Zhivago* portrays ugliness and horror, it is still a David Lean film, which means that it is a feast for the eyes. Some images are simply unforgettable: a vast throng of workers emerging from a tunnel under a red star; a vase of sunflowers weeping; the Goyaesque horrors of the civil war; the ice palace of Varykino.

But what sets *Doctor Zhivago* apart from most cinema is its fusion of powerful images and emotions with a philosophically insightful critique of Communism.

Before the revolution, *Doctor Zhivago* is constructed out of brilliant contrasts: between the grand boulevards and dirty side streets of Moscow, between the glittering world of high society and the drabness and desperation of the common people, between the healthy, neatly-uniformed men heading toward the front and the starved and ragged deserters fleeing it.

But once the Revolution happens, these contrasts are leveled—downwards, of course—until everyone is cold, starving, dirty, and terrified. The Communist slogans promising freedom, bread, and brotherhood all turn out to be lies. Communism delivered famine, not food—slavery and terror, not freedom. Communism did not ennoble mankind. It empowered cynicism, envy, and pettiness.

But many things didn't change. Russia was still governed by autocrats whom the masses feared. There were still haves and have nots. Both before and after the Revolution, one had to ask people "Can you read?" As the civil war ground on, those caught in the middle could no longer tell Red from White.

But the Soviets recreated the old autocracy on a much lower level, in part due to the sheer chaos and cost of the Revolution, in part because the Bolsheviks being materialists were blind to the essence of the civilization they seized, so they were capable of recapitulating it only as a brute farce. It was the old despotism stripped of all aristocratic magnanimity and refinement and infinitely more violent and cruel.

Four main issues separate the Bolsheviks from the old order.

First, they reject private life. "The private life is dead in Russia. History has killed it," says the Red commander Strelnikov. Private life is disdained as "bourgeois," as if men had never sought their own homes, their own families, and their own happiness before capitalism came along.

The problem with killing private life is that most of life happens in private, which brings us to the second contrast between the Bolsheviks and their enemies: theory versus practice, idealism versus life.

The Bolsheviks are idealists. They are theorists. So is Yuri, for that matter. Although he does choose general practice over medical research, he is by inclination a spectator, always gazing at the world, always trying to clear away the frost and fog to see more clearly.

Perhaps true theories never conflict with practice. But we mere mortals have to make do with half-baked theories, which inevitably clash with the mess of life. Fastidious idealists and dogmatic ideologues think they have the truth, however, which puts them on a collision course with practical life, which has lessons of its own to teach.

The conflict between theory and practice throws light on the climax of the movie, in which Yuri chooses to abandon Lara to

Komarovsky. It is a perverse and self-defeating choice. But it is not inexplicable. Yuri is theory. Komarovsky is the mess of life. Yuri is so repulsed by Komarovsky that he is willing to abandon the woman he loves rather than go with him. He may even be condemning himself to death.

What does Yuri do when he decides not to follow Lara? He retreats indoors to *watch* her through a window. Then he smashes out the window *to see her more clearly.*

When private life is suppressed, so are freedom of speech and truth-telling, which is the third gulf between Communism and the old order. Who are you to contradict the Party, which is the avatar of universal truth? And since truth is relative to history, and the party is the historical vanguard, truth becomes identical to whatever lie the party declares expedient. When the Party denies starvation and typhus are in Moscow, but Yuri sees them with his own eyes, he believes his eyes. That makes him a thought criminal. But it is truth-tellers, not liars, who pave the upward path for humanity.

(Robert Bolt clearly admired men who were willing to speak their minds and stand by their convictions, even at the risk of their own lives. Hence his depictions not just of Yuri Zhivago but of T. E. Lawrence and Sir Thomas More. Today, people would place all three heroes on the autism spectrum.)

The real center of the story is not Zhivago but Lara, who is loved by the three principal male characters: Zhivago, Pasha Antipov, and V. I. Komarovsky. But the affair between Zhivago and Lara only happens in the last half of the movie. To give the audience an idea of where the whole story was going, Bolt invented a frame for the story, set sometime in the 1940s, after the Second World War.

Yevgraf has come to a construction site. He is looking for his niece, Yuri and Lara's daughter, who had been lost some time in the 1920s. He is convinced that one of the workers, Tanya Komarova, is the girl he seeks. Then he narrates the whole film to her. At the end, Tanya denies she is his niece. "Don't you *want* to believe it?" he asks. This is the voice of the Party speaking, the party that set up wishful thinking as truth and coerced millions to go along with it. Tonya's reply is: "Not if it isn't true." Yevgraf's only comment is: "That's inherited."

This brings us to a fourth divide between Communism and the old order: hereditary gifts versus blank-slate egalitarianism. At the beginning of *Doctor Zhivago*, we learn that Yuri's dead mother had the "gift" of playing the balalaika. The Gromekos wonder if young Yuri has special gifts as well. At the end of the film, as Tanya walks away, Yevgraf learns she has a talent for the balalaika. "Who taught her?" he asks. "No one taught her," comes the reply. "It's a gift, then," says Yevgraf. These are the last words of the movie. In a way, they are the last words on Communism too. Empowering the gifted, not the mediocre, is the upward path for humanity.

Much of the best anti-communist literature is actually Left-wing: Orwell's *Nineteen Eighty-Four* and *Animal Farm*, for example. But a critique of communism that spotlights hereditary inequality belongs objectively to the Right. I have to credit this to David Lean, whose instincts and convictions were Rightist, since there are only the barest traces of this theme in the novel, and Bolt was a card-carrying Communist.

I find the end of *Doctor Zhivago* deeply moving because it offers a ray of hope, which is made visible in the form of a rainbow. Even though Communism can shatter families and whole civilizations, blood has won out in the end.

The Unz Review, September 25, 2021

The First *Dune* Trailer

If movies can have previews, why can't movie critics release "pre-reviews"? I ask because September 9, 2020 was the release date of the first trailer for the first half of Denis Villeneuve's adaptation of Frank Herbert's *Dune*.

Dune is one of the most anticipated movies of 2020. Trailers can build up a lot of excitement for a film, but they are immediately forgotten when the movie actually appears. Yet due to COVID-19, there is a real chance that more people will see the movie's trailer online than will see the actual film in theaters when it is released in December, and it may take months before the film is released on video and streaming services. Until that time, this and any subsequent trailers will eclipse the film itself.

Hence this little experiment. I want to prereview *Dune* based on the first trailer, plus other information gleaned from interviews and promotional materials. When (and if) you see the film, you can judge my prereview for prescience.

Any *Dune* adaptation is highly significant, because the novel is one of the great works of twentieth-century popular fiction, straddling both the sci-fi and fantasy genres. First published in 1965, *Dune* inspired legions of fans. Herbert wrote five sequels, and after his death his son Brian Herbert, together with Kevin J. Anderson, wrote more than a dozen *Dune* universe books, none of which I have read.

This movie is also significant because *Dune* has already inspired a series of screen adaptations. The first was by Alejandro Jodorowsky, which was highly influential even though it was never filmed.[1] David Lynch's 1984 *Dune* belongs in the category of great flawed films.[2] In 2000, the Sci-Fi Channel did a four-and-a-half-hour, three-part *Dune* miniseries, which I thought was pretty bad, although its sequel, the *Children of Dune* miniseries (2003) is surprisingly good.[3]

---

[1] See "*Jodorowsky's Dune*" in *Return of the Son of Trevor Lynch*.
[2] See "David Lynch's *Dune*," *Return of the Son of Trevor Lynch*.
[3] See "The Sci-Fi Channel's *Dune & Children of Dune*," *Return of the*

Dune also inspired screen homages and rip offs, most notably the vast *Star Wars* "franchise" — which is what the movie industry calls a "mythos."

Beyond that, a *Dune* adaptation is politically important because, as I have argued in "Archaeofuturist Fiction: Frank Herbert's *Dune*,"[4] Herbert's vision is deeply reactionary, antimodernist, and anti-liberal — and for quite compelling reasons.

Based on his movies *Sicario, Arrival,* and *Blade Runner 2049*,[5] Denis Villeneuve is a highly talented director of both science fiction and action films. Thus he was a good choice to direct *Dune*. But will *Dune* be a good movie? Will it be better than the Lynch or the Sci-Fi Channel's versions? (Yes, the Sci-Fi Channel adaptation was inferior to Lynch, but it included plot elements omitted by Lynch but not by Villeneuve, so it is reasonable to compare the two.) Will Villeneuve's film bear any relation to Jodorowsky's *Dune*? This three minute, five second trailer contains many clues.

Perhaps the chief flaw of Lynch's *Dune* is the clunky special effects. The Sci-Fi Channel version's effects also look cheap. Based on the trailer and Villeneuve's other science fiction efforts, this adaptation beats the rivals easily in this department. But this is largely due to advances in technology. The big question is whether Villeneuve's use of the new technology will be tasteful or vulgar. Based on the trailer, I can't yet decide. Aside from the sandworms, most of the effects in the trailer are static images that give one a sense of the *design* of vessels. But the test of effects is how well they move.

Another flaw of Lynch's *Dune* was a lack of grand landscape photography, especially on the watery world of Caladan and the desert planet of Arrakis. Lynch mostly used models without much context. Fortunately, the trailer shows us glimpses of dramatic vistas on both planets. Another flaw of Lynch's Arrakis is that many of the scenes, even in the desert, are dark, gloomy,

---

Son of Trevor Lynch.

[4] See Greg Johnson, "Archeofuturist Fiction: Frank Herbert's *Dune,*" *Counter-Currents*, August 15, 2014.

[5] See *"Blade Runner 2049," Return of the Son of Trevor Lynch.*

and ugly. Deserts are beautiful places, but you'd never know that from the Lynch film. Unfortunately, based on the new trailer, Villeneuve's Arrakis is almost as dark and ugly as Lynch's.

Villeneuve's movie dramatizes the first half of the *Dune* novel. The setting is more than 20,000 years in the future. Mankind has colonized the entire galaxy. No other intelligent life forms have been found. Because of the great distances between planets and the high cost of space travel, the political order is feudal. Noble houses (Dukes, Counts, Barons) rule entire planets, all of them subordinated to the Padishah Emperor on far-off Kaitain.

In addition to the noble houses, the other major powers are secretive initiatic societies dedicated to the development of human capacities.

The Spacing Guild has developed higher mathematics and prescience to traverse space.

The Bene Tleilax brotherhood, who are Sufis, has developed mnemonics and to create "mentats" (human computers, because artificial intelligence is religiously prohibited). They have also perfected genetic engineering techniques and yogic superpowers that allow them to shift shapes.

The Bene Gesserit sisterhood has developed skills in martial arts (the Weirding Way), memory sharing, hyper-observation and abductive reasoning,[6] seduction and sex, religious and political deception, and eugenics. Nobody knows what their ultimate goal is, but their proximal goal—which they are nearing—is breeding a superman, the Kwisatz Haderach (shortener of the way), a Janus-like figure who will be able to access all of his ancestors' memories as well as presciently peer into the future.

The most valuable resource in the universe is the so-called spice mélange, harvested from the sands of Arrakis, also known as Dune. The spice extends life but also expands the mind, thus it is used by the Guild, Tleilaxu, and Bene Gesserit in all their schemes to transcend the human condition.

The plot of *Dune* centers on the struggle of two noble houses, the Atreides and the Harkonnen, for control of Arrakis. But this is no normal aristocratic feud, because the most precious re-

---

[6] Greg Johnson, "Ben Novak's *Hitler and Abductive Logic*," *Counter-Currents*, December 31, 2019.

source in the universe is at stake, and one of the players, Paul Atreides, the fourteen-year-old heir to Arrakis, may well be the Kwisatz Haderach the sisterhood has been aiming for.

In the trailer the two primary characters are Paul Atreides, (played by Timothée Chalamet) and the Bene Gesserit Reverend Mother Gaius Helen Mohiam (Charlotte Rampling), who has come to test Paul's powers on the eve of the Atreides' departure to take control of Arrakis. Their scene and bits of dialogue from it are intercut with flashes of events to come as the Atreides are attacked on Arrakis by the Harkonnen. Paul and his mother are forced to flee to the desert, where they take refuge with the Fremen, the indigenous people of Arrakis.

I wasn't thrilled when I heard that Chalamet was cast as Paul. He does not look as good as Lynch's Kyle MacLaughlin or the Sci-Fi Channel's Alec Newman. He looks too delicate for the action sequences. But it is difficult to find an actor who can pass for a teenager and handle the role. Judging from the trailer, however, Chalamet has some steel in him. He will probably do the character credit.

One of the best sequences in Lynch's film is when the Reverend Mother tests Paul with "the box." We see glimpses of this in the trailer. Lynch's Reverend Mother was played beautifully by Siân Phillips. In the Sci-Fi series, she was played by a Czech actress, Zuzana Geislerová, who would have been forgettable if her stupid hats and heavy accent had not made her ridiculous. (She was much better in *Children of Dune*.) Based on the trailer, Rampling has poise and a great voice. She will do justice to the role.

The only other character in the trailer with significant lines is Duncan Idaho. (Baron Harkonnen and Chani have just a few words.) Although Idaho is a very important character, especially in the subsequent books, Lynch's adaptation left little room for Idaho, who was played by Richard Jordan. In the Sci-Fi miniseries, he was played by the forgettable James Watson. (In *Children of Dune* he was memorably played by Edward Atterton.) Villeneuve has cast the half-Hawaiian bodybuilder/action hero Jason Momoa to play Idaho.

Momoa is a very good choice. The first half of *Dune* contains a number of flight and fight scenes featuring Idaho that were cut by Lynch. These will make excellent action sequences, so Momoa with his heroic physique and martial arts skills will shine in them. As for Momoa's mixed-race ancestry: Duncan Idaho is really the *only* character in *Dune* who is described as not being fully Caucasoid. "Idaho" is an American Indian name, and the character is described as having high cheekbones, a somewhat flat face, and dark, wavy hair like a karakul sheep. Momoa actually looks the part.

Oscar Isaac plays Duke Leto Atreides. This is actually a better choice than Lynch's Jürgen Prochnow and Sci-Fi's William Hurt, since the Atreides are supposed to have a Mediterranean look (brunette, aquiline noses) and descend from the ancient Greek house of Atreus. Isaac, who is of Cuban, Guatemalan, and French ancestry, looks the part. Chalamet, who is half-French, half-Jewish, does so as well.

A beautiful Scottish-Swedish actress, Rebecca Ferguson, plays Lady Jessica, Paul's mother. She looks good, but not as good as Francesca Annis in Lynch's film. Saskia Reeves in the Sci-Fi series was too earthy. Alice Krige (the Borg Queen) was, however, utterly regal in *Children of Dune*.

Just as Kyle MacLachlan looked like he could have been the child of Jürgen Prochnow and Francesca Annis, Chalamet looks like he could be the son of Isaac and Ferguson.

Josh Brolin is a great choice for Gurney Halleck, the Atreides weapons master, who was memorably played by Patrick Stewart in Lynch's film.

I can't complain about Villeneuve casting a Chinaman to play the traitor, Dr. Wellington Yueh, even though he was not described as oriental. Thufir Hawat, the Atreides mentat and Master of Assassins, is played by Stephen McKinley Henderson, who has some black ancestry, but who looks quite white. So even this choice doesn't really stray from Herbert's vision.

As for the Harkonnens: Swedish actor Stellan Skarsgård plays the mad Baron, Vladimir Harkonnen. Dave Bautista plays his brutish nephew Glossu Rabban. Bautista is part Philippino but is in whiteface. The Baron's nephew, Feyd Rautha, does not appear in this movie. David Dastmalchian plays the Harkonnens' twisted mentat Piter De Vries. With his Armenian, Iranian, and European ancestry, Dastmalchian is a strange-looking guy and inspired casting for this role, which was memorably played by Brad Dourif in the Lynch film.

The Fremen leader Stilgar is played by Javier Bardem. He's a great actor and could be the best Stilgar yet, although Steven Berkoff was outstanding in *Children of Dune*.

Unfortunately, at this point Villeneuve's casting goes completely off the rails.

The character of the Imperial Planetologist, Dr. Liet Kynes, is described by Herbert as a natural leader of astonishing nobility as well as a scientific genius. He was memorably portrayed by Max von Sydow in Lynch's film. Villeneuve has decided to cast Kynes as a very black woman (Sharon Duncan-Brewster).

This is such outrageous political correctness that Villeneuve claimed that it was necessitated by his choice of a mulatto actress, Zendaya, to play Liet's daughter Chani, who becomes Paul's love interest. This argument is complete nonsense, however, since Zendaya presumably had a white male parent, so there was no need other than blatant racial appropriation to change Kynes' sex and race. And, of course, it is also racial appropriation to cast his daughter as a mulatto.

But it gets worse. Villeneuve casts two other Fremen with black actors as well. Harah, the wife of Stilgar, is played by Gloria Obianyo. Jamis, who fights with Paul and is killed, is played by Babs Olusanmokun.

This is a very bad sign, for it seems likely that Villeneuve wishes to portray the Fremen, who are the good guys, as primarily non-white. Given that their enemies, the Harkonnens, are depicted with shaved heads and conspicuously white skin, Villeneuve is turning *Dune* into an anti-white race-war prosecuted by non-whites and white race-mixers (Paul, Stilgar). This isn't Frank Herbert's *Dune*. Like every other piece of mainstream entertainment, Villeneuve's *Dune* is just another version of the White Genocide script.

The fact that America has been convulsed for months by people LARPing the same script is producing a great deal of fatigue for blacks and their white saviors. If COVID does not turn audiences away in droves, this blackface desecration of Herbert's vision just might. In the past, I could overlook this kind of casting if other parts of the story were good. I don't think I can do that anymore. This isn't a game. Our race and civilization are dying, and the politicians, journalists, activists, and artists who are promoting the Great Replacement are simply evil. Denis Villeneuve has desecrated *Dune*. This movie deserves to bomb as badly as Disney's *Star Wars*.

The Unz Review, September 24, 2020

Dune, Part I

Denis Villeneuve's *Dune*, Part I is now in theatres. I can't recommend it. It isn't terrible. It is merely mediocre. I found it dull to the eyes, grating to the ears, and a drag on my patience. Villeneuve spends 156 minutes and only gets halfway through the novel. David Lynch told the whole story in 137 minutes. Of course audiences are willing to sit through long movies if they are really good: Peter Jackson's *The Lord of the Rings* trilogy, for instance. But this film isn't in that league.

This is a pity, because Frank Herbert's original novel, published in 1965, is one of the twentieth century's great works of popular fiction, brilliantly synthesizing both the futurism of science fiction and the archaism of fantasy literature. Set more than 20,000 years in the future, *Dune* is the story of two noble houses fighting for control of the planet Arrakis or Dune, which is the sole source of the most valuable substance in the universe, a psychoactive drug known as "spice." *Dune* and its five sequels have been read by millions, inspiring whole universes of fan art and fan fiction, as well as a number of screen adaptations, to say nothing of rip-offs like *Star Wars*.

The first screen adaptation was Alejandro Jodorowsky's failed production, which may have been the greatest movie never made.[1] David Lynch's 1984 *Dune* was a flop, but it is a brilliant movie and remains the best version.[2] In 2000, the Sci-Fi Channel did a three-part *Dune* miniseries which was quite flawed. Its sequel, the *Children of Dune* miniseries (2003), dramatized *Dune*'s first two sequels, *Dune Messiah* and *Children of Dune*. It is excellent, despite its poor special effects.[3]

A *Dune* movie is also politically significant. Frank Herbert's vision of the future was deeply reactionary. He depicts a world where liberal democracy failed and has been replaced by a

---

[1] See "*Jodorowsky's Dune*," *Return of the Son of Trevor Lynch*.

[2] See "David Lynch's *Dune*," *Return of the Son of Trevor Lynch*.

[3] See "The Sci-Fi Channel's *Dune & Children of Dune*," *Return of the Son of Trevor Lynch*.

feudal imperium. In Herbert's imperium, artificial intelligence has been destroyed as oppressive and remains under the iron ban of a syncretic form of Christianity. Computer technology is a great leveler. Without it, humanity must fall back on natural gifts, which are rare. To refine these gifts and make them more common, eugenics is practiced. Biological sex differences are recognized. Bureaucracies are disdained as repressive instruments of equality and fairness. The story of Leto II in *Children of Dune* and *God Emperor of Dune* is opposed to surveillance and empire in favor of freedom and pluralism. Herbert believed that mankind would never be safe unless we could free ourselves from the leveling gaze of a single, universal political order.[4]

Beyond that, Herbert has quite compelling reasons for his belief that liberal democracy will not take mankind to the stars and that mankind can only spread across the galaxy by returning to archaic social forms like hereditary monarchy, feudalism, and initiatic spiritual orders.[5]

Herbert's vision of the future is also gloriously Eurocentric. His imperium is medieval Europe writ large, while his vision of Arrakis and its native people, the Fremen, is based on Arabia, i.e., the Near East—"near" in relation to Europe, that is.

Thus from a Right-wing, European identitarian viewpoint, it would be wonderful to have a really good movie to sell Herbert's vision to a whole new generation.

It is always remarkable when the modern film industry adapts inherently reactionary literature like *The Lord of the Rings*,[6] *Dune*, or—on a much lower level—*The Twilight Saga*.[7] Of course the industry would prefer to churn out stories in which whites, especially white men, are ritualistically humiliated and replaced by nonwhites and strong women. With in-

---

[4] See Greg Johnson, "The Golden Path: Frank Herbert's *Children of Dune & God Emperor of Dune*," *Counter-Currents*, January 12, 2021.

[5] See Greg Johnson, "Archeofuturist Fiction: Frank Herbert's *Dune*," *Counter-Currents*, August 15, 2014.

[6] Reviewed in *Trevor Lynch's White Nationalist Guide to the Movies*, ed. Greg Johnson (San Francisco: Counter-Currents, 2012).

[7] Reviewed in *Trevor Lynch's White Nationalist Guide to the Movies*.

herently reactionary and Eurocentric stories, they have less room for propaganda.

Dune does have an anti-colonialist aspect, but that is Leftwing only if one ignores the fact that ethnic nationalism is anti-imperialist and anti-colonialist as well. *Dune* also involves a struggle for a scarce resource, but that lends itself to vulgar Leftist materialism only if one ignores the fact that the resource's primary use is spiritual and that the imperium is ruled by honor-driven aristocrats and mystical initiates, not by merchants. Thus the best Villeneuve could do to subvert *Dune* is play up these aspects (e.g., in the opening narration), hope nobody asks questions, and stuff the cast with non-whites and strong women, lest Herbert's fans think that race and sex differences actually matter.

Race clearly mattered to Herbert. He envisioned all of his characters as, if not European, at least as Caucasoid. The imperium is European. The Fremen people of Arrakis believed themselves descended from Egyptians. The only character with any hint of non-Caucasoid ancestry is Duncan Idaho, who was described as having high cheekbones and narrow eyes. Idaho, of course, is an American Indian name, so Herbert may have been hinting at some such ancestry. But Idaho also has wavy hair—likened to a karakul sheep—which is not an American Indian trait.

The earlier adaptations of *Dune* have been faithfully Eurocentric, in keeping with Herbert's vision. Villeneuve's new movie puts nonwhites in key roles.

The character of the Imperial Planetologist, Dr. Liet Kynes, was memorably portrayed by Max von Sydow in Lynch's film. Here he is played by a very black woman (Sharon Duncan-Brewster). Villeneuve even invents a scene where she is a bit sassy before being swallowed by a giant sandworm. It isn't quite "Say hello to my little fren'," but that's the vibe they were driving for.

Liet's daughter Chani is played by a mulatto actress, Zendaya. Villeneuve tries his best to make her glamorous, but with her flat nose and big lips, she's a solid five.

Half-Hawaiian bodybuilder/martial artist Jason Momoa

plays Duncan Idaho and actually looks the part.

Doctor Wellington Yueh, despite his name, was not described as Oriental or cast that way in previous adaptations. Here he is played by a Chinaman.

Some minor Fremen characters are also blacked-up: Harah, the wife of Stilgar, is played by Gloria Obianyo. Jamis is played by Babs Olusanmokun.

Given that the villains, the Harkonnens, are depicted as bald headed and pasty white—with part-Filipino Dave Bautista in whiteface as Rabban—I feared that Villeneuve wished to turn *Dune* into a race-war between putatively racist whites and a coalition of non-whites and white race-mixers. But the movie blunts that message by making some of the villains nonwhite as well.

Near the beginning, Villeneuve invents a scene in which the Emperor's herald proclaims the Atreides family stewards of Arrakis. The scene hints at the grandeur of the imperium and the ethos of the Atreides, but its main purpose seems to be to put a very strange looking black man in a prominent role as the Emperor's herald. But the Emperor is one of the bad guys.

Later in the movie, the Oriental doctor Yueh turns out to be a traitor.

At the end of the movie, the young hero Paul Atreides is called out to fight Jamis, a cocky, pigheaded, and deranged black man. Paul tries to avoid the fight, then deescalate the fight, but he is finally forced to kill Jamis. This is not the sort of parable I expected in the present Year of Our Floyd. It makes you feel for Derek Chauvin. Maybe BLM will riot in memory of this miscreant too. George Floyd was no more real a victim than Jamis, and the movie industry has deep pockets.

Dune is an objectively good story. Casting nonwhite actors in white roles doesn't change that. But it is a calculated insult to the author and to white audiences, who are getting mighty sick of it. It is also simply a farce, like casting blacks to play Anne Boleyn or Marshal Mannherheim. When one sees such casting in movie theatres, one should openly scoff. Of course all this diversity casting simply invited the charge that *Dune* is now a "white savior" movie, something that could not be said about earlier adaptations.

How do the performances in this *Dune* compare to earlier versions?

Timothée Chalamet is good as Paul Atreides, but he is not better than Lynch's Kyle MacLachlan or the Sci-Fi Channel's Alec Newman. Unlike the other Pauls, Chalamet actually looks and acts like a teenager.

Oscar Isaac is good as Duke Leto Atreides, far better than Sci-Fi's mumbling William Hurt. My main objection to Isaac is not so much his acting as the script they give him, which depicts him as soft and emotional, more like a democratic politician than a hereditary ruler with the charisma to evoke fanatical loyalty. Lynch's Jürgen Prochnow strikes a better balance between warmth and dignity, but he still fails to bring Herbert's Leto to life. A good portrayal of Leto must answer the question: Why would anyone die for this man?

Rebecca Ferguson is good as Paul's mother Jessica, but not better than Francesca Annis in Lynch's film. As with Isaac, Ferguson spends a lot of time showing her emotions, which makes her more relatable but less formidable. Ferguson's freckled complexion is also distractingly out of place on a high-born woman. Francesca Annis better captures the coolness and strength one would expect of an initiate of the Bene Gesserit sisterhood. The best Jessica of all is Alice Krige in *Children of Dune*.

I had high hopes for Charlotte Rampling as Bene Gesserit Reverend Mother Mohiam. She is good but not better than Siân Phillips in Lynch's film.

I also had high hopes for Jason Momoa as Duncan Idaho, but even in the trailers he looked puffy and out of shape, and his performance is inferior to the best Duncan, Edward Atterton in *Children of Dune*.

I thought Javier Bardem was a good choice for Stilgar, but he looks terrible (his face is far too puffy to be a Fremen), he mumbles his lines, and he lacks the charisma of leadership. The best Stilgar is Steven Berkoff in *Children of Dune*, although he overacts.

Swedish actor Stellan Skarsgård is quite disappointing as Baron Vladimir Harkonnen. He plays the Baron like Marlon Brando's Colonel Kurz in *Apocalypse Now*. Kenneth MacMillan's over-the-top but unforgettable Baron in Lynch's film is more successful at communicating his madness. Ian McNeice in the Sci-Fi miniseries is more successful in communicating his intelligence and urbanity. Interestingly, Villeneuve's Baron is not depicted as a homosexual pedophile. But maybe that side of him will emerge in *Dune* Part II, or maybe it has been omitted entirely, since ascribing such behavior to the villain might strike a bit close to home for Hollywood.

Villeneuve's Gurney Halleck, Dr. Yueh, Thufir Hawat, Shadout Mapes, Piter de Vries, and Rabban are all adequate but not superior to Lynch's cast.

Even though Villeneuve has plenty of time for characterization, the only characters in this film who seem better fleshed out than in Lynch's film are Duke Leto and Duncan Idaho. Most of the other characters are less well-drawn and real than in the Lynch film.

Prophetic dreams and visions play a huge role in *Dune*. Nobody beats David Lynch in that department.

The chief flaw of Lynch's *Dune* are the special effects. The Sci-Fi Channel has cheap special effects too. Villeneuve's special effects are superior, but what really matters is how the technology is used. This brings us to the question of design, where Lynch is again superior. Villeneuve's ships, cityscapes, and interiors are not particularly interesting or imaginative. I liked Lynch's "ornithopter" designs better simply because they didn't look like they could fly, which made them seem far more futuristic than Villeneuve's design. The city of Arrakeen is less detailed, realistic, or interesting than countless pre-digital science fiction worlds, including the original *Star Wars* and *Blade Runner*, which they clearly rip off. So much money and technology went into this movie's sets, designs, and effects, yet very little talent and taste.

A major failing of Lynch's *Dune* is a lack of grand landscape photography. Villeneuve gives us some spectacular landscapes on the watery world of Caladan, but like Lynch, he depicts the desert world of Arrakis as dark, gloomy, and ugly. This is a shocking lapse of taste and simple, basic showmanship. Deserts are beautiful places. Just look at David Lean's *Lawrence of Ara-*

bia. After writing that last sentence, I was astonished to learn that some of *Dune* was actually shot in Wadi Rum, one of the most spectacular Jordan locations used by Lean. You'd never know it from the looks of things.

Lean, by the way, would have been the perfect director for *Dune*. He knew how to create epics. He knew how to photograph deserts, palaces, hovels, and battles, and make every frame look like a great European painting. Imagine if after *Dr. Zhivago* Lean's next project with screenwriter Robert Bolt was *Dune* rather than *Ryan's Daughter*. It would have been poetic, given that a major influence on *Dune* was T. E. Lawrence's *Seven Pillars of Wisdom*.

Technology is supposedly progressing, yet cost-cutting has brought us a world where air travel is slower and less comfortable than 60 years ago, where the Concorde was scrapped, and where movie images contain less detail and depth of focus, to say nothing of beauty. If I were running things, 70mm cameras and supersonic jets would be as standard as seatbelts.

Which *Dune* adaptation is most faithful to the original novel? All three take liberties, but based on the first half of Villeneuve's version, it is the most faithful to Herbert's book. But his fidelity consists in including a lot of chases, fights, and escapes that feel like standard pulp science fiction fare. They make for good action sequences in the film, but they really aren't necessary to reveal character, illustrate deeper themes, or advance the overall story, which is why Lynch dropped them.

Jodorowsky wanted Pink Floyd and Magma to compose the music for his *Dune*. Brian Eno contributed the best music to Lynch's film, but Toto was responsible for most of the score. It is adequate, but it is not Pink Floyd. I don't remember a single note from the Sci-Fi series score. Villeneuve hired Hans Zimmer for his *Dune*. Based on the first trailer, which incorporates Pink Floyd's "Eclipse" from *Dark Side of the Moon*, I had hoped that Zimmer's score would be an homage to Pink Floyd. He tries to do that, but it is mostly oppressive, tuneless electronic noise. I wish Villeneuve had hired Brian Tyler, who did a magnificent orchestral score for the *Children of Dune* miniseries.

Based on his movies *Sicario* and *Arrival*—which are well-scripted, tightly directed, artful, and thoughtful action and science fiction films—I had hoped that Denis Villeneuve would develop into the next Christopher Nolan. But he has disappointed me with *Blade Runner 2049*[8] and now *Dune*. These were gutsy projects, because they invited comparisons with Ridley Scott's original *Blade Runner* and David Lynch's *Dune*. Sadly, in both cases, Villeneuve comes out the lesser director. But in today's film industry, that won't hurt him a bit. He has a bright future as the next Joss Whedon or Zack Snyder, aborted talents who busily churn out high-budget, lowbrow spectacles.

The best way to sum up my feelings about Villeneuve's *Dune* is that, even though he has reserved three fascinating characters—the Emperor, Feyd Rautha, and Alia—for *Dune, Part II*, I'm not the least bit curious to see it.

The Unz Review, October 25, 2021

---

[8] See "Blade Runner 2049," *Return of the Son of Trevor Lynch*.

THE ELEPHANT MAN

David Lynch's second feature film, *The Elephant Man* (1980), is one of his finest works. In many ways, *The Elephant Man* is Lynch's most conventional "Hollywood" film. (*Dune* too is a "Hollywood" film, but a failed one.[1]) The cast of *The Elephant Man* is quite distinguished, including John Hurt, Anthony Hopkins, Sir John Gielgud, Dame Wendy Hiller, and Anne Bancroft. The film was produced by Mel Brooks, who left his name off so that people would not expect a comedy.

The Elephant Man was a commercial success and a critical hit. It received eight Academy Award nominations, including Best Picture and Best Director. It also prompted the Academy to create a new award for makeup the next year. *The Elephant Man* won the British Academy Film Awards for Best Film, Best Actor (Hurt), and Production Design, as well as the French César Award for Best Foreign Film. It is routinely included in critics' "best" lists.

Although *The Elephant Man* is about a hideously deformed sideshow freak, Lynch's treatment is sentimental and compassionate, not lurid and exploitative. Indeed, *The Elephant Man* is wholesome, heartwarming, and quite explicitly Christian, which is surprising given that Lynch, being a longtime devotee of Transcendental Meditation, is more Hindu than Christian.

Yet *The Elephant Man* is unmistakably the work of the director of *Eraserhead*.[2] It is exquisitely shot in black and white by cinematographer Freddie Francis, who later worked on *The Straight Story*.[3] *The Elephant Man* also features Lynch's trademark surreal montages, low-tech special effects, and meticulous sound design, created with his longtime collaborator Alan Splet. Like *Eraserhead*, *The Elephant Man* treats technology as an almost demonic force and depicts urban life as hellish and al-

---

[1] Reviewed in *Return of the Son of Trevor Lynch*.

[2] Reviewed in *Return of the Son of Trevor Lynch*.

[3] Reviewed in *Trevor Lynch: Part Four of the Trilogy*, ed. Greg Johnson (San Francisco: Counter-Currents, 2020).

ienating. Finally, the grotesque subject matter and sentimental manner of treating it are also quite Lynchian.

The story of *The Elephant Man* can be summarized quite briefly. Joseph Merrick (called John Merrick in the film) was born in England in 1862. By the age of five, he began developing abnormally and became shockingly deformed, probably due to Proteus Syndrome. Merrick's skull became massively enlarged and distorted. His right arm became enlarged and useless, but his other arm was normal. His spine was alarmingly twisted, affecting his gait. His body was covered with wart-like growths. He also had difficulty breathing. His head was so massive that he had to sleep sitting up. If he slept normally, he would have been asphyxiated.

Unable to work, Merrick began to exhibit himself as a sideshow freak, which provided a precarious living due to police bans and dishonest carnies. In 1883, a surgeon named Frederick Treves discovered Merrick and exhibited him at a meeting of the Pathological Society of London. Merrick and Treves developed a friendship. Merrick's plight became a *cause célèbre* of British high society. Championed by Queen Victoria herself, Merrick was given a permanent home at London Hospital, where he died at the age of twenty-seven. Lynch's film takes some liberties with the story but conveys the essence.

The opening montage of *The Elephant Man* is pure *Eraserhead*. Like the opening of *Eraserhead*, it is an allegory of a monstrous birth. We begin with the eyes of a woman in a Victorian photograph. Later we learn this is John Merrick's mother. We hear an ominous mechanical humming. Then we see elephants, the mother's face overlaid. The elephants freeze then approach. We hear their lowing and trumpeting. We see a woman thrown to the ground and writhing in slow motion terror, to increasingly distorted sounds. (In *Lost Highway*,[4] Lynch films the transformation of Fred Madison into Pete Dayton in a similar way.) Then we see white smoke rising against a dark backdrop. A baby cries. The sequence is based on the side-show origin myth of the Elephant Man, premised on the idea that a child's

---

[4] Reviewed in *Trevor Lynch: Part Four of the Trilogy*.

development can be shaped by maternal experiences.

Next we see a Victorian circus. The camera focuses on a well-dressed gentleman in a top hat. This is Anthony Hopkins as Dr. Frederick Treves. Although Treves looks like the embodiment of Victorian propriety, he enters the sideshow through an exit door marked No Admittance. This transgressive gesture is repeated a few seconds later. We catch glimpses of standard freaks, such as a bearded lady. Then we meet a horrified woman being comforted by a gentleman. Treves plunges into the darkness from which they emerged.

Treves' destination is the Elephant Man exhibit. When Treves arrives, however, the curtain is closed. The police are shutting the exhibit down for being degrading and "monstrous." The "proprietor," Mr. Bytes, is a fictional composite of the carneys with whom the real Merrick worked. Brilliantly played by Freddie Jones—who was Thufir Hawat in *Dune* and had a cameo in *Wild at Heart*[5]—Bytes is a seedy drunkard and sadist.

Treves is determined to see the Elephant Man and eventually tracks Bytes down for a private showing. In *Blue Velvet*,[6] Sandy is not sure if Jeffrey is a detective or a pervert. Likewise, in *The Elephant Man*, we are led to wonder if Treves is a doctor or a pervert. Bytes has Treves pegged as a pervert—a fellow pervert—and leeringly intimates that they share a common secret. Later Bytes speaks to Treves practically like a pimp: "I move in the proper circles, for this type of thing . . . In fact, anything at all, if you take my meaning."

But when Treves finally sees the Elephant Man, he does not view him with a doctor's objective curiosity, or a pervert's salacious leer. His face registers utter shock. Then a solitary tear appears in his eye.

Treves is still, however, a man of science—and a man of some ambition. Thus he arranges to exhibit Merrick to the Pathological Society of London.

Later, after Merrick has been severely beaten by Bytes, Treves admits him to the London Hospital. Initially, he is placed in an isolation ward near the clock tower, Lynch's gentle homage

---

[5] Reviewed in *Return of the Son of Trevor Lynch*.
[6] Reviewed in *Trevor Lynch: Part Four of the Trilogy*.

to *The Hunchback of Notre Dame*.

At this point, we are thirty minutes into the film and still have not yet seen Merrick's face. Lynch handles this slow reveal masterfully, and once we see Merrick, it takes a while before we see him up close. By taking his time, Lynch not only builds suspense, he also fully humanizes the character before revealing the full horror of his appearance. Also, it should be noted that Hurt's Elephant Man costume and makeup are not as grotesque as the real Joseph Merrick.

Up to this point, Merrick has said nothing either. Treves has assumed he is an imbecile. But this is not true. Eventually, he gets Merrick to speak.

Merrick's presence is opposed by Francis Carr Gomm—the Governor of the hospital warmly portrayed by Sir John Gielgud—on the grounds that the hospital does not admit incurables. Nevertheless, Carr Gomm wishes to meet Merrick, and Treves believes that if the interview goes well, Merrick might be allowed to stay. But the conversation is quite awkward, and when Merrick repeats the same phrases in contexts where they make no sense, Carr Gomm thinks he is an imbecile who has been coached.

But when Merrick recites the 23rd Psalm, and then begins to open up, both Treves and Carr Gomm are thunderstruck. They both had hoped Merrick was an imbecile, because intelligence could only magnify his suffering. But Merrick has not just suffered greatly, he has retained his humanity. He has managed to remain a sensitive and decent human being, a beautiful soul in a hideous material prison, a theme that also harmonizes with the essentially Gnostic outlook of *Eraserhead*. Carr Gomm is overcome with compassion. He vows to find some way to give Merrick a safe haven. The whole sequence is immensely moving.

Carr Gomm writes a letter to the *Times* publicizing Merrick's plight and asking for support, which brings Merrick to the attention of high society and low.

Queen Victoria dispatches her daughter-in-law, Alexandra, Princess of Wales to read her letter to the board of the London Hospital in support of giving Merrick permanent residency.

Upon completing the letter, Alexandra looks directly at the board members and says, "I am sure you gentlemen may be counted on to do the Christian thing." Which they do. When Carr Gomm, Treves, and the stern hospital matron Mrs. Mothershead bring Merrick the good news, he is overcome with emotion, as is any viewer who doesn't have a severely deformed heart.

A prominent actress, Madge Kendal (Anne Bancroft) wishes to meet Merrick. So do the drunkards and floozies who associate with London Hospital's seedy night porter, Sonny Jim (a name reused by Lynch for Dougie's little boy in *Twin Peaks: The Return*).

By day, Merrick receives actresses and society matrons bearing lavish gifts. These are sentimental well-meaning souls who want to marvel at a triumph of the human spirit. By night, he is assailed by raucous drunkards who pay Sonny Jim a few coins to laugh at the Elephant Man.

Mrs. Mothershead, played beautifully by Wendy Hiller, disapproves of both sets of visitors. She sacks Sonny Jim when she finds out about his shows. She also reproaches Treves for allowing the more genteel gawkers, saying that Merrick is once again a sideshow curiosity.

This prompts one of the most touching scenes in the movie. Treves has a sleepless night over the question, "Am I a good man, or am I a bad man?" Treves is a good man, and part of what makes him good is his willingness to entertain such questions. Nobody can watch *The Elephant Man* without admiring the Victorian middle and upper classes: their exquisite manners, their moral earnestness, and their desire to edify and beautify a nation wrecked by Blake's "dark Satanic mills."

Treves' moral crisis is paired with a Lynchian montage of Merrick's night terrors. As with the severed ear in *Blue Velvet*, Lynch's camera approaches then dives into a hole, this time the eyehole in Merrick's hood. We follow pipes to the sound of mechanical chuffing like Merrick's labored breathing. We see men laboring in factories with machines, bringing to mind *Eraserhead*'s Man in the Planet, who is a Gnostic symbol of the spirit's bondage to matter. A leering crowd emerges from the darkness, holding a mirror to Merrick's terrified face, which is intercut with elephant parts. Then he flashes back to the beatings he has received from Bytes. Lynch is a master of putting dreams on film: prophetic dreams, wish-fulfillment dreams, and nightmares.

The contrast between good and bad men is underscored one night when Bytes slips in among the last batch of Sonny Jim's revelers and kidnaps Merrick, taking him to a circus on the Continent. Merrick's health is declining, however, and he cannot perform. A drunken Bytes beats him then locks him in a cage next to some angry, threatening baboons.

It is a terrifying sequence, using an odd technique that crops up in *The Straight Story* and *Twin Peaks: The Return*, in which Lynch places the camera and microphone far from the action, framing it in a vast space and forcing the viewer to strain to see and hear what is happening. It is a return to the static cameras of the early talkies, which often seem like filmed stage plays.

This circus sequence specifically brings to mind Todd Browning's classic *Freaks*, where sideshow freaks band together to avenge one of their own. In *The Elephant Man*, however, they simply liberate Merrick from his cage and put him on a boat at Ostend to carry him back to London.

When Merrick arrives at Liverpool Street Station, he is harassed by urchins who want to know why his head is so big. Fleeing, he accidentally knocks over a little girl. Her mother shrieks an alarm. A large crowd pursues him. The monster is unmasked then cornered in a toilet, where he proclaims the famous lines "I am not an animal. I am a human being! I am a man! I am a man!" Then the police arrive and return Merrick to his home at London Hospital.

Merrick's life is nearing its end. Mrs. Kendal and Princess Alexandra take him to the theatre, where he is enchanted by what appears to be a children's pantomime of *Puss in Boots*. The play montage is pure Lynch, but at his most naïve and winsome, using special effects from the silent era less to depict the story than Merrick's childlike rapture.

When Merrick returns to his room, he completes work on his model of Saint Phillip's Cathedral, then signs it "John Merrick." To Samuel Barber's hauntingly melancholy Adagio for Strings, Merrick says "It is finished," bringing to mind the words of Christ on the cross. Then Merrick looks at a picture of a sleeping child and decides to lie down to sleep like a normal person, which he knows will kill him. As he breathes his last, the camera takes our eyes to the picture of Mrs. Kendal, then the picture of his mother, then the model of the cathedral, rising with the music to focus on the cross on the highest spire. Then we see the stars, and begin to move quickly among them, shades of *Dune*.

Merrick's mother begins reciting lines from Alfred Lord Tennyson's "Nothing Will Die":

Never, oh! never, nothing will die.
The stream flows,
The wind blows,
The cloud fleets,
The heart beats,
Nothing will die.

In the original the first line is a question, but in the movie it is a declarative statement. The poem continues "Nothing will die; All things will change." This flatly contradicts the Christian idea of the immortality of the human soul, affirming instead the essentially pagan and naturalistic idea that all things merely change, one into another, which is also consistent with Hindu and Buddhist ideas that reincarnation is not the transmigration of consciousness from one body to another, but more akin to one flame lighting another before going out.

As she recites, the mother's face appears beyond the stars in a halo of light, which sucks in the white smoke associated at the beginning with Merrick's birth, then finally fills the screen. The End.

There is no evidence that the real Elephant Man killed himself this way. Lynch does not treat it as a death of despair. In fact, Merrick tells Treves that he is happy every day of his life. Near the end of the movie, it is established that Merrick is dying, probably of a problem with his lungs. If abnormal things are growing on the outside, surely they are growing on the inside as well. Maybe Merrick has accepted that death is imminent and decides to end on a happy note and spare himself further suffering.

Lynch treats Merrick's death like an apotheosis, turning him into a patron saint of the unfortunate.

Lynch is masterful in his treatment of the grotesque, which is akin to the sublime because it both attracts and repels us. But there is a false note when Merrick explains people's reaction to him by saying, "We fear things that we don't understand." In what sense do people *fear* the Elephant Man? Is their fear rational or irrational? Do they suffer from a "phobia" like "homophobia," "transphobia," or "Islamophobia"? Should we shame them for cowardice and congratulate ourselves for our bravery?

In truth, most people are not afraid of Merrick. They are simply disgusted and horrified by him. Thus it is false to accuse them of "fear." Moreover, disgust and horror are simple biological reactions to anything unwholesome. Such reactions protect us from dangers: disease, tainted food and water, etc. Thus it is doubly false to claim this is an *irrational* fear: a phobia. Is disgust simply a *disguised* form of fear? Maybe, but it *feels* different, so isn't it a *different* feeling? If disgust is a fear, however, it is not an irrational one.

We are all curious about bad things that befall other human beings: accidents, illnesses, deformities. If we satisfy our curiosity, the result is horror. At this point, however, there are two basic ways to deal with horror: mockery or compassion.

As Anthony M. Ludovici argued in *The Secret of Laughter*, laughter is glorying in one's superior fitness.[7] Forced or nervous laughter, however, is an attempt to reassure oneself that one really is more fit.

But the horror we feel is ultimately based on the recognition that misfortune can befall us all. No, the Elephant Man's affliction is not contagious, thank God. But none of us is immune to

---

[7] Anthony M. Ludovici, *The Secret of Laughter* (London: Constable, 1932); extensive excerpts are reprinted in *The Lost Philosopher: The Best of Anthony M. Ludovici*, ed. John V. Day (Berkeley, Cal.: ETSF, 2003). See Chapter 6, under the heading "Humor."

misfortune of one sort or another. Compassion is the recognition of this fact: one sees oneself in the other and feels for him as one feels for oneself. Mockery is a lie and evasion, compassion an admission of the truth.

As Lynch's career unfolded, he would take us to darker and darker places. He would wring laughter from us over terrible things. But he always sided with the better angels of our nature in the end.

The Unz Review, January 20, 2021

FANNY & ALEXANDER

Ingmar Bergman's *Fanny and Alexander* (1982) is one of his finest works. *Fanny and Alexander* runs 312 minutes—more than five hours. Bergman cut it down to a 188-minute version for theatrical release. The full version was shown as a miniseries on Swedish television but was also released in theaters, making it one of the longest theatrical films in history.

Fanny and Alexander was Bergman's most popular film. It was also highly praised by critics, winning four Academy awards, including Best Foreign Language Film, and three Guldbagge Awards from the Swedish Film Institute, including Best Film.

Bergmann originally intended *Fanny and Alexander* to be his cinematic swan song, thus he made it a summation of his life and work. The story is semi-autobiographical and reprises many of the themes explored in his other films. The result is a life-affirming benediction, a triumph over darkness.

Fanny and Alexander feels like an adaptation of one of those sprawling nineteenth-century novels that you've never read, but it was entirely Bergman's work. The film is set in Uppsala, Sweden in 1907–1909. It depicts *haute bourgeois* life at the very peak of European civilization before the explosion of the Great War.

This is the story of the fabulously wealthy Ekdahl family, headed by the widowed grandmother Helena, a former actress. Helena speaks about how she loved to act, but her greatest happiness was playing the role of a mother, a role she continues to play as she looks out for her three grown sons, their wives, and a growing brood of grandchildren. The Ekdahls are a very close family. They live in vast and sumptuous apartments occupying two floors of the same building, as well as sharing a Swedish country house and a retreat in Provence.

The film begins and ends with lavish celebrations—a Christmas and a christening—that illustrate the customs, manners, and fashions of the time as well as the Ekdahls' unconventional ethos. These sequences are visually dazzling, captured in blazing color. It is pure decorator porn from a director usually associated with austere settings captured in stark black and white.

The prologue and first act take place on the day before Christmas and Christmas morning of 1907. First, the family attends (and some of them perform in) a Christmas pageant at the theater they own. Then there is Christmas dinner—which in Sweden takes place on Christmas Eve—followed the next morning by the family setting off in horse-drawn sleighs for an early service at the cathedral.

The Christmas sequence introduces most of the major characters and a host of minor ones, all beautifully realized. Helena presides benignly over the festivities but fears the passage of time is carrying her from her beautiful life into the "dirty life" of decrepitude and death.

Helena has three sons. The eldest, Oscar, is a sickly, quiet, and introverted actor and the manager of the family theater who is married to the tall and radiant blonde, Emilie, also an actress, who is the mother of their two children, Fanny and Alexander

Carl, the middle son, is a professor. He is a mediocrity and a depressive. He's also a tactless boor, drunkard, and gambler in an unhappy and childless marriage with a German woman, Lydia, whom he abuses.

The youngest son, Gustav Adolf, is an ebullient restauranter married to Alma, the mother of his three children who good-naturedly encourages him in his extra-marital affairs.

Alexander is a wide-eyed boy of ten with a vivid imagination. Although he might not be imagining things when he sees ghosts. Fanny is his shy and quiet eight-year-old sister. Maj is their nursemaid and the object of Gustav Adolf's current adulterous designs. Isak Jacobi, a Jewish antique dealer and moneylender, is an old family friend and former lover of Helena.

The Ekdahls are all highly intelligent and sensitive. With the exception of Carl, they have exquisite manners and tastes. But although they are pillars of the community and uphold most of the social forms, they are also quite unconventional.

When Gustav Adolf puts on a Christmas reception for the cast and crew of the family theater, he tells the waiters in his restaurant to not display the slightest trace of snobbery. When the family sits down to Christmas dinner, they eat in the kitchen, sharing a huge table with the family servants—which makes some of the older servants uncomfortable. These gestures are attempts at aristocratic magnanimity, which seeks to lessen the pains of social hierarchy for those on the lower rungs.

Then there is the matter of extra-marital affairs. Helena, Emilie, and Gustav Adolf are all philanderers, all apparently with the knowledge and the approval—or at least the acquiescence—of their spouses. Helena, Emilie, and Oscar are all theater people, so perhaps such bohemian morals come with the territory. It is, however, rather unrealistic to suggest that the Ekdahls never get burned while playing with the heart's fire. Helena is also something of a feminist, dismissing Strindberg as "that nasty misogynist."

Finally, the close friendship with Isak Jacobi strikes me as unconventional for the time. He is literally at every family function. Yes, they live close to one another. Yes, Isak and the Ekdahls are both in business. Isak's nephew Aron is even in the theater business as a puppet maker. But would this really be enough to overcome the religious and social divides?

The first version of the script—which is very different from the final film—may throw some light on the connection, for Helena Ekdahl's maiden name is given as Mandelbaum, a very Jewish name. This throws light on an odd conversation at the very beginning of the movie, when Helena's maid Ester remarks on how odd it is that they have celebrated 43 Christmases together. Of course it would be odd if Helena had been born a Jew.

Ester, too, is a very Jewish name, but Ester worked as a Christian missionary in China, and, in the first version of the script is said to have warned Alexander that Isak kidnaps gentile children and drinks their blood.

However, if Bergman's original intent was to make Helena Jewish, it seems unfulfilled, since there's nothing particularly Jewish about how Helena is portrayed by the acclaimed Swedish actress Gunn Wållgren.

If any single word describes the Ekdahls, it is "pagan." Although their Christmas celebrations are bookended by a nativity pageant and a church service, everything between is pure pagan revelry and carousing, without a wink of sleep.

Although the Ekdahls are fully aware of the dark and tragic dimensions of life, they flee those terrors by building up the ramparts of what both Oscar and Gustav Adolf call the "little world," the hermetic microcosm, one of the first touches of the esoteric and paranormal that appear throughout film.

When Oscar makes a speech in the theater, he uses "little world" to refer to the theater. When Gustav Adolf uses the phrase at the end of the movie, the meaning is more expansive. The "little world" is the artificial world of beauty and culture that the Ekdahls inhabit with such zest. It is the human realm of meaning that we build to protect ourselves from the chaos and terrors of nature. The theater is thus a microcosm of the microcosm.

On this reading, the theater is not just a symbol and site for fakery, loose morals, and cultural decadence. On a deeper level, the theater is a symbol of the creation of culture in the first place.

The Ekdahls do not lack a feeling for the holy, but when Emilie describes her conception of God, it is a force that lies beyond good and evil and manifests itself in an infinite array of masks. The world-whole in all of its manifestations, good and evil, is sacred. This is an essentially pagan conception of divinity.

The central drama of *Fanny and Alexander* springs from the clash of Christianity and paganism.

In the second act, which takes place in February of 1908, Oscar Ekdahl dies suddenly of a stroke. The whole sequence is deeply touching. A year later, Emilie announces that she is to marry Edvard Vergérus, the bishop of Uppsala.

The bishop's house is starkly different from the Ekdahls'. It is grim and austere, with white walls and sparse, uncomfortable furniture. The bishop's mother and sister are drab and neurotic. His aunt is a fat, vacant invalid played by a female impersonator. The servants are grotesques. Everyone is dressed in grays, blacks, and whites. Bergman is a master of this aesthetic.

Emilie feels unmoored since the death of Oscar, and she is attracted to the bishop (who isn't bad-looking) and thinks that maybe his austere and purposeful life will provide her the stability she is longing for.

Fanny and Alexander take an instant dislike to the bishop.

They were right. As soon as he has the family within his four walls, he reveals himself to be controlling, sadistic, and loathsomely smug. He's an evil stepfather straight from a fairy tale.

The marriage becomes a hell. Emilie wants out but is trapped. She is pregnant, so she will always be tied to Edvard. Moreover, if she abandons him, the law would allow him to keep Fanny and Alexander.

Emilie appeals to Helena, who sets a plan in motion. At this point, the film veers into the bizarre. The bishop is hard up for money and has offered to sell an antique chest to Isak, who had declined. Isak, however, has a change of heart when he realizes that he can use the chest to smuggle out Fanny and Alexander. Isak's visit is played very strangely. He's obviously up to something. The bishop and his sister are both suspicious and rude. But, somehow, he manages to get the children into the chest and close the deal with the bishop.

Then the bishop suddenly explodes in anger, strikes Isak, calls him a "filthy hook-nosed swine," and accuses him of trying to steal the children. Bizarrely, the bishop does not look in the chest but runs upstairs to the children's bedroom. Isak, whom the bishop had thrown to the floor, looks to the sky and cries out. A light illuminates him from above. When the bishop enters the nursery, he sees the children apparently unconscious on the floor. Isak faints, then awakens and has the chest carried away by his workmen. When he opens it in his shop, Fanny and Alexander emerge. The only possible explanation is supernatural. Isak has somehow projected the illusion of the children into their nursery. At this point, Alexander's encounters with ghosts no longer seem like figments of his imagination.

Once the children are out of the bishop's clutches, Gustav Adolf and Carl sit down to negotiate a divorce for Emilie. It is an utterly hilarious scene, and Carl somewhat redeems himself with his cool-headed shrewdness, in stark contrast to Gustav Adolf's typhonic tirades. The bishop, however, dresses up his vengeful priggishness in the garb of spirituality and high principle, so negotiations break down.

Meanwhile, Fanny and Alexander stay in Isak's shop, an Escher-like labyrinth impossibly cluttered with exotic treasures.

There Alexander meets Isak's nephews Aron and Ismael.

Soon after their arrival, Isak reads a story to Fanny and Alexander. He says that it is written in Hebrew, and it will take some work to translate. But once the story begins, his eyes no longer look at the page at all, suggesting that he is simply making it up.

In the parable, a young man travels a crowded and dusty road through a parched wilderness under a blazing sun. Nobody on the road knows where they are going, but they are in a terrible hurry to get there. Suddenly the young man is in a verdant forest. Cool waters flow at his feet. But he is blind to it all and is soon swept back into the mob.

The youth asks an old man about the source of the water. He replies that it flows from a mountain whose top is hidden in clouds. This brings to mind Sinai, from which Moses descended with the divine law. But the cloud is not caused by God. Its cause is entirely natural. Indeed, it is entirely human. It is created by the fears and prayers of men addressed to God or to the void. The fears and prayers become rain, which feed rivers that flow from the mountain.

But most men cannot slake their thirst from the mountain's waters because they will not break from the pointless rat race on the road. At this point, Alexander envisions Christian pilgrims, penitents, and flagellants. The message is that religion springs from man, not God, but it provides real solace, which most men are denied because it can only be found in the solitude of nature, whereas they are caught up in the frantic rat race of organized religion.

This is not the sort of parable a believing Jew would tell.

Aron makes puppets, including an enormous and terrifying representation of the biblical God, something no believing Jew would do either. Aron says he is an atheist, because as a trained magician and puppet master, he has no need of supernatural explanations. He sees how things work. From his side, everything is rational. The magic lies only in the credulity of the audience.

He explains that uncle Isak, however, believes that there are multiple levels of reality, swarming with supernatural beings, and that all of reality, even the seemingly inanimate and profane, is infused with soul and divinity. This is essentially the same pagan outlook professed by Emilie.

Isak's view of the world seems to be more correct than Aron's, for when Aron uses some sort of puppeteer's trick to turn the head of a mummy, as if by sympathetic magic, the bishop's bedridden, imbecilic aunt turns her vomit encrusted face toward the oil lamp by her bedside.

Ismael has a stratospherically high IQ, reads constantly, and remembers everything. But he is locked in his room because he is somehow dangerous. When Aron and Alexander bring him his breakfast, he asks Alexander to stay. Ismael is a sexually ambiguous figure. He is actually played by an actress.

Just as Ismael's appearance straddles both sexes, his mind straddles two worlds. He claims that the barriers between souls are porous, and he can cross them at will. He has the power to read people's thoughts and to project his own thoughts into other people's heads, which he demonstrates with Alexander.

Ismael intuits Alexander's desire to kill the bishop. Embracing Alexander and beginning to undress and caress him, Ismael describes the bishop and his dreams. Then the bishop's aunt overturns her oil lamp. Engulfed in flames, she rushes into the bishop's room, where she throws himself on him. Both die in agony. Problem solved.

The movie ends at the christening party of two baby girls. Emilie has given birth to Aurora. The father is the late bishop. Maj has given birth to Helena-Viktoria. The father is Gustav Adolf. Both children are being welcomed into the Ekdahl clan's dazzling little world, which is starting to look like a free-love commune of rich bohemians.

In the epilogue, Alexander, back in his grandmother's apartment, is knocked to the floor by the ghost of the bishop, who tells Alexander that he will never give him peace. Alexander then picks himself up, goes to his grandmother, and falls asleep in her lap while she reads from Strindberg's *A Dream Play*, which provides the metaphysical explanation for what has happened: "Everything can happen. Everything is possible and probable. Time and space do not exist. On a flimsy framework of reality, the imagination spins, weaving new patterns."

Strindberg's assertion that time and space are not real—particularly for the spirit—can explain the possibility of viewing and changing things across gulfs of space and time. The idea that space and time are not ultimately real, but merely guises by which non-spatiotemporal realities show themselves to us, comes from Swedish mystic Emanuel Swedenborg's *Arcana Coelestia*. Immanuel Kant read the *Arcana Coelestia* after investigating stories of Swedenborg's psychic powers and recognized that Swedenborg's concept of space and time could help explain psychic phenomena. Later, Kant incorporated the "ideality of space and time" into his *Critique of Pure Reason*.

The dramatic conflict in *Fanny and Alexander* is between pagans and Christians. The pagans win when they ally themselves with the Jews. The Jews in question, however, are not believers in the God of the Bible, who is the Christian God as well. Instead, Isak and Ismael believe in the same pantheistic paganism as Emilie. This metaphysics makes possible Isak's and Ismael's magical interventions.

Bergman's treatment of the Jews in *Fanny and Alexander* is interesting in light of his biography. The young Ingmar Bergman was an ardent National Socialist. The war and the Holocaust changed his thinking. It is tempting to read *Fanny and Alexander* as a Swedish pagan and former National Socialist's attempt to envision a rapprochement with the Jews in the form of an alliance against Christianity.

But it doesn't work out that neatly. For one thing, one has to ask if Ismael's homosexual and pedophilic attentions toward Alexander are part of Bergman's vision of utopia or a lingering trace of his darker, youthful views of Jews.

Despite the unsettling elements in the last act, *Fanny and Alexander* is a deeply moving and life-affirming film. It will captivate you as a period drama, draw you in deeper with its complex studies of character, leave you awe-struck as the old gods awaken—with the help of two Jewish Lokis—to shatter the gothic cathedrals, then deposit you back in the flower-garlanded little world of the Ekdahls for another pagan revelry.

The Unz Review, December 28, 2020

HOUSE OF GUCCI

House of Gucci is a highly entertaining combination of comedy, tragedy, and farce, tracing the decline of the Gucci fashion empire from an Italian family business to a global capitalist brand.

House of Gucci would have been the best Martin Scorsese movie in years—if it hadn't been directed by Ridley Scott. It has all the Scorsese touches: lots of Italians (albeit Italian-Italians rather than Italian-Americans), a plush running time, studies of characters who are seldom admirable but always interesting, excellent acting from a distinguished cast, Al Pacino, and a meticulous, nostalgia-infused reconstruction of another era, this time the late 1970s to the mid-1990s, a time that seems impossibly glamorous, wholesome, and white compared with the present.

Gucci was founded by Guccio Gucci in 1921 and passed on to his sons upon his death in 1953. The film considerably simplifies the Gucci family tree, focusing on two of Guccio's sons, Rodolfo (Jeremy Irons) and Aldo (Al Pacino) plus Rodolfo's son Maurizio (Adam Driver) and Aldo's son Paulo (an unrecognizable Jared Leto).

Maurizio is depicted as a nerd who is targeted for seduction and marriage by Patrizia Reggiani. Brilliantly portrayed by Lady Gaga, Patrizia is a social climber from a less wealthy, less distinguished background. Rodolfo dismisses her as a gold-digger, but she wasn't. She stayed with Maurizio even after his father cut him off. But she really was a social climber with a whole cluster of personality disorders. At first, her ambition and lack of scruples served her husband well. She had a child and helped reconcile Maurizio with his father just in time to collect his inheritance. This guaranteed her enormous wealth and prestige. She enjoyed a lavish lifestyle that is only hinted at in the movie.

But Patrizia could not leave well enough alone. She egged her husband on to take a role in the company. Why in God's name would you want to run a company if you are not cut out for it, especially if you already have more money than you could spend in two lifetimes? (When Maurizio Gucci died in 1995, his estate was worth $400 million.) Then Patrizia created a conflict between Maurizio and his uncle Aldo, allying with Aldo's idiot son Paulo. Aldo eventually ended up in jail for tax evasion. Then Patrizia turned on Paulo, first urging him to pursue his own design work then hitting him with a cease and desist for using the family name. Eventually, Maurizio went into business with some shady Iraqis who bought Aldo and Paulo out of the company. Once in charge, Maurizio proved to be a terrible businessman. He cut back on profitable but down-market product lines while expensing his increasingly lavish lifestyle to the company. Eventually, he was forced to sell his shares, leaving the business Gucci in name only.

Patrizia turned Maurizio from a tongue-tied nerd and wallflower to a self-confident jerk. But he resented her interference in his family. He also found her social-climbing increasingly grating. This is beautifully depicted in a scene in Switzerland where Patrizia is reduced to gibbering insecurity by Maurizio's old-moneyed school chums. Finally, Maurizio turned his new-found self-confidence against Patrizia, first separating from her then divorcing. He soon discovered, however, that there's only one thing worse than a scheming wife working "for" him—namely a scheming ex-wife working against him. If you don't already know the story, I won't spoil it for you.

House of Gucci most resembles Scorsese's *Casino*, in which a quasi-autistic nerd marries a *femme fatale*, although in *Casino* the villainess is a junkie and petty grifter, whereas in *House of Gucci*, she is the crazy ex-girlfriend from hell.

House of Gucci is great filmmaking that does not insult the intelligence, taste, or identity of white filmgoers. There are no politically correct messages. There is no tendentious "diversity" casting. *House of Gucci* is Ridley Scott's best movie since *Alien: Covenant* and one of the best movies of 2021. I recommend it highly.

The Unz Review, December 22, 2021

THE INCREDIBLES &
THE INCREDIBLES 2

Brad Bird is the director of three classic animated films: *The Iron Giant* (1999), *The Incredibles* (2004), and *Ratatouille* (2007), as well as the blockbuster sequel *The Incredibles 2* (2018). *The Incredibles* is a superhero film that also pays affectionate homage to the spy movies of the 1960s, especially classic Bond. I also classify *The Incredibles* as a classic of Right-wing cinema because it is explicitly anti-egalitarian and also promotes healthy family values.

Bob Parr is a Nordic bodybuilder who dons cape and mask to fight crime and save lives as the superhero Mr. Incredible. He's enormously strong and virtually indestructible. His wife Helen is known to the public as the superheroine Elastigirl. Her body is infinitely flexible. She can elongate her limbs or flatten out like a parachute or sail. Their superpowers coincide with traditional masculine and feminine archetypes. He's hard and brutal. She's soft and flexible.

The Parrs, however, are forced to hang up their capes when the public turns against superheroes and demands that they be banned. They aren't banned for being vigilantes, mind you. Instead, they keep getting sued: sued for damages inflicted when they battle supervillains, even sued for saving a suicidal man. A sensible society would indemnify superheroes from such lawsuits, for the greater good. But instead, they are forced to stop helping society. Of course banning superheroes does nothing to deter supervillains, whose activities would inevitably increase without opposition. Before you dismiss the whole premise as absurd, ask yourself how it differs from the "defund the police" movement in major American cities.

The Parrs settle down and have three kids, Violet, Dash, and the baby Jak Jak. Both Violet and Dash have superpowers like their folks. Bob has a boring and alienating job in an insurance company. He's gotten fat. Helen is a stay-at-home mom. Bob and his black buddy Lucius, also known as the superhero Frozone, go out once a week and listen to a police scanner, hoping to relive the old times by battling evil.

Bob gets fired from the insurance company and approached by a mysterious defense contractor who needs a superhero to subdue a rogue battle robot, the Omnidroid. Bob handily defeats the Omnidroid and is happy to be a hero again. He begins working out and getting his edge back.

Unfortunately, Bob's mysterious benefactor turns out to be a new supervillain who has been using superheroes as test subjects to refine the Omnidroid. Most of them have been killed in the process. Once the Omnidroid has been perfected, Syndrome plans to unleash it on Metroville, then come to the "rescue" as a new superhero who styles himself "Syndrome." (The "hero syndrome" refers to a form of manipulative behavior in which a person creates a crisis and then comes to the rescue.)

Fortunately, the whole Parr family comes together to use their superpowers to defeat Syndrome and the Omnidroid. Hence Mr. Incredible, who used to work alone, becomes part of a team, the Incredibles.

The music, mid-century modern design, sets, and gadgets of *The Incredibles* teem with delightful homages to the spy films of the 1960s. An homage, of course, has to fall short of an outright rip-off. But major plot elements of *The Incredibles* strike me as an outright rip-off of *Watchmen*.[1] In both stories, superheroes are forced into retirement, hanker for the old life, and return to it surreptitiously. In both stories, they save people from a burning building. In both stories, the villain does not have superpowers, but he uses technological enhancements to make himself powerful and is willing to share those enhancements with anyone who can pay. Both villains also create crises to achieve their ends. Both stories even share a gag with capes. Brad Bird, however, denies having read *Watchmen*, a statement that I find . . . incredible.

Not only are Bob and Helen archetypically masculine and feminine characters as superheroes, they also have a traditional family in which Bob works and Helen stays at home to raise their three children. To underscore just how "problematic" this

---

[1] Reviewed in *Return of the Son of Trevor Lynch's CENSORED Guide to the Movies*.

all is from a feminist viewpoint, at the beginning of the film, we see an interview clip with Helen as Elastigirl: "Settle down? Are you kidding? I'm at the top of my game! I'm right up there with the big dogs! Girls, come on. Leave the saving of the world to the men? I don't think so! I don't think so." I guess she just hadn't met Mr. Incredible yet. And although we can credit the government with forcing Helen out of the superhero profession, there's nothing stopping her from getting some other kind of job. Are we to conclude she just preferred being a mother?

The Incredibles is most famous, however, for its frankly antiegalitarian sentiments, and rejection of equality is the dividing line between the Left and the Right. The government has demanded that superheroes stop using their superpowers and fit in with the rest of us. This means that young Dash Parr can't join the track team, because he is super-fast:

DASH: You always say, "Do your best." But you don't really mean it. Why can't I do the best that I can do?
HELEN: Right now, honey, the world just wants us to fit in, and to fit in, we just gotta be like everybody else.
DASH: Dad always said our powers were nothing to be ashamed of. Our powers made us special.
HELEN: Everyone's special, Dash.
DASH: Which is another way of saying no one is.

Bob is indignant that Dash's elementary school now has a "graduation" ceremony for passing from the fourth to the fifth grades: "It's psychotic. They keep creating new ways to celebrate mediocrity, but if someone is genuinely exceptional, then . . ."

Many viewers think that *The Incredibles* was influenced by Ayn Rand: first, because of the anti-egalitarian sentiments; second, because Ayn Rand herself makes an appearance in the movie as designer Edna Mode, who lives in a hypermodern house with monumental classical Greek décor and smokes cigarettes in a long holder. She's absolutely hilarious and steals the whole show.

But this is a false inference. Ayn Rand is not the only anti-egalitarian thinker. Moreover, Edna Mode is not based on Ayn Rand but on Edith Head, the great Hollywood designer. ("Edna" is a mashup of "Edith Head," and "Mode" is French for fashion.) Brad Bird admits that he read Rand when he was young but denies her influence on the film. Moreover, he openly admits to modeling Edna Mode on Edith Head.

Beyond all that, the movie's philosophy isn't particularly Randian. The main conflict in the film is between those who are *born* with special gifts (including knowledge) and those who lack them. As Helen says to her daughter Violet: "You have more power than you realize. Don't think. And don't worry. If the time comes, you'll know what to do. It's in your blood." The emphasis on heredity and instinct puts *The Incredibles* much closer to Nietzsche than Rand.

Ayn Rand, after all, denied that mankind has any inborn knowledge or skills. She was a firm believer in the blank slate, although with a special twist: she believed that the blank slate could inscribe itself, that "man is a being of self-made soul." (Being one's own cause—*causa sui*—is a metaphysical trait usually attributed to God, not man.)

If Rand believes that human beings are born blank slates, she is committed to the thesis that we are all born equal, i.e., blank. What, then, explains our differences? For Rand, it is will. Some people *try* harder than others. (Don't ask *why* some people try harder than others, because the will is *free*.)

Thus the character in *The Incredibles* who is closest to Rand is the self-made superhero, Syndrome, who makes himself superior with science and technology. Syndrome recognizes, however, that science and technology are ultimately levelers:

> **MR. INCREDIBLE**: You killed off real heroes so that you could . . . pretend to be one?!
> **SYNDROME**: Oh, I'm real. Real enough to defeat you! And I did it without your precious gifts, your oh-so-special powers. I'll give them heroics. I'll give them the most spectacular heroics anyone's ever seen! And when I'm old and I've had my fun, I'll sell my inventions so that everyone can be superheroes. Everyone can be a super!

> And when everyone's super . . . no one will be. [evil laughter]

Of course Rand would not endorse Syndrome's motivations (envy) or actions (murder and mayhem).

The Incredibles really is an incredible film, and not just for kids. It is highly entertaining and often hilarious, with wholesome role models, serious themes, and useful lessons: the traditional family; a clear-cut battle between good and evil; envy, conformity, and democratic leveling versus excellence; the importance of family solidarity; and, above all, no capes. The plot may be derivative, but it is clever, well-paced, and breathes like Egyptian cotton. The dialogue is snappy. The production design and action sequences are dazzling. Michael Giacchino's soundtrack is a note-perfect fusion of Henry Mancini's cool sixties jazz and John Barry's brassy Bond music.

The Incredibles was not just an artistic success. It was also a commercial and critical hit. This created enormous demand for a sequel, which Brad Bird finally delivered in 2018. Sadly, *The Incredibles 2* is not incredible too. It looks great and has many funny episodes, but there's too much going on here, and it never gels into a compelling or coherent plot. The kids might not notice, but the grownups certainly do.

Bird must have been under enormous pressure by Disney to eliminate the "problematic" elements of the first film. There's nothing about excellence versus mediocrity here. Mom and dad briefly swap roles—then again, that's the villain's doing—but the family structure and norms remain unaltered. Bird could always have pled that his movie is set somewhere in midcentury, before the sexual revolution, although the technology is not always consistent with that. There's a cynical wine-aunt, but she's the villain. At a certain point, a whole Tumblr of diversity is dumped into the plot in the form of new superheroes, but they're mostly villains as well. Despite it all, *The Incredibles 2* didn't end up politically correct. Sadly, though, that's the only incredible thing about it.

The Unz Review, September 1, 2021

THE LAST EMPEROR

When I first saw Bernardo Bertolucci's *The Last Emperor* (1987), it struck me as a remake of *Doctor Zhivago*. Both narratives begin in glamorous and archaic empires that fall to communist revolutions. Of course, that could just be due to the fact that the Chinese Revolution was something of a remake of the Russian Revolution. But there are parallels specific to the two films, both of which depict communism as recapitulating the old forms of despotism but as vulgar and brutal farces, stripped of all refinement. Both films also end on a note of hope. But what gives cause for hope is the reemergence of precisely what communism sought to abolish. Thus both *Doctor Zhivago* and *The Last Emperor* are not just anti-communist films, they are *reactionary* anti-communist films. But in the case of *The Last Emperor*, this is hard to square with the fact that director Bertolucci was himself a communist.

The Last Emperor tells the story of Puyi, who became the last emperor of the Qing dynasty in 1908 at the age of two. He was deposed in 1912 after China became a republic. In 1924, he was expelled from his palace, the Forbidden City of Beijing. He then took refuge in Tientsin, where he plotted to regain his throne. Eventually, he threw in with the Japanese, in 1932 becoming the head of state of Manchukuo, the name given to Japanese-occupied Manchuria. In 1934, he was crowned emperor of Manchukuo. In 1945, he was captured by the Red Army. In 1950, he was turned over to the People's Republic of China for trial and rehabilitation. In 1959, he was declared rehabilitated and released. He spent the rest of his life as a worker and citizen in the People's Republic of China. He died of cancer in 1967.

The Last Emperor is based primarily on Puyi's 1964 autobiography, *From Emperor to Citizen*. The script was written by Bertlolucci and his brother-in-law Mark Peploe. *The Last Emperor* was the first Western film to be shot within the Forbidden City. The cast included John Lone as the adult Puyi, Joan Chen as his Empress Wanrong, and Peter O'Toole as his tutor Reginald Johnston. Ryuichi Sakamoto played Japanese agent Masahiko Amakasu and composed the bulk of the music. There were nearly 20,000 extras. *The Last Emperor* was a critical success. It also did well in theaters, despite its 163-minute running time. It won nine Oscars, including Best Picture and Best Director, as well as many other awards.

The Last Emperor works simply as a dazzling, exotic costume drama. It is astonishing to learn that at the dawn of the twentieth century, China was ruled by an absolute monarchy that had not changed much in more than 2,000 years. The emperor was revered as a quasi-divine being who mediated between heaven and earth, a conduit by which higher order infused a world perpetually haunted by chaos. The emperors had multiple wives and were attended by an army of eunuchs, who were not only castrated but had their sexual organs entirely removed, usually when they were children. The only intact man who could sleep in the palace was the emperor. When the emperors died, they were bedecked in jewels and entombed like pharaohs.

But it gets stranger yet. Even though the emperors had absolute power, they were little more than prisoners. They were never alone and were not allowed to do anything for themselves. This is dramatized most effectively on Puyi's wedding night, when he and the empress were attended by six ladies in waiting, who disrobed them as discreetly as possible.

Beyond that, the emperor had no contact with the world other than his courtiers and eunuchs, who used their control of information to shape policies. When a teenaged Puyi took on a Scotsman, Reginald Johnston, as his tutor, he knew almost nothing of world history or geography. The courtiers were so opposed to anything modern that they tried to veto eyeglasses for their nearsighted emperor.

This system became most bizarre when children became emperors. Child rulers are inevitable in monarchies, but they also reduce it to absurdity.

Hereditary monarchy has many benefits. Every social order needs a supreme executive. In normal circumstances, laws can be enforced and policies can be executed by bureaucrats, police, and judges. But in exceptional circumstances, where decisions cannot be based on settled laws and practices, executives need some discretionary power. And when the entire system is threatened by exceptional circumstances, one needs a chief executive who can decide what to do.

Sometimes terrible things have to be done to preserve society. Rioters need to be shot, for instance. But in such circumstances, ordinary policemen and officials fear to do what is necessary because their offices are conditional, and they can be blamed and punished for their missteps. Thus it is important for there to be someone who can take full responsibility during a crisis. Such a decision-maker cannot answer to any other mortal. He must be guided only by his sense of what is required by the common good. And since the common good can sometimes require killing, the decider must be immune from punishment for his actions. In short, the whole political order depends on a decision-maker who is above the law and immune to it.

An executive who can be removed from office, however, cannot employ unpopular measures even to save the nation. Thus the best executive rules for life.

But how does he attain his office? If an executive is elected—especially if the election falls during a crisis—he cannot risk doing anything unpopular either, even if it is necessary to preserve society. Thus the best executive cannot be chosen, for that means he is beholden to those who choose him, not to the public good. The best executive, therefore, must simply be born. (Or he can be chosen by lottery.) Hereditary monarchy is thus one of the best ways to confer the fullest package of executive powers.

Unfortunately, it often confers such powers upon unworthy parties. For when ultimate authority, responsibility, and immunity from punishment are reposed in the hands of a child—who is unable to understand statecraft and make decisions for himself and who cannot be held responsible for his actions, much less the actions of his underlings—monarchy becomes a farce. Decisions have to be made by other people—regents—who lack the ultimate authority or immunity of the sovereign.

The last three Chinese emperors were children when they were crowned. During the reign of the first two—the Tongzhi

Emperor and the Guangxu Emperor—power was largely in the hands of the Dowager Empress Cixi, the mother of the former and the aunt of the latter. When the Guangxu Emperor began to reform China, Cixi overthrew him in a palace coup and went back to running the country. When Cixi was dying, the Guangxu Emperor was poisoned. Puyi was placed on the throne, under the control of Cixi's faction, so that no reforms could take place even after her death.

A new level of farce was reached in 1912, when Puyi's regents abdicated in his name—and didn't even bother to tell him. After all, he was a child. He wouldn't understand. Under the articles of abdication, Puyi remained emperor within the walls of the Forbidden City. The rituals of the court continued unaltered, although they were now completely detached from the mechanisms of government.

Why did this farce continue? Part of it, surely, was superstition. The Chinese seemed unable to shake the belief that the Qing still enjoyed the Mandate of Heaven. Another part of it was the hope that the emperor would be restored, which did happen briefly in 1917. But the main part of it was probably corruption. The court provided a living for thousands. What else was a eunuch going to do in the twentieth century? The Forbidden City was a vast treasure house, which the courtiers were systematically plundering. When the teenaged Puyi ordered an inventory of the treasury, it was burned to the ground to cover the theft.

But the corruption of the Qing court came from the very top. What is corruption anyway? The purpose of government is to serve the common good. Every office should play that role. Of course, every office is staffed by officials, and every official is a mere mortal, who has his own private ends.

The only office where there is no divide between private and public interests is a hereditary monarch. His whole life, from birth to death, is dedicated to the public good. Thus he serves as an example to everyone else. But when the monarch is a puppet of scheming courtiers serving who knows what ends while merely going through the motions of serving the public good, it only makes sense for more humble functionaries to start looking out for themselves as well.

Of course they keep going through the motions of government. But their hearts are not in it. The regime has been hollowed out. It no longer serves its purpose. A hollowed-out regime can last a long time if it is not tested. When it is tested, we see whether its functionaries are willing to pull together and do what is necessary for its survival. But China was in the throes of a century of humiliations. Eventually, under the stress of foreign interventionists, domestic rebellions, ambitious politicians, and rogue generals, the regime simply collapsed.

The Last Emperor begins in 1950 when Puyi arrives at a Chinese Communist prison. But as the film unfolds, we learn that he was basically a prisoner since the age of two, when he was made the emperor.

It is astonishing that the communists did not kill Puyi. Mao's regime was the bloodiest in human history. What would have been one more life? Yes, the communists believed that man is born good, does wrong only because of society, and can be reformed. But murdering their opposition was quicker and easier. There's never been any shortage of Chinese.

Perhaps Puyi was spared for propaganda purposes. If he could be reformed, then anyone could. But Puyi was not the only Qing to be spared by the Red Chinese. His father, Prince Chun, died in Beijing in 1950—in a palace, not a prison. Many descendants of the Qing royal clan live in China to this day. Perhaps they were protected by the Mandate of Heaven after all, or at least a lingering belief in it.

It was to break with such traditions that the Cultural Revolution was launched, but on Bertolucci's depiction, it simply ended up recapitulating the old regime as farce. One of the most spectacular scenes of *The Last Emperor* is Puyi's coronation, in which thousands of Chinese nobles assemble to kowtow to the new emperor. At the end of the movie, we see hysterical Red Guards parading thought criminals through the streets and demanding they kowtow to Chairman Mao.

The end of *The Last Emperor* is enigmatic. The elderly Puyi buys a ticket to visit the Forbidden City as a tourist. Thinking he is alone, he tries to sit on this former coronation throne. A young boy in the red kerchief of the Pioneers stops him. Puyi tells him that he was once the emperor of China. To prove it, he rummages under the throne's cushions and finds a cricket cage that he had hidden there. The cricket cage first appears during the coronation, when it is presented to Puyi by an official, Chen Baochen. When Chen opens the cage, the cricket emerges. Its crouched posture makes it look like it is kowtowing to the emperor too. When the boy opens the cage, the cricket reemerges. When the boy looks back at the throne, however, Puyi has disappeared. This is, of course, pure fantasy. Crickets only live a couple months. So this is a magic cricket.

How do we interpret this ending? First, we can ask what the cricket means. The cricket represents the reemergence of something that has gone into hibernation for a very long time. The kowtow, of course, is a symbol of imperial authority, brought back by the Red Guards. But is such authority good or bad? If Bertolucci were a liberal, he should say it is bad. But Bertolucci is supposedly a Marxist, and Marxists never had any problem with state power and its symbols.

Second, we can ask what it means to end with magic as such. Ultimately, Bertolucci doesn't view history through Marxist lenses. Instead, he views it aesthetically. And as an aesthetic spectacle, he finds communism lacking. The most visually spectacular parts of the film are from Puyi's childhood: his meeting with Cixi who pronounces him the new emperor, his coronation, and his wedding. In Tientsin and Manchukuo, Puyi and his court embraced modern dress and décor, with equally spectacular results. Bertolucci portrays the People's Republic of China, however, as utterly drab and vulgar, and not just the prisons. At the end of the Red Guard scene, we are serenaded by massed accordions and treated to some proletarian ballet. Even as degenerate drug addicts, the Qing at least had style.

One can criticize communism from the Left, but by turning history into an aesthetic spectacle and ending with a poetic flourish, *The Last Emperor* repudiates communism from the Right.

The Unz Review, September 29, 2021

LAWRENCE OF ARABIA

David Lean (1908–1991) directed sixteen movies, fully half of them classics, including three of the greatest films ever made: *The Bridge on the River Kwai* (1957), *Doctor Zhivago* (1965), and, greatest of them all, *Lawrence of Arabia* (1962). *Lawrence of Arabia* is repeatedly ranked as one of the finest films of all time, and when one compares it to such overpraised items as *Citizen Kane* and *Casablanca*, a strong case can be made for putting it at the very top of the list. I am hesitant to speak of "*the* greatest" anything, just because I have not *seen* everything. But when I think of some of my personal favorites—*Vertigo*, *Network*,[1] *Rashomon*[2]—I can't honestly rank any of them higher than *Lawrence of Arabia*.

Everything about this film is epic: from its nearly four-hour running time and its 70-milimeter widescreen image with astonishing detail and depth of focus—to the magnificent settings in Jordan, Morocco, and Spain—to the music by Maurice Jarre—to the cast of thousands crowned by such stars as Peter O'Toole, Alec Guinness, Omar Sharif, Anthony Quinn, Jack Hawkins, José Ferrer, and Claude Rains.

Lean had to go big, simply to do justice to the story. *Lawrence of Arabia* is about one of the most remarkable men of the last century, Thomas Edward Lawrence (1888–1935) and his role in the Arab revolt against the Ottoman Empire during the First World War.

Based on Lawrence's sprawling narrative of the revolt, *Seven Pillars of Wisdom*, the script by Robert Bolt (*A Man for All Seasons*, *Doctor Zhivago*) is a supremely masterful screen adaptation. (Michael Wilson, who worked on the script of *The Bridge on the River Kwai*, also receives screen credit, but the final script is Bolt's.) The timeline is simplified, and certain characters are amalgamated, both to save time and heighten dramatic conflicts, but the truth of the story is conveyed.

---

[1] Reviewed in *Trevor Lynch: Part Four of the Trilogy*.
[2] Reviewed in *Return of the Son of Trevor Lynch's CENSORED Guide to the Movies*.

Like Lawrence's book, the movie has several layers. First of all, it is a historical narrative. Second, it offers lessons in political philosophy. (The word "wisdom" in the title should have been a warning.) Lawrence was a nationalist, not an imperialist. To fight the Turks, he favored aiding Arab nationalists rather than spending British lives to conquer territory and resources in Mesopotamia. But, against Lawrence's own intention, *Seven Pillars* also makes a case for empire, a case that Lean's film clearly reinforces. Third, there is a strong element of Nietzschean self-mythologization: what Aleister Crowley calls "auto-hagiography" and the Arabs call "blasphemy."

On the symbolic plane, Lawrence overthrows the three Abrahamic faiths by rejecting their doctrines and reversing or rewriting their central stories with himself as the hero. The movie takes this process further, both reflecting upon the process by which Lawrence became a legend and perfecting it: cinema as apotheosis. I want to focus on the latter two layers. Thus I will skip huge stretches of the story and leave those for you to discover on your own.

T. E. Lawrence was one of five illegitimate sons of an Anglo-Irish Baronet, Sir Thomas Chapman, and an English mother, Sarah Junner. Highly intelligent, Lawrence read history at Jesus College, Oxford from 1907 to 1910. From 1910 to 1914, he was an archaeologist in the Holy Land, working with such eminent figures as Leonard Woolley and Flinders Petrie. Woolley and Lawrence also gathered intelligence for the British in the Negev Desert in early 1914.

When the World War broke out, Lawrence enlisted. Fluent in French and Arabic and knowledgeable of Arab history and culture, he received a military intelligence post in Cairo. In June of 1916, when Sharif Hussein, Emir of Mecca, led an Arab revolt against the Ottomans, Lawrence was sent to Arabia to gather intelligence. The rest is history.

The movie begins with Lawrence's death in a motorcycle accident in 1935, at the age of 46. After a memorial service at St. Paul's Cathedral attended by the crème of the British establishment, a priest asks if Lawrence "really belongs here," which introduces the theme of Lawrence as an outsider. The first half of the movie can be seen as an affirmative answer to that question.

Then we flash back nearly twenty years to Lawrence in Cairo. From the start, Peter O'Toole plays Lawrence as slightly autistic and ambiguously gay. He also has a masochistic side. He likes to extinguish matches with his fingers. "The trick . . . is not minding if it hurts." It is a small exercise in self-overcoming, a hint of greater things to come.

Lawrence's commander, General Murray, despises him as an overeducated misfit, but a civil servant Mr. Dryden (a composite character played by Claude Rains) values his intelligence and language skills. Dryden "borrows" Lawrence for an intelligence gathering mission to Arabia. He is to meet Prince Faisal (Alec Guinness), the son of Sharif Hussein, and evaluate his leadership potential.

Lawrence tells Dryden that he thinks this mission will be "fun." Dryden says that the only people who find the desert fun are Bedouin and gods. His unstated premise is that Lawrence is neither. Lawrence flatly declares, "No, it will be fun." If Dryden is right, and Lawrence is not a Bedouin, that implies that Lawrence thinks of himself as a god. To underscore Lawrence's funny idea of fun, he lights a match. But this time Lawrence blows the flame out.

Crossing the desert to find Faisal, Lawrence's guide Tafas is killed by Sharif Ali (Omar Sharif) for drinking at his well. You see, Tafas is from the wrong tribe. This prompts a bit of political philosophy delivered with autistic frankness that borders on the suicidal, given that it is spoken to a man holding a smoking gun: "As long as the Arabs fight tribe against tribe, they will be a little people, a silly people, greedy, barbarous, and cruel." A nation comes into being when tribes of the same people put aside petty differences and rivalries and embrace a common government, including the rule of law, for a higher good. Throughout his adventures in Arabia, Lawrence's dream of a rising Arab nation is stymied by tribal rivalries and blood feuds.

Out of autistic principledness, Lawrence rejects Ali's help in finding Faisal, preferring to risk it on his own.

When Lieutenant Lawrence reaches Faisal, he is ordered by his British military advisor, Colonel Brighton, to say nothing, observe, and report back to Dryden. But Lawrence is irrepressible. As an autist, Lawrence can't keep his ideas to himself, which intrigues Faisal. Brighton counsels a strategic withdrawal to Yenbo, where the British can resupply him. Faisal wants the British fleet to take the port of Aqaba, but Brighton refuses. It is too well-defended. When Brighton leaves, Faisal bids Lawrence to stay. Faisal naturally fears the English have designs on Arabia, but he is forced to depend upon them: "We need the English, or—what no man can provide, Mr. Lawrence—we need a miracle."

This prompts Lawrence to spend a night brooding in the desert. The next morning, Lawrence suggests to Ali that the Arabs should take Aqaba themselves. Aqaba's guns point toward the sea, because an attack from the land was deemed unlikely. Ali points out that such an attack would require crossing the Nefud Desert, a waste that even the Bedouin avoid. Lawrence proposes crossing the Nefud with fifty men—all members of Ali's tribe—then raising more troops from the Howeitat tribe on the other side. Ali agrees.

When Lawrence tells Prince Faisal that he is "going to work your miracle," Faisal replies "Blasphemy is a bad beginning." Lean films Lawrence's nocturnal meditations as something more than just a brainstorming session. Now we know that it was a step toward apotheosis.

As Lawrence and his followers make their last push across the Nefud, one of the men, named Gasim, falls off his camel in the dark. When his riderless camel is noticed, Lawrence wants to go back to rescue him. But Ali and the Arabs say they dare not risk it. Gasim's time has come. "It is written," meaning that it is the will of God. Lawrence declares "Nothing is written"—meaning that the will of God is nothing in the face of the will of man—then he goes back on his own to search for Gasim. As he departs, Ali rages at Lawrence's "blasphemous conceit" and says he will not be at Aqaba. Lawrence replies that he will make it to Aqaba: "*That* is written"—by Lawrence himself.

In the space of a single conversation, Lawrence rejects the written laws handed down by Moses and Muhammad. He overthrows God and lays down his own laws. Blasphemy indeed.

But Lawrence's blasphemy is not punished. It is rewarded. When he rescues Gasim, the Arabs begin to idolize Lawrence.

As Lawrence sleeps, Ali burns his uniform. The next day, the Arabs dress him the white and gold robes of a sharif of their tribe, conferring noble status on him. It is proclaimed, "He for whom nothing is written may write himself a clan." Because Lawrence is a bastard in England, he cannot inherit his father's name or title. For Ali, that means he is free to choose his own name. He is free to found his own family, clan, or dynasty. He is free to be somebody's ancestor, not somebody's heir. This is the privilege that descends on all men who bring victory in battle. It is how aristocracies everywhere are born. The Arabs call him "Aurens." Now Ali wishes to style him "El Aurens," which is the equivalent of the German "von." Lawrence is beginning to enter — and alter — Arab society.

The night before Lawrence's men and the Howeitat are to strike Aqaba, a shot rings out. One of the Howeitat lies dead, killed by one of Lawrence's men. The Howeitat demand justice, but if they execute the killer, his own tribesmen are bound to avenge him. Tit-for-tat violence will destroy the alliance. Arab tribalism is about to snatch defeat from the jaws of victory.

But Lawrence has a solution. *He* will execute the prisoner. He will take the blame. He, not the Howeitat, will bear the brunt of the blood feud of the dead man's tribe. Thus the alliance of the two tribes can be maintained for the attack on Aqaba. Lawrence is offering himself as a scapegoat to prevent tribal conflict from spinning out of control.

Of course, in a sense Lawrence can't really serve as a scapegoat, because he knows that he is no danger of actually being punished by Gasim's tribe for executing him. He has already been hailed as a sharif by Gasim's own kin.

The scapegoat here functions as a symbol of the political enemy in Carl Schmitt's sense. If the Arab tribes are to become an Arab nation, they must find a way to take the enmity between them and place it on an outsider. If the Arabs are to become a political "us" they must have an external enemy, a political "them" against whom to define themselves. Lawrence wants it to be the Turks, but he knows that a people in need can create an enemy in its own midst, then externalize it. Lawrence is willing to fill that role in a pinch.

Ironically, though, Lawrence's gesture also undermines nationalism and makes a case for empire. In Xenophon's *The Education of Cyrus*, book 3, we learn of how enemy tribes can be unified not by a common enemy but by a common "friend." Two enemy peoples in the Caucasus, the Armenians and the "Chaldeans," are locked in perpetual warfare. Neither group is strong enough to defeat the other, so their costly conflict can only be terminated by a third party.

Cyrus occupies and fortifies the highlands between the Armenians and Chaldeans. He pacifies them by offering to ally himself to whichever tribe is wronged by the other. Then he delivers the fruits of peace by brokering mutually enriching economic exchanges between the two tribes in place of mutually impoverishing conflict.

None of this would be possible without a third power, an outsider who is above their conflicts and benevolently disposed toward them. This was the legitimating ideology of the Persian empire; hence Cyrus became known as the "prince of peace." Lawrence plays the same role in brokering peace between the tribes. It is, of course, but a small step from hero to emperor. Contrary to the principle of national self-determination, sometimes only an outsider will do.

When Lawrence and the rest of us see the face of the condemned man, it is a punch in the gut. It is Gasim, the man Lawrence risked everything to save. Lawrence asks Gasim if he is guilty. "Yes." Then Lawrence puts six bullets in him. When he flings away his gun in disgust, a mob converges on it, as a holy relic. Lawrence is becoming a legend. (In reality, Lawrence executed a different man. By making Gasim the killer, the screenwriter not only made the story more economical, he also increased its dramatic power.)

After Aqaba is taken, Lawrence basks in victory for a few moments by the seaside, where Ali throws him a garland of flowers, stating "The miracle is accomplished. . . . Tribute for the prince, flowers for the man." Lawrence replies "I'm none of those things, Ali." When asked what he is then, Lawrence says,

"Don't know." But he's being coy. If he has worked a miracle, he's a god, or on his way to becoming one.

When the telegraph equipment in Aqaba is smashed by the excitable Arabs, Lawrence proposes taking the news to Cairo by crossing the Sinai desert. "Why not? Moses did it." To which Auda abu Tayi, the leader of the Howeitat (Anthony Quinn in his most compelling role) replies, "Moses was a prophet and beloved of God." But Lawrence is doing more than imitating Moses. He's already tossed away the written laws of Moses and Muhammad. Now he's reversing Moses' journey by going back into Egypt.

When Lawrence arrives in Cairo, he's dressed in Bedouin robes and caked with filth. But Lawrence walks into military HQ like he belongs there. He was an outsider even when he wore the uniform, but now it's obvious. Naturally, he is not welcomed until he is recognized as one of their own. He looks like a beggar. He has gone through hell. But when he reports that he has taken Aqaba, everyone from the top brass to the lowest guardsman knows a good thing when he sees it.

General Murry has been replaced by General Allenby, a far shrewder leader superbly played by Jack Hawkins. Allenby promotes Lawrence to major on the spot. Brighton declares it a "brilliant bit of soldiering" and recommends Lawrence be put up for a commendation. Dryden says, "Before he did it, sir, I would say it couldn't be done." When Allenby summons the lowly Mr. Perkins into his office and asks his opinion of Aqaba, he says "Bloody marvelous, sir." We know Perkins is a lowly fellow because we only see his boots, stamping to attention as he enters and leaves.

Allenby proposes a drink at the officers' bar. The beautifully filmed and choreographed sequence is one of the movie's most memorable. The British HQ was filmed in a magnificent palace in Spain. The music is Kenneth Alford's splendid march, "The Sound of the Guns." (Alford also composed the "Colonel Bogey March," which became an unlikely hit record after Lean and composer Malcolm Arnold used it in *The Bridge on the River Kwai*.) Allenby, Lawrence, and company sweep through the halls and down the grand staircase—past rank after rank of smartly uniformed officers and sentries, standing at attention and saluting—into the sumptuous bar, where all the officers spring to attention until Allenby puts them at ease and begs their permission to drink there, as a guest of Major Lawrence. It is a perfect image of how hierarchy is oiled by magnanimity, manners, and good humor. We pretty much know where David Lean stands on the empire vs. nationalism question. The British Empire has seldom seemed better oiled and more glamorous on screen.

But it is precisely the British ability to look past appearances and to recognize the talents and achievements of an outsider and misfit like Lawrence that made this victory possible. As Allenby and Lawrence continue their conversation in the courtyard, the camera follows Lawrence's eyes to the galleries above, which are lined with onlookers. Again, we see a legend forming. When Allenby takes his leave and Lawrence returns alone to the bar, the officers briefly stand silent then burst out in acclaim. When the priest at Saint Paul's asks, "Does he really belong here?" he means at the very center of one of the world's great empires. Here we see that the answer is yes. It is an enormously moving climax, and we're only at the Intermission.

In the first half of the movie, Lawrence makes himself a legend in service of Arab nationalism. In the second half, he meets a rival myth-maker, Jackson Bentley, a fictional American journalist based on Lowell Thomas and played by Arthur Kennedy. Bentley's goal is to use the Arab anti-colonial revolt and the romantic figure of Lawrence to build American sympathy for the war. Prince Faisal replies: "You are looking for a figure who will draw your country toward war. Aurens is your man." Amusingly, Bentley tells Faisal, "I just want to tell your story." The bastards still say the same thing today.

When Lawrence and the Arabs attack a Turkish train, we see apotheosis in action. A victorious Lawrence stands on top of the train to receive the acclaim of the tribes. A wounded Turk shoots him. Lawrence falls to the sand, where he takes stock of his wound. When a bloodied Lawrence returns to the roof, the tribes are ecstatic. Lawrence prances on the roof of the train like a model on a catwalk, whirling in his robes, drinking up the adulation of his followers.

Looking down through the camera's eyes, we see only Lawrence's shadow across the sands and the cheering crowd. Looking up, we see only his silhouette against the sky. Bentley eagerly snaps pictures, which the Arabs correctly believe will steal their virtue. Bentley *is* stealing—and selling, and exploiting—Lawrence's virtue, his power.

The juxtaposition of the three-dimensional Lawrence and his two-dimensional shadow and silhouette, along with the journalist's camera, is a subtle commentary on myth-making. Lawrence is becoming one of the shadows projected on the walls of the cave of public opinion.

In my review of John Ford's *The Searchers* (elsewhere in this volume), I comment on Ford's framing effect of moving from silhouette to three-D and back to suggest that the domestic world is less real and more fragile than nature, again an analogue to Plato's Allegory of the Cave. Lean uses the same contrasts to similar effect. Lean carefully studied *The Searchers* before filming *Lawrence* to understand how Ford shot his spectacular Monument Valley settings. He may have taken other inspiration as well.

Sated with loot and desiring to take the winter off, Lawrence's Bedouin allies melt away. But the British campaign rolls on. Lawrence has been asked to besiege Deraa, but he only has fifty men left, the original number he set out with toward Aqaba. Having worked a miracle once before, he presses on. "Who will walk on water with me?" he asks. More blasphemy. But not even Lawrence can motivate fifty men to take a town garrisoned by thousands of Turks.

So Lawrence proposes to go into Deraa alone. Of course with his fair complexion, golden hair, and blue eyes, he's going to have a hard time passing, but for some reason Lawrence *wants* to draw attention to himself—even though he is the most wanted man in the Empire, with a bounty of twenty-thousand pounds on his head. The whole mission makes no sense, and some suspect that it is wholly fictional. Only Ali accompanies him.

Lawrence is arrested, beaten, and most probably raped by a sadistic Turkish general, then thrown into the street. Lawrence's feeling of invincibility is shattered. He wants to return home and bury himself in an ordinary life. "I'm only a man." Ali is incredulous, objecting "A man can do whatever he wants!" Lawrence retorts, "But he can't want what he wants." Meaning that we may be able to reshape the world according to our desires, but we can't reshape our desires. Then he pinches his white flesh and says, "This is the stuff that decides what he wants." Is he referring to his race, which made it impossible for him to pass as an Arab? Is he referring to his sexuality? (Lawrence was most definitely a masochist and most probably homosexual.) Whatever his meaning, Lawrence is doubting his outsider magic.

Lawrence meets with Allenby in Jerusalem and asks to be relieved. "I'm an ordinary man, and I want an ordinary job. . . . I just want my ration of common humanity." Allenby has seen these mood swings before and handles Lawrence shrewdly. "You're the most extraordinary man I've ever met." Lawrence agrees rather too readily. "Not many people have a destiny, Lawrence. It is a terrible thing for a man to funk it [i.e., lose his nerve] if he has."

This is Lawrence's Garden of Gethsemane moment, when he seeks to renounce or flee his superhuman destiny. But that proves impossible. It is not long before the old Lawrence is back. *He* is going to deliver Damascus to the Arabs. The scene ends dramatically with Lawrence standing in front of a painting of Phaeton falling headlong from the solar chariot declaring emphatically that the Arab tribes "will come *for me*."

Of course, at Deraa he's learned the limits of his charisma. So he demands a great deal of money from Allenby as well, to buy allegiance. When Lawrence sets out for Damascus, he has a paid bodyguard of notorious cutthroats, all of them wanted men.

Lawrence's goal is to beat Allenby to Damascus and install an Arab National Council. He almost loses the race when he comes across an Arab village sickeningly massacred by the retreating Turks. The cutthroats urge "no prisoners." Ali reminds Lawrence of Damascus. When one of Lawrence's men charges the Turks and is gunned down, Lawrence unleashes a massacre. This is his Phaeton-like fall. Faisal prophesied it earlier in the film when he said that for Lawrence, mercy is a passion. For Faisal it is merely good policy. "You may judge which is more reliable." Clearly, Faisal's motive was more reliable in the end.

Despite the massacre, Lawrence beats Allenby to Damascus, occupies key facilities, and declares an Arab National Council in charge. Allenby's response is shrewd. He orders the British army to quarters, including the medical and technical staff. He's going to let the Arabs muck things up, out of tribal pettiness and general backwardness. Eventually, they will get tired of playing at government and leave. Which is pretty much what happens. "Marvelous looking beggars, aren't they?" Allenby remarks as he sees the Bedouin begin to slip back to the desert.

The movie ends with Lawrence, now a full colonel, being sent home so the politicians can take over. Along the road, he passes a troop of Bedouins leaving Damascus and more British coming in. A dispatch rider on a motorcycle passes him and speeds ahead, foreshadowing his death. It looks anticlimactic, but that's history.

It also looks like a defeat, but it wasn't entirely. Prince Faisal held on. He was willing to accept British engineers to run things, but he insisted on flying an Arab flag and declaring himself king. Faisal was eventually run out of Damascus by the French, but he became king of Iraq, which was pretty much a British oilfield with an Arab flag until his grandson was machine-gunned by revolutionaries. His brother became king of Jordan, where his descendants rule to this day. It wasn't what Lawrence wanted, but without his efforts, the Arabs would have had to settle for a lot less. Lawrence's sense of mission wavered from time to time, but he didn't fail the Arabs. Ultimately, they failed themselves.

Visually, *Lawrence of Arabia* is one of the most beautiful films in the history of cinema. It has been studied obsessively by other filmmakers but never equaled. Every new viewing discloses new influences. (For instance, surely Faisal's silent, red-robed guardians gave George Lucas an idea or two.) If a picture is worth a thousand words, *Lawrence of Arabia* is worth a million. Better, then, that you see it for yourself.

What did Lawrence do after Arabia? There were stints at the Foreign Office and the Colonial Office. But having made history, he found office work boring. So he turned his talents to making legend, writing *Seven Pillars of Wisdom* and delivering lectures to enormous audiences. He also filled his ration of common humanity by joining the Royal Air Force under an assumed name. Apparently he found it relaxing to take orders from fools. When his enlistment was up, Lawrence left the RAF in March of 1935. He had his fatal accident before he could begin the next chapter in his legend.

We can only imagine what Lawrence would have thought of Lean's film. I think it is insightful, but it isn't necessarily pleasant to be spiritually X-rayed. However, if Lean is right about Lawrence's ambitions, I think he would have been pleased to see his apotheosis finally made complete.

The Unz Review, May 31, 2021

THE LIFE & DEATH OF COLONEL BLIMP

One of my all-time favorite movies is *The Red Shoes*, Michael Powell's 1948 Technicolor feast about a ballet impresario played by the great Anton Walbrook and his ecstatic, obsessive, and ultimately destructive relationship with his art—and one artist in particular. So you can imagine how eagerly I sought out Powell's first foray into Technicolor, 1943's *The Life and Death of Colonel Blimp*, also starring Walbrook.

My interest was further sharpened when I read some of the critical notices. No less than Martin Scorsese praised *Blimp* as a masterpiece. Andrew Sarris called *Blimp* "England's answer to *Citizen Kane*"—an over-praised movie, to be sure, but still an intriguing comparison. Anthony Lane of the *New Yorker* said *Blimp* "may be the greatest English film ever made," which is high praise indeed when one considers that Alfred Hitchcock and David Lean were in the running. *Empire* magazine ranked *Blimp* #80 in its list of the 500 Greatest Movies of All Time, and it is #45 in the British Film Institute list of the Top 100 British Films.

I am sad to report, however, that *Blimp* is the worst "great" movie I have ever seen—worse even than *Casablanca*, which it displaced in my ranking. To be clear, there are many films that are worse than *Blimp*, but they are seldom heaped with praise by directors and critics. *Blimp* is so bad, in fact, that I long hesitated to give it even a negative review, for two main reasons. First, I didn't want to watch it again. Second, I don't want to encourage anyone else to watch it, and negative reviews often have that perverse effect, because people wonder if it is "really that bad." Well, it really is. Take my word for it. *Blimp* isn't even entertainingly bad, like many midnight movies. But it is at least *interestingly* bad, hence this review.

The idea for the story of *Blimp* came from Powell's previous film, *One of Our Aircraft Is Missing* (1942). Then-editor David Lean thought a scene should be cut because it did not advance the plot, but he did remark that it contained the dramatic seed of a whole new film about the conflict between youth and old-age, specifically in a military setting.

This idea grew into the story of a British officer, Clive Wynne-Candy, who fought in three wars, fell in love three times with beautiful women (all played by the same actress), and at the end of his career clashes with the younger generation, who could use his wisdom and experience, although they can also teach him a thing or two.

As an elevator pitch, it is intriguing idea for a serious film, with plenty of opportunity for dramatic conflict and romance centering on deep, archetypal symbolism: the adventure and horror of war, youth versus old age, the eternal feminine, and those intriguing threes.

Unfortunately, during the "development" process, Clive Wynne-Candy was amalgamated with the cartoon character of Colonel Blimp, created by David Low. Low's Blimp is a dim-witted, jingoistic, reactionary blowhard who speaks in hilarious clichés, vacuities, and contradictions: "Gad sir! Mr. Lansbury is right. The League of Nations should insist on peace—except, of course, in the case of war."

But Clive Wynne-Candy is neither a colonel nor named Blimp. Nor does he die, for that matter. And although his opinions are old-fashioned, he is neither stupid nor contemptible. Which makes the Blimp makeover seem rather dumb and dishonest: a cynical attempt to boost the movie by name-checking a rather different cartoon character. But the cynicism does not stop there.

Powell's creative partner, screenwriter Emeric Pressburger, was a Hungarian Jewish refugee who hated the Nazis—and apparently all Germans, whom he regarded as mere stand-ins for Nazis—and wished to put his talents to work stirring up and sustaining another World War.

Thus Powell and Pressburger teamed up to make a whole series of anti-Nazi or just anti-German propaganda films: *The Spy in Black* (1939), *Contraband* (1940), *49th Parallel* (1941), *One of Our Aircraft Is Missing* (1942), *Blimp* (1943), *The Volunteer* (1943), *A Canterbury Tale* (1944), and *A Matter of Life and Death* (1946).

According to Powell, Pressburger fancied himself the "British" answer to Dr. Goebbels. He also thought *Blimp* was his finest work. He was delusional on both counts, for *Blimp* is very clumsy propaganda, which is fortunate, because its intended message is pure evil.

The only thing "Blimpian" about *Colonel Blimp* is the script, which is bloated with undramatic hot air, yielding a running time of nearly three hours. Of course, if the original story idea had been developed into a compelling drama, it could have run three hours with no complaints.

My hypothesis is that once the original idea—with its span of four decades, triple romance, and struggle between youth and experience—was fused with a cartoon buffoon, Pressburger felt relieved of the necessity of any serious dramatic character development or storytelling. Hence the characters become mere caricatures and the plot becomes as thin as a clothesline on which Pressburger strings his messages.

Usually, these messages are conveyed by a cast member making a speech, often looking straight into the camera. It is flat, undramatic, and often deadly dull. Since Pressburger was pretty much indifferent to what came between, the story is cluttered with pointless characters, childish and cutesy dialogue, scenes contrived merely for superficial color and charm, and bizarre, psychologically implausible changes of character.

For instance, the central relationship of the movie is the forty-year friendship of Clive Wynne-Candy, played by Roger Livesey, and Prussian officer Theo Kretschmar-Schuldorf, played by Anton Walbrook. When they first meet in Berlin in 1902, they are fighting a duel with sabers because Clive has insulted the honor of the German military.

The preparations for the duel take up a great deal of screen time because Pressburger had developed a pedantic fixation on a Prussian dueling manual. But when the duel actually starts—at last, some action!—the camera cuts to the exterior of the building, which renders the rehearsal of the rules pointless and makes a complete mockery of the duel's dramatic buildup, such as it is. It is practically a textbook example of an anticlimax. Amazingly, Scorsese praises this perverse stunt as brilliant and even imitated it in *Raging Bull*.

Clive's love for three women of three different generations, all played by Deborah Kerr, could have been developed into a great romance. But Clive's feelings for all three women are more narrated than shown. Indeed, I was completely taken by surprise when Clive announced his love for the first of them, Edith.

There is a bit more feeling in Clive's relationship with the second woman, Barbara, whom he marries. But when she dies, we learn of it only from a newspaper clipping flashed on the screen. Would it have killed Pressburger to have actually written a scene?

When Clive's loyal servant Murdoch dies in the blitz, we learn about it the same way. Why not just flash the whole script up and dispense with the cast entirely? Why treat these opportunities for drama and genuine feeling in such a cold and perfunctory way while cluttering up the script with pointless inanities?

Unfortunately for Pressburger, drama, characterization, and the rest are necessary to sell propaganda. Generally, the worse the propaganda, the better the story has to be. If Pressburger had been a better storyteller, the world would have been a much worse place.

So what was Pressburger's message?

The story begins in 1902. Clive Wynne-Candy has won the Victoria Cross in the Second Boer War. He dashes off to Berlin when he learns that the Germans are spreading dastardly lies that the British interned innocent Boer civilians in concentration camps, where many of them died. Of course this dastardly lie is true. Why is Pressburger eager to hide that fact? Because real British concentration camps for civilians would be a real moral equivalency between the British and the Third Reich.

Pressburger is keen on selling the idea that the British establishment consisted of innocent, overgrown children, complete with silly nicknames and schoolboy pranks, given to sports and hunting. They fight wars the same way: as gentlemen, loath to do anything dishonorable, unsporting, or not "cricket." They are also quick to forgive their enemies, no matter how dastardly.

After World War I, Clive finds Theo in a British prisoner of war camp, listening to an orchestra concert, because although the Germans are butchers, they are cultured butchers. Once Theo is released, Clive invites him to dinner at his London mansion. His fellow guests are top military brass and important civil servants who assure Theo that they want nothing more than to get Germany up on her feet in no time. Nothing about lost territories, starvation blockades, or onerous reparations. Message: Germany had no reason for resentment against England.

Theo interprets this magnanimity as weakness and reports it to his fellow German officers. He's so villainous that you expect him to click his heels and twirl the tip of his moustache.

We also learn that England has fought a clean war, Germany a dirty one. But England won because "right is might." This too is interpreted by the Krauts as weakness.

Pressburger's message is that the Second World War happened not because the Allies were too cruel to the Germans but because they were far too kind. In the current war, the British need to renounce their alleged high-mindedness and mercy. Next time, no more Mr. Nice Guy. When Germany goes down again, the Brits need to keep her down, forever.

By the time World War II breaks out, however, Theo has had a mysterious change of heart, which he talks about endlessly without making it psychologically plausible. He is no longer a dastardly, resentful Kraut. He is now an anti-Nazi who has taken refuge in England. A talented storyteller could make this transformation plausible, even inevitable, but the only reason it happens in *Blimp* is because Pressburger now wants Theo to make anti-Nazi propaganda speeches.

Theo and Clive are reunited. Clive is about to make a propaganda speech on the radio, but at the last minute it is nixed by the government. Theo has read the speech and explains why. Clive had planned to expatiate on what a dirty war the Germans were fighting, yet again. This was fine. But then Clive mentioned that he would prefer to lose than to stoop to German methods. Theo makes an impassioned appeal to Clive to drop the English gentleman routine, because Nazism is the most dastardly idea in human history, which must be defeated by any means necessary, including war crimes.

At the end of the movie, Clive has been retired from the regular army and has gone to work for the Home Guard (the British militia). But he still has a few lessons to learn. The Home Guard is having an exercise, which begins at midnight. The Old Guard like Clive follow the rules, but the New Guard decide to launch the war a little early, storming Clive's club—a symbol of the British establishment—and taking him prisoner. After all, it's what zee Germans would do. Suitably humiliated, Clive stands in front of his bombed-out mansion—another symbol of the destruction of the old order—and salutes the young whippersnappers in their victory parade. The end.

The younger generation is portrayed as brash, fast-talking, and vulgar. They all seem to be proles. Women wear uniforms and sport male nicknames. Big band music blasts from jukeboxes. Engines throb and roar. In short, they are portrayed as Americans. It would be laughable if it weren't so repulsive.

Pressburger seemed to regard colonials as barbarians who would be more receptive to his message of total war. In one scene during the First World War, an Australian is brought in for some "enhanced interrogation" of German prisoners. After all, it's what zee Germans would do.

These barbarians would probably claim they didn't trust anyone over thirty, but they believed everything they heard from the Pressburgers of the world and happily incinerated whole German cities at their behest.

I don't know what's more obscene: Pressburger egging the Brits on to commit war crimes—or the pretense that they needed to be egged on in the first place. Britain's Blimps never hesitated to fight dirty—and they never lost any sleep over it either.

Churchill did everything he could to sabotage *Blimp*, flattering himself that the overly scrupulous Clive Wynne-Candy was meant to be a parody of him. Churchill certainly showed the world that was untrue.

The movie opened to largely negative reviews. Critics were absolutely right to complain about the long running time, which really means they found it dramatically empty and boring. But they were rightly impressed by the film's technical qualities. The sets, costumes, art design, and Technicolor cinematography are dazzling. But they simply underscore the fact that everything that makes *Blimp* bad comes down to Pressburger's script.

Blimp was, however, a success with the British public, although some criticized it for being insufficiently bellicose because it had *one* good German in it. Apparently, they nodded off before it became clear that the purpose of the one good German was to justify anti-German war crimes.

Pressburger's target audience was the British upper class. He acknowledged what they all knew: that there are good Germans and that the English and Germans are kindred peoples sharing a common culture. He acknowledged all that, then argued that the British should *still* stop at nothing to defeat the Germans, then crush them forever.

Blimp was not seen in America until after the war, and then only with increasingly drastic cuts. A restored version was released in theatres in 1983. The movie's unfathomably inflated critical reputation began then. I hope this review will contribute to the Hindenburg-like revision it so richly deserves.

The Unz Review, August 2, 2021

THE MAN WHO SHOT
LIBERTY VALANCE

John Ford's last great film *The Man Who Shot Liberty Valance* (1962) enjoys the status of a classic. I find it a deeply flawed, grating, and often ridiculous film that is nonetheless redeemed by raising intellectually deep issues and by an emotionally powerful ending that seems to come out of nowhere.

The stars of *The Man Who Shot Liberty Valance* are John Wayne and Jimmy Stewart, both fine actors given the impossible job of playing men in their 20s, even though they were aged 54 and 53 at the time. It just doesn't work.

There's also too much buffoonery. Ford thought that drunkards and men with funny voices were hilarious. In *The Man Who Shot Liberty Valance*, we get *two* funny drunkards and *three* men with funny voices, including Andy Devine and Strother Martin. There is also a great deal of scene-chewing overacting and overbroad parody that often seem downright cartoonish.

The film is poorly paced as well, burning through screen time and my patience with dramatically needless details of frontier kitchens and political conventions.

Beyond these lapses of taste, *The Man Who Shot Liberty Valance* also contains Left-liberal messages on race. For instance, Devine's Marshal Link Appleyard is married to a Mexican woman. Oddly enough, the same actor's character in Ford's *Stagecoach* (1939) is married to a Mexican as well. In real life, Andy Devine was married to a white woman. Bucking the color bar must have been Ford's preference.

Wayne's character Tom Doniphan has a loyal negro sidekick named Pompey (Woody Strode). Pompey even endures the indignity of being refused service at the saloon, but Doniphan stands up for him, although he does refer to him as "my boy Pompey."

At the very center of the film is a scene in which newly-minted lawyer Ransom Stoddard (Stewart) teaches reading and civics to a class of white adults, plus Pompey and a brood of

Mexican children. (All the children in Shinbone are nonwhite, a poignant sign that white civilization has not yet been established there. Now such classrooms are signs of white civilization in decline.) Lawyer Stoddard teaches that the fundamental law of the land is the Declaration of Independence, which holds that "All men are created equal." The Declaration, of course, is not the fundamental law of the land. That would be the Constitution, which says nothing about all men being created equal.

Ford was known as a patriot and an anti-communist, but on race, his politics were aligned with the Hollywood progressive consensus. Ford did not, however, identify with outsiders against America's WASP ethnic core because he was Jewish. Instead, he did so as an Irish Catholic, born John Martin Feeney.

Judging from Ford's cavalry trilogy—*Fort Apache* (1948), *She Wore a Yellow Ribbon* (1949), and *Rio Grande* (1950)—the West could not have been won without the help of golden-hearted, silver-tongued Irish drunkards. These stereotypes seem rather broad and offensive today, but Ford—a heavy drinker himself—obviously regarded them affectionately and thought their inclusion to be progressive.

I list these problems up front, because I don't want you to be surprised or deterred by them. For in spite of its flaws, *The Man Who Shot Liberty Valance* is a worthwhile film. As the title suggests, this is a movie about violence, specifically the relationship of violence to manliness and civilization. The film's message is deeply anti-liberal. Indeed, although Ford could not have known it, *The Man Who Shot Liberty Valance* illustrates many of Carl Schmitt's criticisms of liberalism. Thus I include it among the classics of Right-wing cinema.

The movie opens with a train pulling into the town of Shinbone in an unnamed state in the American Southwest. Shinbone is conspicuously bright, clean, and attractive. Everything looks brand-new. The only thing old and dusty is the stagecoach, a victim of progress suitably abandoned at the undertaker's parlor. Shinbone was built on a soundstage. Ford was known for shooting on location because he loved sweeping vistas and gritty authenticity. But Shinbone's cleanliness and newness—its clear artificiality—were quite deliberate representations of progress and the end of the frontier.

Senator Ransom Stoddard and his wife Hallie (Vera Miles) are met by the former Marshal, Link Appleyard. They have arrived to attend the funeral of their old friend Tom Doniphon (John Wayne), who is being interred in a pauper's grave at public expense. As a sign of the changes in Shinbone, we learn that Doniphon will not be buried with his gun, because he had not carried one in years. When the local newspaper editor demands to know why a sitting Senator is attending the funeral of a pauper, Stoddard agrees to tell the tale.

We flash back some decades. Ransom "Rance" Stoddard, fresh out of law school, has gone West, not so much to seek fame and fortune as to improve the place by bringing law, literacy, and progress from back East. Outside a much rougher version of Shinbone, the stagecoach in which Stoddard is riding is robbed by outlaw Liberty Valance (Lee Marvin) and his gang (including Lee Van Cleef and Strother Martin). When Stoddard objects to the rough treatment of a woman, Valance beats him severely then sends away the coach, leaving him to his fate.

Played to cartoonish excess by Lee Marvin, Liberty Valance is a cold-blooded murderer and thief. He's also a drunkard and a petty bully. The entire town of Shinbone lives in terror of him. He's the kind of man who needs killing, so decent people can plant crops, raise children, and sleep at night.

It seems odd that an American movie would have a villain named Liberty. Isn't America the land of liberty? But Liberty Valance is not really an American. He's a man of the Wild West. America is a Republic with laws. The West is the state of nature. Liberty Valance represents the liberty of savages in the state of nature, where one man's liberty is exercised at the expense of another's. Savage liberty must die so civil liberty can be born. Thus it is appropriate that Liberty Valance is a hired gun of the cattle interests, who oppose statehood and the coming of law and order.

Stoddard is rescued by Tom Doniphon, who owns a small horse ranch outside Shinbone, and brought into town. For no sensible reason except that he likes her, Tom awakens Hallie, who works as a waitress at a local eatery, to help tend to

Stoddard's wounds.

Tom quickly pegs Rance as a greenhorn and a tinhorn. He doesn't know how the world works, but he talks like he does. When Tom tells Rance that he'd better get a gun if he wants justice, Rance launches into a speech:

> But do you know what you're saying to me? You're saying just exactly what Liberty Valance said. What kind of community have I come to? You all seem to know Liberty Valance. He's a no-good, gun-packing, murdering thief, but the only advice you give me is to carry a gun. Well, I'm a lawyer! Ransom Stoddard, Attorney at Law. And the law is the only . . .

Jimmy Stewart was brilliant casting because he's obviously in love with his own voice.

Rance doesn't see any difference between force used by criminals and force used by decent men against criminals. He's an idealist who apparently thinks the laws can magically enforce themselves. In John Wayne's most often-imitated line, Tom calls Rance "Pilgrim," which pretty much sums up his combination of moralism and utopianism. He's a spindly, priggish, progressive zealot. He reminds me of Barack Obama.

Rance settles in Shinbone, working alongside Hallie in the kitchen of the eatery owned by Swedish immigrants Nora and Peter Ericson. Rance's role in the community, however, is distinctly feminine. In a land where men wear guns and settle problems for themselves, he refuses to wear a gun and expects the law to settle disputes . . . somehow. Thus in the Ericsons' restaurant, Rance wears an apron while washing dishes and occasionally waiting tables. (Obama also allowed himself to be photographed in an apron.) When Rance learns that Hallie can't read, he takes on another stereotypically female role: schoolmarm.

When an apron-clad Rance brings Tom his dinner in the restaurant, Liberty trips him then mocks him. Tom is enraged. It is his steak, after all. Tom demands that Liberty pick it up. Tom is the toughest guy in town, the only one who is not afraid of Liberty. A gunfight almost ensues until Rance, still clad in an apron, picks up the steak for them, ranting about the absurdity of men killing one another over matters of pride. This too is an attitude more commonly associated with women. Ford clearly thinks that manliness is connected with a willingness to fight over matters of honor.

Rance begins to have some doubts, however, when it becomes clear that the local law enforcement, Marshal Appleyard, is a fat, effeminate coward. Devigne's squeaky voice is well-employed, but Ford labors the point endlessly, to the point of cartoonishness.

When Rance allies with the local newspaper editor, funny drunk Dutton Peabody (Edmond O'Brien), to fight the cattle barons and appeal for statehood, Liberty is hired by the ranchers to intimidate the townspeople. At that point, Rance furtively buys a gun and sneaks off to practice shooting. Why the deception? Because he can't really reconcile it with his self-image and the image he has established with the public.

There's also a love triangle in the mix. Tom is in love with Hallie. Everybody sees it. But he hasn't screwed up the courage to propose. It is his one failure of nerve as a man. When Rance enters the picture, Hallie begins by tending his wounds like a mother. Then she works with him in the kitchen like a sister (both in aprons). Then he schoolmarms her along with a brood of Mexican children. Rance is pretty much zilch as a man, certainly nobody Tom would regard as a rival. But when Hallie begs Tom to stop Rance from getting himself killed in a duel over honor, the big lug realizes that he is in danger of losing his girl.

When Rance (still wearing his apron) faces Liberty Valance, Liberty toys with him, shooting a jar first, then wounding his arm, then taunting him to pick up the gun again. Rance does so, takes aim, and shoots Liberty dead. Hallie rushes to tend Rance's wounds. But Rance is no longer a child. He has faced death in a duel over honor. He's a man now. When Tom sees them together, he knows that he has lost Hallie. He gets staggering drunk and burns his own house down in self-pity.

Rance Stoddard enjoyed some esteem for his good heart and his skills as a teacher and a lawyer. But his refusal to carry a gun put him in the category of women and children when it came to defending the community. However, when he shot Liberty Valance, he became a man and a hero. It also launched his political career.

But none of this sits well with Rance's puritanical idealist streak. He feels that he bears the "mark of Cain" and is perhaps unworthy of public office. So Tom takes him aside and tells him a story. Tom was watching the confrontation with Liberty, and when Rance raised his gun to fire, Tom shot Liberty dead with a rifle. Tom is willing to take the guilt—and also the glory—to salve Rance's morbid conscience. "It was cold-blooded murder," says Tom. "But I can live with it." It is telling that Rance can't live with killing in self-defense.

I wonder, though, if Tom's story is even true. Did it really happen, or did he make it up to spare Rance's feelings? True or false, Tom is astonishingly generous. If the story is true, Tom saved Rance's life and lost the woman he loved in the bargain. If the story is false, Tom is admitting to murder simply to make Rance feel better, perhaps because he hopes to promote Hallie's happiness even after losing her.

This is an enormous risk for Tom. If Rance shot Liberty, it was self-defense. But if Tom killed Liberty, he could hang for it. For Tom's sake, Rance is forced to keep the secret. Oddly enough, his conscience allows him to return to politics, where he enjoys an illustrious career: governor, senator, ambassador to England. Granted, he no longer thinks his public esteem is based on killing, but shouldn't he be bothered that it is based on a lie? Perhaps he can live with the lie by telling himself that he is doing good things for the people. But couldn't he say the same thing about killing Liberty Valance?

The deeper truth that Rance evades is that, for civilization to come to the West, *somebody needed to shoot Liberty Valance*. It doesn't really matter who. When Dutton Peabody nominates Rance to represent the territory in Washington, he explains how the West was won. First, it was held by merciless Indian savages. Then it was settled by cattlemen, whose law was the gun. The cattlemen did what was necessary, namely kill and subjugate the Indians. Then came the farmers and businessmen, who need fences and law and order. Liberty Valance is a hired gun of the cattle interests. His type was necessary to deal with the Indians. But now he has outlived his usefulness and stands in the way of progress. Progress requires a new kind of man: Ransom Stoddard, attorney at law. And isn't it poetic that Rance Stoddard is the man who shot Liberty Valance?

The possibility that the story is false is supported Ford's frank exploration of noble and ignoble lies later in the movie. Although the newspaper editor has pried the story out of Rance by insisting on his "right to the truth," once the tale is told, he burns his notes and tells Rance he will not print the truth. "This is the West, Sir," he says, "When the legend becomes fact, print the legend." What he really means is when facts are *replaced* by legend, print the legend.

But why replace the truth with legend? What's wrong with the truth? The superficial truth deals with who shot Liberty Valance: Tom or Rance? If Tom shot Liberty, he can't be punished now because he's dead. Rance, of course, kept the secret. Perhaps there would be legal consequences for that. But the real need for deception has to do with the deeper truth: *somebody* needed to shoot Liberty Valance so that civilization could come to the West, just as the Liberty Valances of the world were needed to shoot the Indians. This truth needs to be concealed because it does not sit well with liberalism.

Liberalism seeks to do away with force and fraud in human affairs. This is a noble aspiration shared by anti-liberal thinkers as well. Liberal theorists are famous for constructing accounts of how civil order can arise from the state of nature without force or fraud, by means of a social contract between rational agents. It is only because liberals think that political legitimacy depends on the *immaculate conception* of liberal order, without resort to force and fraud, that they are forced to print the legend. Liberalism does not banish force from politics, and especially from the foundation of political order. It merely banishes honesty about force.

Rance Stoddard is a brilliant and scathing portrait of liberalism. When Rance's priggish, effeminate idealism clashes with the grim reality of the state of nature, Tom Doniphon needs to rescue him again and again. If Rance really shot Liberty Valance, it was only by discarding his initial belief that there is no difference between Liberty and Tom—and only by taking Tom's advice to buy a gun. If Tom shot Liberty Valance, the repudiation of liberalism is even deeper, for Rance has the law on his side but isn't up to the task of defeating Liberty, so Tom has to commit cold-blooded murder.

Liberalism, in short, depends on illiberal men and extralegal violence for its very survival. But, instead of questioning their own ideological premises, liberals simply lie about this fact. Ford doesn't dispute the benefits of law and order. He just thinks they would be better secured by men who are more honest about the role of violence in founding and maintaining them.

This is an amazing message for a Hollywood film. I have no doubt that this is Ford's intended meaning. Everything about this film, both its virtues and its flaws, is 100% John Ford. He was one of Hollywood's most meticulous *auteurs*, a fact that is somewhat hidden by the formulaic quality of all his films. Ford started making movies in the silent era, when they were everyone's entertainment, which meant that every film had to have something for everyone, including a love story and some crude comic relief, usually involving booze. Of course one could level the same sort of criticisms at Shakespeare.

I chalk the film's flaws up to the self-indulgence of old age. Ford was pushing 70, and his hard-working, hard-drinking life was catching up with him. Perhaps we can credit the film's virtues to another trait of old age: impatience, because time is short, which leads to greater frankness, even though it might ruffle some folks' feathers.

I don't want to spoil the movie's brilliant and heartbreaking final scene, so I will leave you with these words. Since men like Liberty Valance need killing to create political order, nothing is too good for the man who shot Liberty Valance. It is a burning indictment of liberalism that such men lie unsung and unstoried in paupers' graves.

The Unz Review, March 25, 2021

THE MATRIX RESURRECTIONS

Larry and Andy Wachowski's *The Matrix* (1999) is a science fiction classic. The setting is a devastated Earth in the far future. The premise is that humanity has been enslaved by artificial intelligences. Human beings spend our lives in what are essentially coffins while mechanical vampires drain our energy. We don't know it, because we are asleep, dreaming that we are in a radically different world. This is the Matrix. Today we would call it a multiplayer online game.

Like many dystopias, *The Matrix* is actually too optimistic. The Wachowski brothers thought the human race would have to be forced into the pods. They didn't imagine we would *choose* them. But eventually, gaming addicts will build coffins for themselves as in *The Matrix*, where they can loll about catheterized, diapered, and fed intravenously, so the game never ends. To sustain themselves, they'd gladly share their body heat.

The image of the human race both enslaved and deluded about its condition by an illusory world created by malevolent powers goes back to Plato's Allegory of the Cave in the *Republic*. It is echoed in Descartes' *Meditations* and the Marxist concept of ideology.

Plato, Descartes, and Marx all believed that emancipation is possible. But there's no way to think yourself out of the Matrix. If you managed to wake yourself up, you'd discover that you are a naked, flabby blob in a pod full of pink goo, hooked into a machine that both nourishes and drains you.

Plato posited a sunlit world outside the cave where one could live and plan to return and liberate one's fellows. Outside the Matrix, however, the Earth is devastated and shrouded in perpetual clouds. You wouldn't have a chance.

Thus it isn't clear how the resistance movement of the Matrix started or how it can end. To begin, the resistance needs a *deus* not *from* the machine but *outside* of it altogether: perhaps a seed of unenslaved humanity living in a place called "Zion" near the Earth's core.

Getting people to join the resistance is a hard sell. You can persuade people to quit a job or a relationship by arguing that "it isn't really you." But imagine telling people that everything about their world, including the people they love, including their very selves, is fake. The real world is a hellscape where they are living corpses, imprisoned in coffins, fed upon by parasites. Which world would you choose?

Thus it is nice that the resistance gives people a choice: the first choice they ever really had. If they take the red pill, they will trade everything and everyone they knew and loved for life in a post-apocalyptic hell. If they take the blue pill, they will go back to sleep in the Matrix. Naturally, only deeply alienated people would take the red pill.

However, the ultimate goal of the resistance is to crash the Matrix for everyone, whether they like it or not. But it is not clear how the human race could survive such an event. There's Zion, but that promised land probably isn't big enough for everyone.

The Matrix works as the story of the hacker Neo (Keanu Reeves) awakening to the truth and joining the resistance. But as far as the larger project of liberating humanity goes, the creators of *The Matrix* had written themselves into a corner, and they should have quit while they were ahead. The story could not stand up to too much scrutiny about where the resistance came from and where it was going.

The first sequel, *The Matrix Reloaded*,[1] was a clever movie with a bleak message: the resistance itself is an illusion, created by and subordinate to the Matrix. Of course that's a useful lesson in a world of coopted and manufactured oppositions. The problem is that on the basic premises of the films, there can't really be a *true* opposition. Which means that no matter what happens, the machines will always be in control.

The second sequel, *The Matrix Revolutions*,[2] was pretentious, incoherent garbage in which Neo and the heroine Trinity (Carrie-Anne Moss) both die. It sounds like a bleak ending, but look

---

[1] Reviewed in *Trevor Lynch's White Nationalist Guide to the Movies*.
[2] Reviewed in *Trevor Lynch's White Nationalist Guide to the Movies*.

on the bright side: if the hero and heroine are dead, at least there won't be another sequel, right?

Wrong. For, as this new movie has the brass to explain, Warner Brothers needed more money, and money has the magic power to resurrect dead franchises over and over again. Hence *The Matrix Resurrections*. What could possibly go wrong? Look how well it worked for *Star Wars*!

The Matrix is objectively more useful to the pro-white Right than the anti-white Left, but you have to look past the casting to see that. In *The Matrix*, the bad guys are all clean-cut white men. The good guys look like the Left: a coalition of non-whites and white misfits. But just bracket that out for a minute. Imagine the movie with a monoracial cast and you'll see that the story itself is not anti-white. Only the casting gives that impression.

In today's world, what is the closest thing to the Matrix? The mass media, including gaming. In today's world, who are the parasites who control the media? They are overwhelmingly Leftist and disproportionately Jewish. (The Wachowskis are not Jewish, but Anglo and Polish in descent.) In today's world, the race-conscious Right are the advocates of realism—racial, sexual, and political—whereas the Left are advocates of social constructionism, utopianism, gender fluidity, and delusional happy talk. (Both Wachowski brothers have "changed their sex." Larry is now known as Lana, and Andy now styles himself Lilly.)

In today's world, who are the slaves of the Matrix? The answer is tricky, because almost everyone is deceived and exploited to one extent or another. But whites, especially straight white men, are at the bottom of the progressive stack. Whites are targeted with relentless hate propaganda, including the casting of *The Matrix* itself.

Thus it was natural for race-conscious whites to see *The Matrix* as an allegory for our situation and to appropriate the "red pill" as a symbol of our awakening. To my knowledge, the first use of the red pill in this manner was in Michael Polignano's speech "My Awakening Too" from May of 2004.[3]

---

[3] Michael Polignano, "My Awakening Too," in *Taking Our Own Side* (San Francisco: Counter-Currents, 2010).

One of the ambitions of *The Matrix Resurrections* was to somehow "take back the red pill" from the Right. The movie accomplishes nothing of the kind, so I suspect that this was just another cynical attempt to promote a movie by getting race-conscious whites to hate it online. (See my article on the *No Time to Die* trailers, in this volume.)

The Matrix Resurrections is directed by "Lana" Wachowski, but after a few minutes, I thought this was the work of Jar Jar Abrams, since it follows the pattern of his cursed *Star Wars* movies.[4]

Because the Mouse needed money, Abrams was tasked with resurrecting *Star Wars*. Since the purpose was money, and since he held the fans in utter contempt, there was no question of creating an original story within the larger *Star Wars* mythos (what the money people call a "franchise"). So Jar Jar decided to simply coast on nostalgia. He dusted off the original cast members (who were long past their discard dates) and put them in scene-by-scene, sometimes shot-by-shot rip-offs of the original trilogy, this time as farce. Since he had no idea what made the original trilogy popular, he took the 70-IQ cargo cultist route of imitation, thinking that would be safer. He also junked the plots up with so many inanities and gags and leaps of logic that he delivered running times of 138 and 142 minutes, which simply highlighted the vapidness of the stories. Not only did he insult the intelligence, taste, and values of the fans, he bored them silly.

"Lana" follows the Abrams playbook to the letter. *The Matrix Resurrections* is garbage: pretentious, incoherent, boring, and deeply insulting to its audience. But "Lana" goes Abrams one better: he breaks the fourth wall; he goes "meta"; he thinks that brazenly flaunting the greed and cynicism of the whole enterprise will somehow redeem it. But it doesn't. Self-conscious, ironic garbage is still garbage.

I like to think that the Wachowskis were sincere when they made *The Matrix*. It probably never occurred to them that they

---

[4] My review of *Star Wars: The Force Awakens* is in *Return of the Son of Trevor Lynch*. My review of *Star Wars: The Rise of Skywalker* appears in *Trevor Lynch: Part Four of the Trilogy*.

were far closer to the machines than the plucky resistance fighters. Judging from *The Matrix Resurrections*, however, "Lana" no longer has any illusions. He's quite comfortable with his role as deceiver and parasite. If you are a fan of *The Matrix* and still think that objective reality matters—if you'd like to be liberated from illusion—if you are not comfortable with being a pod-dwelling, bamboozled milch-cow for soulless parasites at Warner Brothers, I have a red pill for you.

The Unz Review, December 30, 2021

MILK

You have to give the Left credit. They never take a day off. The eye of Sauron never blinks. They are frenzied and relentless in their attempts to overthrow our civilization. They softened us up for a long time, rotting away our character and identity by promoting vice, cynicism, and nihilism—all while playing the victim. Now that we are too weak to resist and too deracinated to care, they have launched a ferocious campaign of iconoclasm against our forefathers' heroes: Christopher Columbus, Thomas Jefferson, Robert E. Lee, etc. Once they have finished destroying us in effigy, the next logical step is destroying us in person, i.e., open genocide against whites, rather than the stealth genocide they instituted in the 1960s with multiculturalism and race-replacement immigration.

But Leftists don't just tear down idols. They are also both shameless and tireless in molding new idols from human excrement. George Floyd is just the latest and most ludicrous in a long line of fake heroes, saints, and martyrs: Lenin, Stalin, Martin Luther King . . .

Jewish gay rights advocate Harvey Milk (1930–1978) is one such figure. Milk was the first openly gay elected official in California as a member of the San Francisco Board of Supervisors. In 1978, Milk and San Francisco Mayor George Moscone were murdered by Dan White, a mentally unbalanced former member of the Board of Supervisors.

White had resigned his position impulsively then asked to be reinstated. Milk lobbied against his reinstatement. White was white, male, heterosexual, Catholic, his high school valedictorian, a Vietnam veteran, a former policeman, and a former firefighter celebrated for his bravery. He represented everything Milk loathed. Milk worked with him when he was on the Board, but he was hoping to replace him with another Leftist. Moscone agreed.

Moscone was not homosexual, and Milk was not killed because he was homosexual, but such details did not stop Milk from being touted as a martyr for gay rights and the recipient of an ever-increasing, ever more absurd list of honors and tributes.

For instance, in November of 2021, as part of the ongoing anti-white cultural revolution, the United States Navy launched the USNS *Harvey Milk*. My first reaction was that the ship should have been named after the Village People, because at least they sang about being "In the Navy." But it turns out that Harvey Milk had been in the Navy, receiving an "other than honorable" discharge for being homosexual. Here, at least, Milk was arguably a victim because he was gay.

But we used to name ships after heroes, not victims. Naming a ship after Harvey Milk is still an "other than honorable" gesture. It is less about honoring Harvey Milk than dishonoring the US Navy. Apparently, five other ships will also be named after woke icons. I don't even want to know their names.

To my mind, the most absurd Milk tribute is the opera *Harvey Milk* by "American composer and cantor" Stewart Wallace, which casts Harvey Milk as a baritone and Dan White as a tenor and includes such characters as Dianne Feinstein and (of course) "concentration camp survivors."

There is, however, a genuinely worthwhile tribute to Harvey Milk: Gus Van Sant's 2008 biopic *Milk*, starring Sean Penn who won the Best Actor Oscar for his whiny nebbishy portrayal of the man himself. *Milk* was released to universal critical acclaim, but I gave it a hard pass when it was in theaters, since no critic would dare expose it if it were bad. Years later, I gave *Milk* a chance when it popped up on cable.

Milk is a well-made but typical biopic, complete with montages set to contemporary pop music. I don't know how accurate it is, and I honestly don't care enough to look into it too deeply. I know it omits Milk's endorsement of Jim Jones and the People's Temple and his penchants for manic and emotionally abusive behavior. I must note, however, that if the movie is a whitewash, a lot of unflattering facts still show through.

Milk is portrayed as neurotic, abrasive, duplicitous, and aggressively Jewish. He is portrayed as an active player in the Leftist takeover of the San Francisco government which eventually ruined America's most beautiful city. He wasn't above outing fellow homosexuals for personal political advantage (which is merely hinted at in the film). He cynically instructs his followers to start a riot, so he can pop up and play the peacemaker before the news cameras. In debates, Milk was an aggressive prick. His speeches began with the line, "My name is Harvey Milk, and I'm here to recruit you," which is shown to be self-defeating, since it played into the hands of fundamentalist Christians pushing a ballot proposition to fire homosexual teachers to prevent them from "recruiting" children into homosexuality. As soon as he got elected to office, Milk began throwing his weight around, making demands and issuing threats. He dated a drunkard with clear borderline tendencies who embarrassed him in public and later hanged himself.

The movie begins in 1970 with Harvey Milk, a closeted Republican in New York City, turning 40 and feeling that he has done nothing to be proud of. (This film offers hope to late bloomers.) Milk and his then boyfriend Scott Smith (James Franco) decide to move to the Castro District of San Francisco. Harvey morphs into a hippy, but he has the capital and the skills to open a small business, Castro Camera.

The shop not only is a source of income, it becomes a power base. It is a place to interact with the public and network. Later, it serves as a meeting place for political discussions and organizing. Milk's first foray into politics was organizing gay shop owners in the Castro. He also began directing business to friendly straight shop owners and away from hostile ones. (Although it is not shown in the film, when Milk organized the Castro Street Fair, it brought large crowds to the district. Skeptical merchants were won over by booming sales.)

When Milk first ran for City Supervisor in 1973, he was an angry, abrasive hippy with a narrowly sectarian gay agenda and an energetic but amateurish campaign. He lost. When he ran again in 1975, he cleaned up his appearance, sought to build coalitions, and became more diplomatic. He lost again but came closer to power. In 1976, he ran for State Assembly and lost to Art Agnos, who later became Mayor of San Francisco.

Agnos is shown dispensing valuable advice to Milk, whose speeches were angry rants about gay victimhood. He needed to articulate a more positive vision and offer policies to improve the lives of everyone. Milk took this advice to heart. Later he ran a campaign against dog poop, to clean up San Francisco's parks.

In 1977, Milk ran for City Supervisor yet again. This time, he brought in a professional campaign consultant and sought establishment endorsements. He won.

But it would not have happened without San Francisco changing the election rules. Instead of the whole city voting on a common roster of candidates, the city was divided into districts. The establishment's goal was to elect a more "diverse" (i.e., Leftist) Board of Supervisors by creating districts that would favor strongly Leftist constituencies. That year, Chinatown put a Chinaman on the Board. A heavily black district elected a black woman. Milk's district included the Haight and the Castro. He was a shoo-in.

At every step of his political career, Milk was courageous, tireless, and masterful at motivating others to work for him. Once he paired these virtues with the right packaging, message, and objective political conditions, he succeeded.

The peak of Milk's career was his 1978 campaign against Proposition 6, a ballot initiative backed by fundamentalist Christians demanding that homosexuals be purged from public schools lest they "recruit." Milk argued that closeted homosexuals should come out to their friends, neighbors, coworkers, and families. He believed that fewer people would vote for Proposition 6 if they actually knew a homosexual, whereas it would be easier for them to victimize essentially invisible and anonymous people. It was a gamble, since homosexual vanguardists tend towards exhibitionism and delight in antagonizing "breeders." ("I'm Harvey Milk, and I'm here to recruit you.") Maybe Milk was counting on closeted homosexuals to be less provocative and thus soften the gay image.

Many prominent politicians, including Ronald Reagan, opposed Proposition 6, which was defeated by a margin of 2:1, so it is hard to know how much Milk's efforts contributed. Nevertheless, in a talk called "Toward the Tipping Point,"[1] I argued that

---

[1] Greg Johnson, "Toward the Tipping Point: Making Our Ideas Viral," *Counter-Currents*, October 21, 2015.

Milk's strategy might pay off for nationalists once we reach a certain percentage of the electorate. For instance, in Sweden nationalists are a quarter of the electorate, yet they are essentially invisible in their communities, which allows their enemies to control their image and demonize them. In countries where nationalists have the strength of numbers and can organize counter-measures to the firing and harassment of their supporters, they should consider nationalist "coming out days" to increase their exposure and humanize themselves.

I won't lie: there's a lot to cringe at in *Milk*. But if you are interested in identity politics and retail political organizing, it offers food for thought as well.

The Unz Review, November 30, 2021

MISHIMA:
THE LAST DEBATE

Yukio Mishima (1925–1970) was one of the giants of Japanese letters as well as an outspoken Right-wing nationalist. On November 25, 1970, Mishima shocked the world when he and members of his private militia, the Tatenokai or Shield Society, took hostage the commander of the Japan Self-Defense Force's Ichigaya Camp. Mishima then delivered a speech to the assembled soldiers and press, exhorting the Japanese to turn away from American-imposed consumerism back to their traditional aristocratic culture, which prized honor above life and comfort. Then, to show that he really meant it, Mishima committed ritual suicide along with one of his followers, Masako Morita.

Mishima: The Last Debate, directed by Keisuke Toyoshima, focuses on an event that took place on May 13, 1969: Mishima's debate with the radical student protest group, the All-Campus Joint Struggle Committee or Zenkyoto, which had mounted violent protests against the government, the educational system, and the American occupiers. Interestingly enough, Zenkyoto was anti-communist as well as anti-capitalist and anti-American. They drew more inspiration from phenomenology and existentialism than from Marxism.

Mishima despised Marxism and probably would not have debated communists. But Zenkyoto's third positionist stance overlapped significantly with his own Right-wing nationalism. Thus he accepted the invitation to debate in the hope of winning over some of the students. This was not a Quixotic hope, given that the Shield Society consisted mostly of college students.

The debate took place in Lecture Hall 900 of the University of Tokyo in front of an audience of 1,000 including Mishima's Tatenokai security detail. The event lasted two hours and was filmed by the broadcaster TBS. The footage was long thought lost. When it was rediscovered, it was given to Toyoshima to create a documentary, which runs for 1 hour, 51 minutes and incorporates 45 minutes of debate footage plus contemporary news footage of student unrest and recent interviews with debate participants and eyewitnesses, as well as academics and two prominent novelists. The novelists are Mishima's friend Jakucho Setouchi, a Buddhist nun who was 97 years old at the time of the interview, and Keiichiro Hirano, an outspoken admirer of Mishima. The film is fundamentally respectful of Mishima and all other participants in the debate. The documentary premiered in Japan in late 2020, and only now has a version subtitled in English leaked onto the internet.

Mishima's performance in the debate is masterful. Dressed in a black polo and white slacks, he is conspicuously fitter and more stylish—and even more youthful—than the students, who are half his age but often look frumpy, slovenly, and defensive. Mishima is remarkably diplomatic and respectful in dealing with the students, even when they are rude and abrasive. He is relaxed throughout: smoking, laughing, and cracking jokes with the audience. He seeks to find common ground and then bring the students around to his way of thinking.

Mishima could win on charisma alone, but his arguments are even more impressive. He knows his phenomenology and existentialism better than the students yet keeps his remarks firmly grounded while his interlocutors often float away in abstractions. At the 29-minute mark, Mishima answers a question about the status of the "other" in his thought that is the high point of the film. He begins by saying that he hates Jean-Paul Sartre—probably because he was a communist—then explains Sartre's phenomenology of the obscene as objectification in *Being and Nothingness*—bringing the house down with a joke about the Prime Minister—before arguing that non-objectifying relationships with others are fraught with the potential for enmity and violence, which of course give rise to the political. He states that when he wished to move away from a literature that merely objectified others, he had to choose an enemy, which for him is communism. It is a rather deft transition from abstract philosophy to concrete Rightist politics.

There's a good deal of back and forth between Mishima and a hippy actor and director named Masahiko Akuta, who shows up with his infant daughter in his arms. Akuta is often quite muddle-headed and overly abstract. He frequently comes off as a phony. But Mishima patiently tries to interpret Akuta's remarks and respond to them. Akuta is also quite rude at times, but Mishima never takes umbrage.

When Akuta brings his arguments down to earth, it is usually in the form of accusations premised on goofy cosmopolitan pieties. "You are nothing without Japan," he asserts, to which Mishima replies by inventing the "yes" meme in 1969: "That's me." When Akuta accuses Mishima of being unable to transcend being Japanese, Mishima says, "That's okay." As Akuta waxes cosmopolitan, Mishima just responds, "Ah so," holds out the microphone, and lets Akuta dig himself into a deeper hole.

Mishima defends his Japanese identity as simply a fact, as a destiny that cannot be avoided. His only choice in the matter is to own up to it or not. In Heidegger's idiom, being Japanese is Mishima's "thrownness," and owning up to that fact is "authenticity." By contrast, Akuta's claim that one can transcend one's nationality is inauthenticity: phoniness. We do not create our identities, nor can we recreate them, but try telling that to an actor. Mishima is quite comfortable with philosophical abstractions, but being a novelist, he is also masterful at making them concrete. At one point, he tells the audience that if they don't know what it means to be Japanese, they need to go abroad for a spell.

Mishima makes frequent reference to the emperor, telling the students that he would have joined their movement if they had mentioned the emperor just once. At one point, he states that the students are wrong to think the emperor is "bourgeois." The bourgeois ethos places life and comfort above all else, whereas the aristocratic ethos embodied by the emperor puts honor above life and comfort. Mishima recounts how the emperor presided over the graduation ceremony of his elite high school, remaining as rigid as a statue for three hours. Mishima wished to communicate that there is an aristocratic critique of bourgeois society from above, not just the Marxist critique from below.

The documentary ends with Mishima's suicide, which includes actual footage from Mishima's final speech plus the announcement that he and Morita had killed themselves. I did not know that this footage existed, and although it was brief, I found it surprisingly moving. I hope it will be the seed of its own documentary. Many of the soldiers who heard Mishima are alive today. I would like to know their thoughts after more than fifty years.

I was also quite amazed to see interviews with three members of the Shield Society, all of them in their 70s, as well as to learn that they still meet every November 25th to honor Mishima and Morita. As one would expect, they are a very dignified lot.

Several things are remarkable about Mishima's debate. First, it is carried on at a very high level of abstraction, with remarkable earnestness. Today's student radicals are inane and infantile by comparison. Second, Mishima's performance is impressive in both substance and style. Third, it is astonishing that such a meeting took place at all, although in the 1960s, George Lincoln Rockwell was invited to speak on American university campuses. Such events would never happen in academia today. If they were scheduled in the first place, they would rapidly be shut down by angry mobs.

At the beginning of the debate, Mishima says he is there to test whether words can still bridge the gap between opposed political camps. It was possible at the University of Tokyo in 1969. It scarcely seems possible today, but the documentary itself proves that it is. When Toyoshima was offered the project, he had a one-sided and negative image of Mishima. Thus when he viewed the footage, he was shocked at Mishima's graciousness, humor, and fair-mindedness. I think he tried to emulate these qualities in the film, with great success, since it is scrupulously decent and respectful in its portrayal of all parties. *Mishima: The Last Debate* is an excellent documentary. I recommend it highly to anyone interested in Mishima, Japanese culture, and radical politics, where the extremes really can meet from time to time.

The Unz Review, July 27, 2021

THE *NO TIME TO DIE* TRAILERS

Everybody has a time to die, including James Bond. Bond has cheated death countless times, but this time his number may be up. If so, the death certificate will list COVID-19.

No Time to Die, the twenty-fifth Bond film from Eon productions, stars Daniel Craig in his fifth and final outing as Bond. *No Time to Die* was supposed to have been directed by Danny Boyle (*Trainspotting*) who was to share script-writing duty with his *Trainspotting* collaborator John Hodge. I thought this was a fantastic team. But they left the film because of creative differences.

Boyle was replaced by Cary Joji Fukunaga, the half-white, half-Japanese American director of the first season of *True Detective*. The script is by Fukunaga with Neal Purvis and Robert Wade, plus Phoebe Waller-Bridge, who was brought in to add wokeness, which does not bode well.

The cast brings back Christoph Walz, Ralph Fiennes, Léa Seydoux, Ben Whishaw, and Naomi Harris to reprise their roles from past films. Rami Malek plays the villain Safin, which is an inspired bit of casting.

But there are bad portents in the music department. Fukunaga associate Dan Romer left while scoring the film over creative differences and was replaced by Hans Zimmer, who has done a large number of undistinguished but workmanlike scores. Billie Eilish's theme song is one of the worst Bond songs ever, and there's stiff competition.[1] These lapses of taste alone do not bode well for the film.

No Time to Die was filmed from April to October 2019 in Italy, Jamaica, Norway, the UK, and the Faroe Islands at the cost of $250 million. The release was scheduled for April 2020 but because of COVID-19 was postponed twice, first to November of 2020, then to April 2021.

That's a very long time to wait to recoup such a huge investment, and if further delays are necessary, the financial burdens

---

[1] Greg Johnson, "Bond Songs: From Best to Worst," *Counter-Currents*, February 28, 2020.

will only mount. This could very well be the first straight-to-video Bond movie, which financially would be a very far cry from the box office receipts of *Skyfall* ($1.111 billion) and *Spectre* ($879.6 million).

A commercial flop won't necessarily kill the Bond franchise, but it could put it on extended hiatus, as well as dry up potential talent and funding. It might be the final straw for Eon Productions, led by half-siblings Barbara Broccoli and Michael Wilson, who might just pull a George Lucas and sell the franchise to one of the studio conglomerates. We know how well that worked out for *Star Wars*, which Disney ruined with cynical, formulaic remakes and obnoxious ultra-Left propaganda.

Of course, Eon Productions has its own history of cynical remakes and Leftist propaganda, and, judging from the two trailers for *No Time to Die*, and other publicity materials, Bond's death certificate may list political correctness as a co-morbidity.

In July of 2019, the world learned from alleged "leaks" and "inside sources" that *No Time to Die* would feature a black, female 007 played by Lashana Lynch (no relation). This was simply a cheap, dishonest publicity stunt calculated to mislead readers who initially thought that the character of James Bond had been turned into a black woman. But the merest glance below the headlines indicates that, no, Bond is still a white man, but at the beginning of *No Time to Die*, Bond has retired from MI6 so his *number* 007 had been reassigned to a black woman.

If Eon wants to generate even more buzz about this film, perhaps they will reveal that Bond's office has been reassigned to a gay Chinaman and his parking space has been reassigned to a crippled lesbian.

This kind of cynical publicity has been a feature of the Bond franchise for decades. For instance, it is often claimed that the new Bond girl will be a "strong, independent woman" — unlike all the rest. Of course, virtually every Bond girl from the start has been strong and independent. The Bond franchise is also notorious for sex and race replacement, casting Judy Dench as M who dressed down Pierce Brosnan's Bond as a "sexist, misogynist dinosaur." Eon has also blacked up the recurring characters of Felix Leiter and Miss Moneypenny, and every few years, they float the rumor that a black male James Bond is in the offing. They keep doing this because there hasn't been a backlash—yet.

Hilariously enough, though, Lashana Lynch made the rounds in the media taking the farce with deadly seriousness. She pretended that having the number 007 is a great achievement for someone black and female (and trans, by the look of her), as if her character were more than just an empty collection of PC "firsts" which she was qualified to play for reasons other than being a black trans woman. Lynch vows, moreover, to play the role *authentically*, the comic potential of which was explored in countless racist "Ms. Bond" memes.

This pushback was completely predictable, for Eon's stunt was not just calculated to mislead but also to offend. White people are increasingly sick of the Great Replacement, both on the silver screen and in the real world. So Eon basically dared racist web wags to go after Lashana Lynch.

They were probably hoping to replicate the troll storm that greeted another black trans woman, Leslie Jones, when she was cast in the 2016 SJW remake of *Ghostbusters*, a campaign that led to Milo Yiannopoulos being permanently banned from Twitter. This was, of course, great publicity for *Ghostbusters*, since it promoted black, feminist, and SJW solidarity against evil racists and anti-feminists. It wasn't enough to prevent *Ghostbusters* from bombing, however.

If Eon's publicity agents are worth their salt, they were trying to provoke the same reaction. Who knows, maybe they created the prototypes for the Ms. Bond memes. While internet racists gleefully "trigger the libs," the "libs" have figured out how to trigger internet racists and use them to sell more of their filth.

Since *No Time to Die* did not appear in November due to the second wave of COVID-19, Eon decided to squeeze a little more buzz out of the Lashana Lynch stunt, this time focusing on how bravely she endured the pushback from "toxic" and "racist" Bond fans who were scandalized by the idea of her having Bond's old number. The poor dear even had to take a break from social media for a whole week.

Of course, not one in a thousand people is dumb enough to care about Bond's *number*. What offended them was the tiresomeness of the Great Replacement, the fraudulence of this particular stunt, the emptiness of Ms. Lynch's historic "achievement," and how seriously she seemed to be taking it.

The whole thing smacks of desperation. Is this the best case they can make for this film?

Now let's look at the trailers and see what they reveal.

The first trailer was released December 4, 2019. Lashana Lynch is disturbingly prominent. She's dark black, sweaty-looking, ugly, arrogant, and threatens to shoot Bond. In all fairness, though, she's not nearly as scary-looking as Grace Jones. When Bond returns to MI6 headquarters, his name is not recognized by the black fellow at the desk. Then we see Bond flanked by Lynch's 007 and Miss Moneypenny, both black. "The world's moved on," says Lynch in a voiceover, and that means the Great Replacement. It is that disgustingly blatant. And the reaction of many white normies has been visceral rejection.

Let's hope they cut together all the anti-white bits and put them up front. But the question is: Why? Why the ritualistic humiliation and replacement of a white hero? Obviously, because the Great Denigration and Great Replacement of whites is the central ideology—the Satanic anti-religion—of our time. The sad truth, though, is that the filmmakers do not do this to appease blacks but to appease other whites, especially their fellow white people who dominate the movie business.

The second trailer, released on September 3, 2020, is an enormous improvement. It dials back the wokeness to almost zero. (Why did they do that? Was there some pushback?)

If I had only seen the second trailer and had been spared the Lashana Lynch publicity stunt, I would be enthusiastic about seeing this movie. I am strongly prejudiced, though. Daniel Craig is my favorite Bond, and I think *Casino Royale* and *Skyfall* are two of the best Bond films of all time. If the script of *No Time to Die* is on a high enough level, Craig can carry the show, and no woke monkey business will be able to sink this film.

Furthermore, as a Bond fan with a long memory, I also have low expectations. Bond movies were promoting race-mixing and gender-bending back in the sixties. I am a fan in spite of all that. And even the worst woke elements of *No Time to Die* will probably not compare with *Live and Let Die* (1973) or *A View to a Kill* (1985), in which our hero ends up in bed with Grace Jones.

As a reviewer, I will of course make time to see *No Time to Die*, no matter what. But I am reasonably optimistic that I will actually like it. If it is woke garbage, I will certainly let you know.

But there's a real question as to whether the white men who are the core of Bond's fan base are going to see *No Time to Die* or stay away in droves. "Go woke, go broke" was wrecking movies long before the death of George Floyd set off months of black rioting. Now a lot of white men who might have been amused by Lashana Lynch are experiencing Negro fatigue.

Beyond that, white men are increasingly embittered. Bitterness is a wild card, because it leads to spite. A spiteful man will even harm his own interests to avenge himself. He can't be reasoned with, predicted, or controlled. A critical mass of white men like that are going to be a problem for more than just the movie business.

The Unz Review, December 1, 2020

NO TIME TO DIE

No Time to Die is an excellent Bond film. It belongs in the company of *Casino Royale* and *Skyfall* and quite self-consciously reaches for the heights of *On Her Majesty's Secret Service*, which is arguably the best Bond film ever.

I was especially looking forward to *No Time to Die* because—although it is very much a minority opinion—my favorite Bond actor is Daniel Craig. (Timothy Dalton is my next favorite, although he only played the role twice and only one of his films, *License to Kill*, is first-rate.) Neither Craig nor Dalton is the best-looking Bond, but they are both excellent actors who give the character some soul. Fleming's Bond is arguably a sociopath, but one can't say the same about Dalton's Bond and especially Craig's.

No Time to Die is Craig's fifth and final Bond film and seems to bring the Bond saga to an end. But fear not, there will always be new Bond films. The whole series could be "rebooted," but it would be far preferable to simply do "prequels." I very much hope Tom Hardy is the next James Bond and that Christopher Nolan takes a turn or two as director.

The story arc of Craig's five Bond films is now clear: from orphan with half-understood entanglements with surrogate parents in *Casino Royale* and *Quantum of Solace*, to a return to his ancestral home with a surrogate family (Judy Dench's M and Albert Finney's Kincade) in *Skyfall*, to an encounter with his foster brother—including sibling rivalries and cuckoldry—in *Spectre*, to Bond's attempt to form a family of his own with Madeline Swann (Léa Seydoux) in *No Time to Die*. It is the family themes—especially in *Casino Royale*, *Skyfall*, and *No Time to Die*—that allow Craig to tap into and communicate real emotional depth and power.

There are many strong performances in this film. The best is Daniel Craig's. Léa Seydoux is also excellent as Madeline. Rami Malek is a very effective villain. It is odd casting an Egyptian as a Russian, but it is not the first time it has happened (see *Doctor*

Zhivago). The script by longtime Bond writers Neal Purvis and Robert Wade is well-constructed, making use of aspects of Fleming's Bond mythos that have not yet been incorporated into the movies. Some aspects of the villain's ultimate plot left me puzzled, but that is a minor problem. Half-white, half-Japanese America Cary Joji Fukunaga is an artful and effective director. The movie is well-paced, despite the long running time, and the action sequences are extremely well-done and often grittily realistic, especially the aftereffects of explosions on Bond. There's some humor—especially Ana de Armas as Paloma who is cutely awkward—but no camp. I usually don't notice Hans Zimmer's music at all, but in *No Time to Die*, it is sometimes excellent, including a passage near the end that made me think of Arvo Pärt. (His best score remains *Interstellar*.) The theme song by Billie Eilish is a snoozer, which is sad, because the themes for *Casino Royale*, *Skyfall*, and *Spectre* were so good.

Of course the big question is whether or not *No Time to Die* is "woke." Relax. The answer is: No, not by the standard of other Bond films, which have a long history of diversity casting and race-mixing. There was a media manufactured "scandal" about casting a very black woman, Lashana Lynch, as the new 007. But she merely got Bond's number when he retired. As Bond points out in the film, "It's just a number."

In some ways, *No Time to Die* is actually less woke than earlier Bond films. I am sure nobody will complain of a "spoiler" if I reveal that Bond doesn't end up sleeping with Lynch's character, which is interesting, since Bond has bedded black women in the movies starting fifty years ago with *Live and Let Die*. In *A View to a Kill*, he ended up in bed with Grace Jones, who is far scarier than Lashana Lynch.

As I predicted in my article on the trailers for *No Time to Die*, the claims that this movie is especially "woke" were simply a cheap publicity stunt, perhaps intended to trigger racists on the internet to give the movie free publicity. You've been had. But don't be angry. Just be flattered. They did it because they know we have power.

The Unz Review, October 7, 2021

RED RIVER

Howard Hawks' *Red River* (1948) is one of the greatest Westerns. *Red River* has it all: charismatic performances by John Wayne and Montgomery Clift, a solid ensemble cast to back them up, a beautifully economical script, dramatic black-and-white cinematography, and a surprisingly good score from Dimitri Tiomkin, who had always struck me as a hack.

All of these elements are masterfully drawn together by Hawks. His sense of pacing and visual drama never fails. He grabs your attention with stark contrasts between dark and light, vast landscapes and closeups. He'll sweep you up in action, then stop you dead in wonder.

Red River is the story of the first cattle drive on the Chisholm Trail from Texas to Abilene, Kansas. In Hawks' hands, however, a movie about an episode in the history of America's livestock business becomes mythic, epic, and philosophical. The frontier strips away the trappings of civilization and displays human nature and the origins of society naked in all their glory and squalor. Like such great Westerns as *The Searchers*, *The Man Who Shot Liberty Valance*, and *Once Upon a Time in the West*, *Red River* is an origin story about the transition from savage to civil society.

This transition is particularly problematic for Americans, since our default programming is liberal individualism that prizes equality, personal freedom, contractual obligation, private life, and comfort above things like adventure, conquest, honor, and glory, to say nothing of holiness and truth.

Unfortunately, as *Red River* shows, you can't carve civilization out of the wilderness by following liberal principles—although it is increasingly evident that liberalism can wreck any society that takes it too seriously. Liberalism forces us either to cover up the illiberal origins of our society or to destroy it in a fit of self-loathing. (But there's another option as well: to embrace the truth about our origins and stop immolating ourselves before the Moloch of liberal norms.)

Red River begins in 1851. A wagon train is headed to California. Pioneers banded together because there is strength in numbers, and strength was needed to confront the dangers of the frontier, including merciless Indian savages. But practically the first thing we see is a wagon pulling away from the safety of the train. Thomas Dunson (John Wayne) has decided to strike south for Texas and found a cattle ranch.

The leader of the wagon train doesn't want Dunson to go. They are all safer sticking together. Dunson understands that, but this appeal to rational self-interest falls on deaf ears. He has a vision, and he is willing to accept the risks to follow it. The leader says Dunson agreed to go to California. Dunson says he signed nothing, and as we will soon see, promises on paper mean nothing to him anyway. The leader says that Dunson is too good with a gun to lose. Dunson replies that he's also too good with a gun to keep. In the end, it comes down to the threat of force.

Dunson has fallen in love on the trail with Fen (Colleen Gray). He wants to leave her behind as well. Founding a ranch is hard, dangerous work. She's not strong enough. "But what about the nights?" she asks. Good question, but in Tom's mind, starting a cattle ranch requires cows for the bulls but not women for the men. Tom promises to send for her when it is safe and gives her his mother's bracelet (which he himself was wearing) as a token of his pledge.

This opening scene establishes that Tom Dunson is not a man to be reasoned with. Once he makes up his mind, he is immovable. Being open to persuasion, of course, is one of the principles of parliamentary democracy.[1] Dunson, however, is quick to reach for his gun to silence his critics. He's a budding tyrant, not a liberal democrat. But, as it turns out, it takes a tyrant to found a great ranch in the wilderness.

Dunson turns south with his sidekick Groot (Walter Brennan) plus two cows and a bull to start his herd. A few hours later, the wagon train is massacred by Indians. Dunson and Groot see the smoke in the distance and prepare to defend

---

[1] Greg Johnson, "Notes on Schmitt's *Crisis*—and Ours," *Counter-Currents*, July 19, 2020.

themselves. They kill the raiding party sent after them, but the two cows are slaughtered. Dunson also recovers his engagement bracelet from one of the braves, who surely killed Fen to take it.

The next morning, they come upon a boy named Matt Garth (Mickey Kuhn) leading a cow. He is the sole survivor of the massacre. He's gibbering from the horror. Dunson snaps him out of it with a brutal slap. It's a rough beginning, but Matt and his cow become the co-founders of a great ranch, the Red River D. "D" for Dunson.

When Tom finds the spot he wants to settle down on, he is greeted by two Mexican riders, who inform him that this land belongs by grant and patent from the King of all the Spains to one Don Diego, who resides 400 miles to the south. Groot thinks that's too much land for one man. So does Tom. Groot is a Lockean, who believed that when we appropriate property from the state of nature, we should leave as much and as good for others.

Tom, however, has no such notions. He wants to build his own empire. When one of Don Diego's emissaries draws his gun, Tom kills him and tells the other to inform Don Diego of the new arrangement. When Tom releases the cow and bull, he says that wherever his herds roam will be his land. The herd will appropriate for him. (The Hungarians have a similar land-appropriation myth.) There's no talk of leaving as much and as good for others.

Flash forward to 1865. The Red River D has become the largest ranch in Texas. Tom has killed six more men to protect it, but other ranches have started in the area.

Matt has grown into a man superbly played by Montgomery Clift. Matt is the son Tom never had. But there is a strange intimacy between them. Matt now wears the engagement bracelet Tom gave to Fen. They share cigarettes with one another. When Tom starts putting his brand on other ranchers' cattle, Matt jokes that pretty soon his will be the only rump around there without Tom's brand. Tom says, "Bring me the iron." There's more than just a hint of pederasty here. This is what happens on the frontier when women are left behind as too weak.

The Civil War has ended. Matt has returned to Texas, quite practiced in the use of his gun. It goes without saying that he fought for the South. Texas is in crisis. There's no market for beef in the defeated South, so Tom decides to drive his herd a thousand miles to a railhead in Missouri, to ship them north. They will face obstacles from men as well as nature. Indians and murderous gangs of rustlers stand in their way. It will be a brutal march, but Tom Dunson is a man of enormous will. He will make it happen.

As the drive progresses and obstacles mount up, Tom wears out cattle, horses, and men. The men become sullen and restive, and Tom becomes increasingly obsessive and tyrannical: Captain Ahab in a saddle.

Tom has no sense of being on equal footing with other men. He doesn't listen to them. When the men learn that they can drive the herd to Abilene, Kansas and avoid the Missouri border gangs, Tom will hear none of it. His mind is made up.

Although the story began with Tom quitting the wagon train, when three men propose to quit the drive, Tom guns them down. When three more desert, Tom sends a gunslinger to retrieve them. One is killed and two return. Tom then says he is going the hang the deserters.

But this time, he has gone too far, and Matt leads a mutiny. They will take Tom's herd to Abilene and leave Tom behind. Tom vows to kill Matt, and Matt believes him.

Tyranny might have been necessary to create the ranch and start the drive. But men are not animals, and Matt's more democratic style of leadership is necessary to finish it. As the men move closer to civilization, they begin taking on some of its features. And in this case, who can blame them?

In the last act of *Red River*, Matt completes the drive. When his scouts find a wagon train ahead, complete with women and coffee, Matt changes the drive's course to meet them. The men clearly need a break, and they are low on supplies. Tom never would have considered it. When the wagon train comes under Indian attack, Matt abandons the herd and rides to the rescue. Tom never would have bothered.

But in many ways, Matt is like Tom. When Matt meets a a beautiful woman, Tess Millay (Joanne Dru) in the wagon train, it is clearly love at first sight. She wants to leave with him, but he refuses. She's too weak for the road ahead. She's been wounded by an Indian arrow, but beyond that, she's a woman. Matt leaves her with Tom's engagement token.

Meanwhile, Tom has gathered some gunmen and set off in pursuit of Matt. He knows he is getting old. He knows that Matt is the closest thing he will ever have to a son. He knows that if he kills him, there will be nobody to carry on his vision once he has gone. But his wrath is too great. He is like Wotan in Wagner's *Siegfried*, who knows that his grandson Siegfried is his only hope for the future but still warns the lad not to tempt his wrath, lest it bring both of them to ruin.

Tom's wrath is his thumotic side expressing itself. Up to this point, Tom has shown immense willpower, but it is all in service of building a ranch. He's a titan of industry, but at bottom he's just a merchant. Now we see Tom willing to throw away everything he has built to avenge a very personal betrayal. It is one of John Wayne's greatest performances. When Tom finally catches up to Matt, he is genuinely terrifying, striding straight through the milling herd toward Matt, murder in his eyes.

It is an amazing buildup to one of cinema's most anticlimactic and farcical resolutions. The mythic and heroic thrust of *Red River* points toward a bloody end: the unstoppable force of Tom Dunson versus the unmovable object of Matt Garth. Tom's wrath is too great to be turned aside by words. One of them has to die. The only really happy ending possible is Matt killing Tom. It is terrible to have to kill one's tyrant father, but it is the only way to secure a future. It would be a powerful coming-of-age story.

Instead, however, Matt allows Tom to shoot at him. Is he used to this kind of abuse? Is Matt acting the role of Jesus, letting his father expend his wrath on him? But Matt can't stop bullets or rise from the dead, so it seems like madness. Normally, it would mean Matt's death. So our storyteller—with flawless anti-tragic instincts—contrived to have Tom wounded by one of Matt's friends, so his aim is off. Then Tom begins beating Matt until Matt fights back. At this point, both are so tired that it is clear that nobody will die today. The duel to the death over honor has been replaced by a scuffle in the dirt.

Having averted tragedy, the movie then plunges headlong into farce. Tess Millay breaks up the fight by firing off a gun. Tom and Matt are breathless, bloody, and sprawled on their asses amid a peddler's pots and pans. But they seem most stunned by the fact that they are being scolded like naughty children by a woman waving a gun around.

Tess's ravings are a classic case of dismissing the masculine struggle for honor—which basically encompasses the whole field of human history—as just a childish game. There's no question that Tom's resolution to kill Matt is unhinged, but it isn't silly. Neither is most of human history. But, to borrow a line from Camille Paglia, if Tess Millay had her way, we'd still be living in grass huts.

When Tom met Tess while pursuing Matt, he offered her half his fortune to bear him a real son who could replace Matt. There's a lot going on here: Matt cuckolding Tom by taking up with a woman, Tom cuckolding Matt to father an heir to displace him, Tess saying she'll take the offer if Tom calls off his vendetta, which reveals that Tess will only marry Tom because she's in love with Matt, and who knows how many layers of love, jealousy, and spite. But now Tom suggests that Matt should marry Tess after all.

This reminds me of another Wagner story. In *Die Meistersinger*, Hans Sachs renounces the much younger Eva so she can marry Walter, a knight closer to her age. One of the core themes of both stories is what Erik Erikson called "generativity": older generations promoting the wellbeing of younger generations to ensure the survival of the species.

At the heart of generativity is renunciation. Life has to go on, and if the old do not relinquish power to the young, then none of us has a future. But still, I find Tom's sudden transformation from embittered, power-mad killer to great big softie too quick. Nothing we have seen in the movie so far makes this change plausible.

Red River is an entertaining and emotionally powerful epic about the conquest of a continent. But in the last few minutes, it whisks us straight from barbarism to decadence: from frontier patriarchy to schoolmarm matriarchy. You can criticize it as drama, but you can't fault it as a history of America.

The Unz Review, November 24, 2021

THE RED SHOES

Michael Powell's *The Red Shoes* (1948) is his greatest work and one of my all-time favorite films. *The Red Shoes* is a work of art about art. The central characters of *The Red Shoes* are ballet impresario Boris Lermontov (brilliantly played by Anton Walbrook), ballerina Victoria Page (acted and danced by Moira Shearer), and composer Julian Craster (Marius Goring, who was much too old for the role and looks ridiculous whenever he smokes a cigarette but is otherwise adequate).

Page and Craster are young talents who are drawn into the creative vortex of Lermontov's company, rise quickly to stardom, then fall in love with one another and fall out with Lermontov. A happy ending seems, however, to be in the offing until the screenwriter contrives a perversely tragic finale in which Vicky Page dies. Both Lermontov and Craster live on, but they are utterly destroyed as human beings.

The Red Shoes doesn't just *dance around* its subject—focusing on personalities, the creative process, and backstage romance—it actually puts ballet on the screen, most spectacularly in the form of a seventeen-minute original ballet based on Hans Christian Andersen's fairytale "The Red Shoes," with music by Brian Easdale, set design by Hein Heckroth, and choreography by the great Robert Helpmann and Léonide Massine, who also dance in the ballet and play the roles of Ivan Boleslawsky and Grischa Ljubov in the film.

The core of *The Red Shoes* is the character of Boris Lermontov, loosely based on the great Russian ballet impresario Sergei Diaghilev and unforgettably brought to life by Anton Walbrook. Lermontov is brilliant, charismatic, and utterly devoted to ballet, which he regards as his "religion." He can be domineering, autocratic, brooding, and sometimes brutally frank. But his most outstanding traits are the elegant manners, sensitive diplomacy, and affectionate fatherliness with which he manages his team of highly strung and egotistical artists.

A great deal of the charm of *The Red Shoes* is watching Lermontov's creative family in action: Page, Craster, and Grischa as well as designer Sergei Ratov (played by the great German actor Albert Bassermann) and conductor Livingstone "Livy" Montague (played by Esmond Knight). Each day ends as one by one they bid him a fond "Goodnight, Boris."

Two of the best scenes—where Craster rehearses an orchestra, correcting a wrong note in the process, and where he introduces his original music for *The Red Shoes* ballet—were actually based on episodes in the process of creating the movie itself.

The Red Shoes is about the relationship between art and life. Early in the film, they are likened to one another, because they are both compulsions:

> **LERMONTOV:** Why do you want to dance?
> **VICKY:** Why do you want to live?
> **LERMONTOV:** Well, I don't know exactly why, but I must.
> **VICKY:** That's my answer too.

But if art and life are both compulsions, then they can conflict with one another. Even in the best of circumstances, artistic excellence can only be achieved by dominating the body and its desires, sublimating some, suppressing others. As Lermontov puts it, artistic excellence can only be achieved by a "great agony of body and spirit."

But beauty and excellence can easily become all-consuming obsessions that don't just dominate life but destroy it, a danger represented by the red shoes. In one of the best scenes in the movie, Lermontov summarizes the story of *The Red Shoes* ballet to Craster, who will compose the music:

> The ballet of *The Red Shoes* is from the fairy tale by Hans Andersen. It is the story of a girl who's devoured by an ambition to attend a dance in a pair of red shoes. She gets the shoes, goes to the dance. At first, all goes well, and she's very happy. At the end of the evening, she gets tired and wants to go home. But the red shoes are not tired. In fact, the red shoes are never tired. They dance her out into the streets. They dance her over the mountains and valleys

through fields and forests, through night and day. Time rushes by. Love rushes by. Life rushes by. But the red shoes dance on.

Lermontov is practically in a state of rapture when he completes his synopsis.

"What happens in the end?" asks Craster.

"Oh, in the end, she dies," says Lermontov, as if it were an afterthought.

The Hans Christian Andersen tale is more about sin and addiction to sensual pleasures, whereas in the film the red shoes represent the sacrifice of life to the obsessive pursuit of beauty.

Later in the film, after the successful debut of *The Red Shoes* ballet, Lermontov explains his ambitions for her career and offers Vicky a Mephistophelean choice:

> **LERMONTOV:** I want to create, to make something big out of something little, to make a great dancer out of you. But first, I must ask you the same question: What do you want from life? To live?
>
> **VICKY:** To dance.

Near the end of the film, Lermontov comforts a heartbroken Vicky with the words, "Life is so unimportant" — unimportant compared to art, that is.

Part of life is love, marriage, and family. Lermontov is particularly dismissive of ballerinas who allow these considerations to interfere with their art. First, it leads him to dismiss his prima ballerina Irina Boronskaja (Ludmilla Tchérina):

> I'm not interested in Boronskaja's form anymore . . . nor in the form of any other prima ballerina who's imbecile enough to get married. . . . She's out, finished. You cannot have it both ways. The dancer who relies upon the doubtful comforts of human love will never be a great dancer. Never.

(This episode seems to be based on Diaghilev's decision to fire

Vaslav Nijinsky when he got married.)

Lermontov then begins to groom Vicky to replace Boronskaja. When Lermontov learns that Vicky and Julian have fallen in love, he tries to break them up, driving Craster to quit on the assumption that Vicky will stay. But instead she leaves as well.

It is tempting to believe that Lermontov was acting out of sexual jealousy. His body language with Vicky in one scene is quite intimate. Also, before he learns of Vicky's relationship with Craster, he seems to wish to ask her on a date, although it may simply be to discuss business. Earlier in the film, Vicky thinks that Lermontov has invited her on a date, which she eagerly accepts, dressing up like a princess. But it turns out to be just a business meeting. Only when it becomes apparent that Lermontov is entirely focused on his work does she notice Craster. Craster accuses Lermontov of jealousy. He agrees, but says it is not sexual. He may be telling the truth. After all, there's no hint of sexual interest in Boronskaja, yet he rejects her for getting married as well. It might indeed be just about his single-minded devotion to ballet.

In another brilliant, brooding scene, Lermontov comes to the realization that he has been a fool. (Note that Lermontov, always the impresario, adjusts the lighting, finds his mark, and assumes a pose before inviting people into a room.) Then Lermontov decides to approach Boronskaja, who is still happily married, and lure her back on stage. Boris has obviously concluded that art and life—in particular, married life—need not conflict. A year later, he manages to lure Vicky back on stage to dance *The Red Shoes* again.

Then Emeric Pressburger's script goes seriously off the rails. Or, rather, the red shoes dance the story off a balcony and onto the rails. The original Andersen tale has a gruesome end. The girl, unable to take off the red shoes, asks the executioner to chop off her feet, which go dancing off in the red shoes. The girl, thus freed of sin, ends up going to heaven, which is a happy ending of sorts.

Fixated on contriving an ending that is both gruesome and unhappy, Pressburger simply forgets about Lermontov's character development toward accepting that his ballerinas can have private lives. He also turns Julian Craster into a petty, jealous villain—something not foreshadowed in the least. Then they drive Vicky to suicide.

The whole setup is absurd. Vicky has come to Monte Carlo on vacation. On the spur of the moment, she agrees to dance *The Red Shoes* again. We are asked to believe that Craster's new opera is to premiere in London the same day that Vicky dances *The Red Shoes* again in Monte Carlo. Why was Vicky in Monte Carlo on her husband's big night?

Then we are asked to believe that Craster leaves his premiere and travels all the way to Monte Carlo on the *suspicion* that his wife will be on stage again. He shows up in her dressing room to the sound of villainous music, dressed in a black leather trench coat (in Monte Carlo, in the summer). Is Julian a Nazi now? Then he demands that she return with him that very moment to London without going on stage.

Vicky refuses. Julian storms out. Lermontov villainously exults in triumph. Then Vicky, who is trying on the red shoes for that night's performance, goes mad and hurls herself off a balcony, then gets hit by a train. The train seems like overkill, but there's still enough life in her to beg a distraught Julian—who just happened to see her plunge to her death, even though it would have been impossible from his vantage point—to take off the red shoes.

I can't think of a more arbitrary, ramshackle, and dissatisfying end to an otherwise great movie. It is a testimony to just how good the rest of the film is that viewers put up with it.

When the producers of *The Red Shoes* saw the finished film, they thought they had an expensive flop on their hands and decided to cut their losses by stinting on the premiere and promotion in the UK. However, the film became a hit in the US, largely due to word of mouth and a few independent theatre owners who loved it. *The Red Shoes* ended up nominated for five Academy Awards, winning for its music and art direction. It went on to be one of the highest grossing British films ever.

Initial reviews were tepid and desultory, but the film's reputation among filmmakers and critics has grown steadily over the years. It is widely hailed as a masterpiece and included in many "best of" lists.

Despite the flawed ending there are many reasons why I return to *The Red Shoes* again and again: Michael Powell's extraordinary visual imagination, the colorful characters and outstanding cast that bring them to life, cinematographer Jack Cardiff's lush Technicolor, Brian Easdale's vivid music, the dazzling ballet sequences, and the glimpses of London, Paris, and Monte Carlo before the fall, which provoke nostalgia for a world I have never known.

But above all, I love *The Red Shoes* as a portrayal of the world of European high culture: an aristocratic, inegalitarian world devoted to the pursuit of beauty and excellence—a world whose basic principles contradict those of democracy and mass commercial entertainment. Try it for the entertainment. You'll stay for the art. And some of you will return out of obsession.

The Unz Review, August 23, 2021

THE SAILOR WHO FELL FROM GRACE WITH THE SEA

Yukio Mishima's 1963 novel *The Sailor Who Fell from Grace with the Sea* is one of his darkest works. Set in post-war Yokohama, it is the story of Fusako Kuroda, a thirty-three-year-old widow who runs a boutique selling Western luxury goods, and her thirteen-year-old son Noboru Kuroda.[1]

Fusako's world is entirely feminine, bourgeois, modern, and Western. She is also deeply lonely. Then she meets Ryuji Tsukazaki, the second-mate on a steamship. Ryuji is ruggedly masculine. Contemptuous of safety and hungering for risk, Ryuji took to the sea out of romantic longings for adventure and glory. But he too is lonely.

Ryuji and Fusako spend a few passionate days together, then he returns to the sea. But they can't forget one another, and when Ryuji returns to Yokohama some months later, he proposes marriage, which Fusako joyfully accepts.

Fusako's son Noboru is also attracted to Ryuji. He is a fatherless boy, cocooned in Western, bourgeois luxury. Ryuji represents the exact opposite. Noboru sees the sailor as archetypically masculine and heroic.

But Ryuji constantly disappoints Noboru. First of all, he is just *too nice*, whereas Noboru longs for hardness. But the last straw is when Ryuji decides to marry Noboru's mother and quit the sea. Fusako even starts dressing him in smart English suits and training him to work in her boutique.

Sounds like a soap opera plot easily resolved into a happy ending. But this is Mishima, so it is much, much weirder. When we are first introduced to Noboru, he is a peeping Tom, who watches his mother masturbate. Then he watches her make love with the sailor. Noboru also fancies himself a genius and belongs to a small circle of precocious thirteen-year-old Nietzsche-

---

[1] Alex Graham, "Yukio Mishima's *The Sailor Who Fell from Grace with the Sea*," *Counter-Currents*, December 4, 2017.

an sociopaths. This plot element reads like a mashup of Hitchcock's *Rope* and *Lord of the Flies*.

The gang starts out by killing and dissecting a cat, then they decide that the sailor can only be restored to his fallen heroic status by being cut up as well. We never actually see this happen, but everything is clearly driving toward it, and it mounts into one of the most suspenseful, gripping, and horrifying final chapters in literature.

Sailor is powerful because it is constructed around deep conflicts: primal family dramas as well as the clashes between land and sea, civilization and the wild, the masculine and feminine, the bourgeois pursuit of happiness vs. the heroic pursuit of glory, and Japanese tradition vs. Western modernity.

Sailor is a slender, compulsively-readable volume that most people can devour in an afternoon. It cried out for translation and then for a film adaptation. The translation came rather quickly, in 1965. I can't help wondering how Kurosawa would have directed *Sailor* in the Yokohama of *High and Low*,[2] or how Hitchcock or Michael Powell would have handled it in a Western setting. But the film adaptation of *Sailor* ended up in the hands of a very different director and appeared in 1976.

I avoided the film of *Sailor* for a long time, for two reasons. First, the book may be a masterpiece, but I found it intensely disturbing, and I didn't really want to see it on film. Second, the film is not set in Japan but in England, which I thought would undermine one of the deep dramatic conflicts in the book, which is between Japanese tradition and specifically *English* modernity.

Mishima puts all the pieces in place for a very happy ending. Fusako has found a husband, and Noboru has found a father figure. If the novel were set in England and written by Jane Austen, the happy ending would have been a wedding. But this is Mishima's novel, set in Japan, so all our hopes are dashed in the most perverse way possible because, to quote Nietzsche, "Man does not strive for happiness; only the Englishman does that."

I am sorry I hesitated to watch *The Sailor Who Fell from Grace with the Sea*, for it is a very good film. *Sailor* was the directorial

---

[2] Reviewed in *Trevor Lynch: Part Four of the Trilogy*.

debut of John Lewis Carlino, who had a long and distinguished career as a screenwriter, including John Frankenheimer's *Seconds*, Mark Rydell's film of D. H. Lawrence's *The Fox*, the fascinating sociopathic buddy film *The Mechanic* starring Charles Bronson and Jan Michael Vincent, and Anthony Page's *I Never Promised You a Rose Garden*. Carlino went on to direct only one more film, *The Great Santini* (1979), his adaptation of Pat Conroy's novel of the same name.

Fusako and Noboru Kuroda become Anne Osborne and her son Jonathan, played by Sarah Miles and Jonathan Kahn. Industrial Yokohama becomes quaint Dartmouth, in Devon. Fusako's Western import boutique becomes a select antique shop. And the sailor, Ryuji Tsukazaki, becomes an America, Jim Cameron, played by Kris Kristofferson.

The casting and acting are uniformly good. All three main characters are convincingly brought to life, with almost no friction transforming them into whites. Miles' performance as the mother is the best. Some might claim Kristofferson is wooden and inarticulate, but that's how the character is supposed to be played. He does, however, convey genuine warmth and humanity. There is real sexual chemistry between Miles and Kristofferson.

The gang of sociopathic schoolboys becomes even more realistic and chilling in the English context due to their posh accents, public school uniforms, and constant bullying and backbiting.

Carlino masterfully adapts Mishima's story to the screen. It is easy, because Mishima's novel is short, and there's quite a bit of dialogue. Moreover, Carlino chooses the exact right bits of interior monologue to dramatize. The most repulsive scene in the book is the killing and dissection of the cat. Carlino handles it admirably, removing the grossness but not the horror. Finally, he fully realizes the almost unbearable suspense Mishima generates in the last pages.

A few things don't quite fit, though. For some reason, I did not find it odd that an upper-middle-class Japanese widow would casually enter into a sexual relationship with a sailor in 1950s Japan, but it seemed very odd for an English widow of her class, even in the 1970s.

The settings, moreover, are very different from the novel. Yokohama is urban, industrial, and gritty. This underscores the difference between the wild beauty of the ocean and the ugliness and artificiality of urban life. Dartmouth, however, seems small, quaint, and very beautiful, and it is surrounded by scenic countryside and seacoast.

Scenes that in the novel take place indoors or in seedy industrial settings are filmed outdoors. There is a great deal of stunning landscape photography. The interiors of the Osborne house and shop are also beautifully appointed, and the camera lingers on the details like decorator porn. The music is middlebrow classical.

In fact, the whole film is shot like a *Masterpiece Theatre* period drama, only with nudity, masturbation, sex, voyeurism, animal cruelty, and murder. If Carlino's aim was to be unsettling, he succeeded wildly. Like the novel, the film is brilliant, troubling, and difficult to enjoy—but it is well worth the effort.

Unz Review, September 14, 2020

THE SEARCHERS

The Searchers (1956) has been acclaimed not just as one of John Ford's greatest films, and not just as one of the greatest Westerns, but as one of the greatest films of all time. This praise is all the more surprising given that *The Searchers* is a profoundly illiberal and even "racist" movie, which means that most fans esteem it grudgingly rather than unreservedly.

I think *The Searchers* is absurdly overrated, for it is far from flawless. But it is still a great work of art that plumbs deep themes and stirs deep feelings. It should be seen by everyone, even people who generally don't watch movies. (Spoiler Alert: I am going to talk about the whole story, so bail out here if you want to see the film with fresh eyes.)

Although *The Searchers* is set in Texas in 1868, Ford's treatment goes beyond the historical to the mythic and epic. The movie begins in a dark room. A door opens on a magnificent Monument Valley landscape. The silhouette of a woman appears in the doorway. As she steps forward, into the light, she moves from being two-dimensional to three. It is like watching a specter, a shade, taking on an embodied form. It has the feel of a creation myth.

But what is being created? The answer seems to be civilization, and it is a very different myth than the one told by liberal social contract theorists. The opening also suggests that the interior realm of family and domesticity is less real than the exterior world. It certainly proves to be less harsh and far more vulnerable.

A rider approaches across the desert. This is a lawless land, where every stranger is regarded with apprehension. The wife is joined on the porch by her husband, then her daughters, then her son, all scanning anxiously. The figures are shot from a low angle. They move with dignity. They barely speak. The whole feel is monumental, epic.

As the rider comes closer, they recognize him as a long-lost member of the family: Ethan Edwards, played with searing charisma by John Wayne. After eight years of fighting, first with the Confederacy then as a mercenary for the Emperor Maximilian in Mexico, the wanderer Ethan has come to the ranch of his brother Aaron, Aaron's wife Martha, and their three children, Lucy, Ben, and Debbie.

Ethan clearly aims to stop fighting and make a home there. He gives his sabre to Ben and a Mexican medal to Debbie. He presents Aaron with a substantial amount of money to "pay his way." But Ethan's attempt to return to society and enjoy the fruits of peace does not last a single day, for there's trouble afoot.

The next morning, Ethan goes off with a group of Texas Rangers to recover the stolen cattle of a neighboring rancher, Lars Jorgenson. When they find the cattle slaughtered with Comanche lances, Ethan concludes that the cattle theft was a diversion to pull the men from the ranches, leaving them vulnerable to attack. The party splits up, riding to defend both the Jorgenson and Edwards ranches.

When Ethan arrives back at his brother's ranch, he finds it in flames. Aaron, Ben, and Martha are dead. Lucy and Debbie have been abducted by a band of Comanches led by a warrior known as Scar. After a brief funeral, Ethan and a group of Rangers go in search of the girls.

After a battle with the Indians, the party splits in two. Most of them return home, while Ethan continues the search accompanied by Lucy's fiancé Brad Jorgenson (Harry Carey, Jr.) and Martin Pawley (Jeffrey Hunter), an orphan who was adopted by the Edwards and considers the kidnapped girls his sisters. When Ethan finds Lucy dead, a distraught Brad charges into the Indian camp and is killed. The searchers are thus reduced to Ethan and Martin, so we need to pause a bit and examine both characters.

Who is Ethan Edwards? He is a warrior and a wanderer in wild spaces: the space between warring civilizations and the space between civilization and savagery. He lives in the state of nature, not civil society. In the state of nature, there is no overarching power to enforce the peace, so a man needs to know how to protect himself. Thus Ethan knows how to thread his way between hostile peoples, negotiate treaties with enemies, strike bargains with crooks, and deploy both trickery and violence in a fight. He knows Spanish, Comanche, and probably some other Indian tongues.

Ethan fought on the side of the Confederacy out of loyalty. (He won't swear another oath to the Texas Rangers.) Once the Confederacy was defeated, he fought for the Emperor Maximilian for money. But war is a young man's game. Ethan is getting too old for it. Thus, he wants to take his earnings and make a home for himself with his brother's family in Texas.

Ethan is a dark character. He has done dark deeds. He fits "any number of warrants," which doesn't necessarily mean he is guilty of anything. But the local Rangers would rather be his friend than his enemy. On two occasions, the Ranger Captain Clayton chooses to ignore Ethan's possible crimes because they need his help. They sense that Ethan is like them: a guardian of peace and family life, even though he has known precious little of them himself.

For instance, when a fight breaks out at a wedding at the Jorgenson home, Ethan shoos Mrs. Jorgenson inside because he doesn't think a woman should see such things. When Ethan finds the bodies of Martha and Lucy, both of whom were presumably raped, he spares others the sight. He has peered into the abyss so that others don't have to.

Ethan doesn't wish to remain in the state of nature. But he understands that he may never see civil society. He may have to give his life so that others will see it. He may have to do things that render him unfit for civil society, so that others can enjoy it in innocence and peace.

At one point, Mrs. Jorgenson says, "A Texican's nothin' but a human man out on a limb . . . This year and next and maybe for a hundred more. But I don't think it'll be forever. Someday this country will be a fine good place to be . . . Maybe it needs our bones in the ground before that time can come . . ."

Texas is a pagan land that demands human sacrifices before it becomes a decent place to live. This is why Ethan interrupts the Christian burial of his family to begin the search for the killers. Texas is not yet ready for such niceties. It needs more blood and bones, and Ethan is ready to lay down his own.

Ethan is a man in a hurry. The proximate reason for haste is that with each passing minute, the girls are closer to rape, torture, and death. The deeper cause is that he's over the hill, so his time is short. Thus he's rude and abrasive. He treats weakness with contempt. He is focused on action and has no time for social niceties. He is cold and ruthless, using Martin as bait to trap and kill the treacherous merchant Futterman. He is also increasingly savage. He shoots out the eyes of a dead Indian, because mutilated men "can't enter the spirit land" but must "wander forever between the winds." He scalps another Indian corpse for the same reason. He even slaughters buffalo simply to starve the Indians.

Ethan's search for Debbie quickly takes on the quality of an obsession. He barely knew the girl. She was eight years old when he returned from eight years of wandering. But she is all that remains of his family, and he searches for her for five years, long after most men would have given up. He is Odysseus, who returns home for a day, then becomes Captain Ahab.

There's a lot to dislike about Ethan Edwards, but he's the only man who could have rescued Debbie. As in *The Man Who Shot Liberty Valance*, Ford wants to confront liberals with the fact their civilization could not have been built without illiberal men and illiberal deeds.

The central hangup of most critical writing about *The Searchers* is that Ethan is a "racist," even a "virulent" one. "Racism" is a recently invented sin, a bogus moral concept that means hating people "for no reason whatsoever" except the fact that they are "different." A racist, in the words of Jim Goad, means "a vicious loser who hates people with different continental ancestry . . . merely to compensate for being an inadequate psychopath and to avoid taking responsibility for his own problems." Racists, we are always told, are "ignorant," for apparently to know Indians or blacks or Mexicans is to love them.

Ethan clearly isn't a racist in this sense. First of all, he is not ignorant of the Comanches. He knows their language and their myths. He respects them as enemies. He clearly hates them. But he doesn't hate them because they are merely "different" or because he is a "loser." He hates them because of their treachery, violence, and cruelty. They butchered his family after raping the women, something they did to countless other white families.

Critics are also exercised over the fact that Ethan would rather kill Debbie than allow her to stay with the Indians. Surely this is an expression of irrational "racism" and "hate." But is it? Plan A was always to rescue Debbie. At one point during their search, Ethan and Marty encounter some white women and girls rescued from Comanche captivity. They have clearly been driven mad by the experience. "Hard to believe they are white" says their rescuer. Ethan says, "They're not white anymore." Arguably, this is a fate worse than death. At this point, Ethan formulates Plan B: to kill Debbie if he can't rescue her.

Ethan also knows that once Debbie reaches puberty she will be raped. Maybe she will be killed then. Maybe she will be made into a squaw. Ethan would rather die than suffer that fate. He wants to spare Debbie from it. This isn't racism and hate. It is an act of love in a terrible situation.

Martin Scorsese was deeply influenced by *The Searchers*. In *Taxi Driver*, Scorsese modeled the characterization of the pimp Sport (played by Harvey Keitel) on Scar. Scorsese saw the relationship of Sport and the teenage prostitute Iris (Jodie Foster) as an exploration of how someone like Scar would establish his hold on a captive like Debbie. (Screenwriter Paul Schrader originally made the pimp black, which was true to life. The producers thought it would be too "racist" to have a black pimp, so Scorsese had a Jewish actor play him as an Indian.)

The Searchers is based on Alan Le May's 1954 novel of the same name, which is based on the true stories of James W. Parker and Brit Johnson, both of whom searched for years to rescue female kin kidnapped by Indians. In the novel, the conflict is neatly racial: whites versus Indians. But in Ford's movie, these neat lines are blurred in two important cases.

First, Ford makes Martin Pawley one-eighth Cherokee. He first appears riding a horse bareback, then neatly dismounts while it is still trotting. He's also late to dinner. Later we see that he is highly emotional and impulsive, although he is still a teenager. When he is a little older, he does not fight "fair" in a fistfight. All this suggests that he has a bit of Indian wildness in him.

Ethan rescued Marty as a child after his parents had been killed by Comanches. He was adopted by Aaron and Martha and regards the Edwards as family. When Ethan sees him, he blurts out that he could be mistaken for a half-breed. In truth, he cannot. Played by Jeffrey Hunter, Marty has strikingly handsome Caucasian features, with a dark tan—but no darker than Aaron—and flashing, pale blue eyes. Ethan also rejects Martin calling him "Uncle Ethan," because they are not blood kin.

Second, the Comanche chief Scar is played by a German actor, Henry Brandon. Like Marty, he has handsome white features, a dark tan, and pale blue eyes.

I don't think Ford was trying to lessen the racial conflict in the movie so much as to create additional dramatic conflicts. Blood loyalties drive the whole story: Ethan wants to avenge his dead kin and rescue or kill Debbie. Scar wants to avenge his two dead sons killed by whites. But there are other loyalties. Marty is not blood kin to the Edwards, but he was raised by them and feels loyalty to them, a tie that Ford brings into sharper relief with a taint of Indian blood. Scar, by contrast, has white blood and Indian loyalties.

Ethan himself recognizes that blood kinship is not everything. The rescued whites who have gone mad in captivity may be racially white, but they no longer belong to white society. Which opens the disturbing possibility that some whites can embrace "going native." When Ethan and Marty finally find Debbie, she claims that the Comanches are now her people, but she also tries to save Marty and Ethan from them. When Ethan sees she has gone native, he tries to shoot her. It looks like he will shoot Marty as well to get her. But he is wounded by a Comanche arrow.

When Ethan and Marty reach safety, Marty tends to Ethan's wound, and Ethan informs him that he is disowning Debbie and leaving his property to Marty. Clearly, he is giving up the search. Earlier, Ethan offered Marty some of his property to settle down and marry Laurie Jorgenson. Clearly, he doesn't think a taint of Cherokee blood makes him a bad match for Laurie. Blood matters a great deal in this world, but so does loyalty, and sometimes it cuts across the lines of blood and race. When Laurie suggests that it might be better for Debbie to die than stay with the Comanches, it is obviously not because she has a horror of miscegenation. Instead, she has a horror of rape.

The characters of Marty and Laurie bring us to the main faults of *The Searchers*. They are incredibly annoying: less characters than caricatures. Perhaps these characters could have been saved by good acting, but both Jeffrey Hunter and Vera Miles as Laurie are committed over-actors. Marty is annoyingly whiny and buffoonish, and Laurie tends to be shrill. There is a great deal of childish flirting and bickering. It is often painful. But the worst thing about it is that Ford left nothing to accident. He clearly wanted it exactly this way, which is a terrible lapse of taste.

George Lucas claimed that Ethan's return to the flaming ruins of the ranch influenced the scene in *Star Wars* where Luke Skywalker returns to the moisture farm after the Stormtroopers have destroyed it. Anakin Skywalker's massacre of the Tusken raiders in *Attack of the Clones* clearly takes some inspiration from *The Searchers* as well. I wish to suggest the terrible possibility that Lucas also copied Luke's annoying whining from Marty and the juvenile bickering between Luke, Leia, and Han from similar scenes in *The Searchers*.

The character of Marty does develop, making *The Searchers* something of a coming-of-age tale. Marty starts out as a callow teenager who is simply sucked into the vortex of Ethan's maniacal charisma and drive. By the end of the film, he is man enough to defy Ethan then fight off Laurie's would-be groom, a grinning, drawling buffoon about whom the less said the better.

The end of *The Searchers* baffles the critics who see Ethan as simply a racist hater. A short time after Ethan almost kills Debbie, Scar's Comanches show up in Texas. The Rangers, along with the US Cavalry, go in search of them. Marty insists on going into the camp alone, to rescue Debbie. He kills Scar, then the Rangers and Cavalry attack. Debbie runs off. Ethan scalps Scar's corpse, then goes looking for Debbie. She flees from him in terror, but he rides her down, dismounts, scoops her up, and says "Let's go home, Debbie."

What happened? Obviously, Ethan has had a change of heart.

But it makes perfect sense. He wanted to kill Debbie when she wanted to stay with Scar. But Scar is now dead, his people will be killed or captured, and Debbie has run *away* from the Comanches. So she has had a change of heart too. Now Ethan *can* rescue her, so he does. But that was Plan A all along.

The final scene of *The Searchers* is utterly heartbreaking. Returning to the epic laconicism of the opening, it is entirely without words. Ethan, Marty, and Debbie return to the Jorgenson ranch, where the family is gathered on the porch. Then we see through the door of the darkened Jorgenson home. Mr. and Mrs. Jorgenson welcome Debbie and take her inside while Ethan watches. Then Marty and Laurie pass Ethan and enter together. Two new families are forming. As they enter the dark interior, their figures become two-dimensional silhouettes. They are entering the realm of shades, the happily ever after. Ethan stands for a moment, then turns and walks away. He will not enter the domestic world that he has given everything to secure. He is a mutilated man who will wander between the winds and know no peace. Then the door closes, and we see only darkness.

The Unz Review, April 16, 2021

TAXI DRIVER

It began with Dylann Roof. Since then, the Molotov cocktail of autism, involuntary celibacy, gallantry, vengeance, and mass murder has exploded with such regularity that I keep dusting off a boilerplate article to condemn it whenever the perpetrators are connected with White Nationalism. But even with Roof's case, I felt that I had seen this all before. Then I remembered where: *Taxi Driver*.

Taxi Driver is Martin Scorsese's breakout film and remains one of his greatest achievements, alongside *Raging Bull*, *Goodfellas*, and *Gangs of New York*.[1] *Taxi Driver* is an unforgettable portrait of Travis Bickle, an alienated loner in an urban hellscape who decides to die in a hail of bullets and thus seeks out opportunities to dispense vigilante justice. Despite his best efforts, however, Travis accidentally survives and is hailed as a hero for rescuing a child prostitute from a pimp.

Any movie involving vigilantism is inherently anti-liberal, which makes it grist for Right-wing viewers and reviewers, regardless of the vigilante's or the director's intentions. Liberalism is the idea that we can be governed by laws, not men. Vigilantism takes place when the legal system breaks down and citizens feel the need to take action themselves. But *Taxi Driver* is even more Right-wing today because this is the age of the Alt-Right and "incel" spree killer.

Taxi Driver fuses urban grittiness and emotional power with daring avant-garde cinematic techniques. Even though it was made on a shoestring budget, everything about this film is first-rate: the script by Paul Schrader (who went on to write and direct *Mishima*[2]); the performances, especially Robert DeNiro as Travis Bickle and Jodie Foster as Iris, a twelve-year-old prostitute; the cinematography of Michael Chapman; and the lyrical but also menacing musical score by Bernard

---

[1] *Gangs of New York* is reviewed in Trevor Lynch's *White Nationalist Guide to the Movies*.

[2] Reviewed in Trevor Lynch's *White Nationalist Guide to the Movies*.

Herrmann (his last, before dying of a heart-attack, aged sixty-four).

Taxi Driver was a commercial and critical success. It won the Palme d'Or in Cannes in 1976, as well as many other nominations and awards. *Taxi Driver* is also regularly featured on critics' "best" lists.

So who is Travis Bickle? Travis Bickle is a twenty-six-year-old honorably discharged Marine from someplace where they wear cowboy clothes. He has drifted away from home and family to New York City at its low-point in the sleazy seventies: corrupt, crime-ridden, teetering on the brink of bankruptcy, and swarming with rats, junkies, pimps, hookers, and other vermin. *Taxi Driver* was shot during the heatwave of 1975. You can practically feel it. There was a sanitation strike. You can practically smell it.

Travis suffers from insomnia. And we know from *Fight Club* how crazy lack of sleep can make you.[3] His insomnia might have something to do with his diet of junk food and steady consumption of alcohol from paper bags and flasks. He also pops pills from prescription bottles. We don't know if they are uppers, downers, or anti-psychotics.

To while away his sleepless nights, Travis has been hanging out at porn theaters and all-night eateries, but at the beginning of the film, he takes a job driving a cab. He is looking for long, exhausting, draining hours, so he can finally sleep.

Travis is also desperately lonely: "Loneliness has followed me my whole life, everywhere. . . . I'm God's lonely man." He tries to connect with his fellow cabbies. But, being on the nightshift, they are almost as weird and asocial as he is.

One day, Travis becomes infatuated with Betsy (Cybill Shepherd), a campaign worker for Senator Charles Palantine, who is running in his party's presidential primary. (His party is not stated, but he's clearly supposed to be a Democrat.) Betsy is beautiful. Travis believes she is lonely too. After watching her for a while, he walks into the office and asks her on a date. Betsy accepts. Travis is strange, but he's not bad-looking and

---

[3] Reviewed in *Trevor Lynch: Part Four of the Trilogy*.

has an off-kilter charisma.

Travis blows it on their second date, however, when he takes her to a pornographic movie. It is painfully awkward. After that, he is reduced to increasingly desperate stalking behavior. He is convinced that Betsy needs saving from her lonely, hellish existence, and he becomes increasingly indignant that she does not want to be saved.

The choice to take Betsy to a dirty movie makes it abundantly clear that Travis has issues. So does a bizarre greeting card that he sends to his parents. He has a shaky grasp of socially appropriate behavior.

Travis spends too much time alone. He broods and ruminates. He tells Wizard, one of his fellow drivers played by Peter Boyle, "I got some bad ideas in my head." Travis does not, however, come off as delusional. Instead, he is angry at the sleaze and injustice that surround him: "All the animals come out at night. Whores, skunk pussies, buggers, queens, fairies, dopers, junkies. Sick, venal. Someday a real rain will come and wash this scum off the streets." He becomes increasingly vengeful. He starts thinking that maybe *he* will be that rain, a hard rain.

One wonders, though, why Travis continues to subject himself to this world. Not every city is as dystopian as New York. He could also focus on better neighborhoods and better fares. But he doesn't. The truth is that Travis is a glutton for punishment. He has a masochistic, self-defeating personality.

Travis does not fantasize about making the world a better place for himself. He doesn't feel he has a future. Instead, he fantasizes about dying honorably. He is what I call an "honorable defeatist."[4] He feels doomed to failure, so to salvage some sense of agency and worth, he wants to take control of the process and destroy himself over a matter of principle.

When I first saw *Taxi Driver*, I assumed Travis suffered from post-traumatic stress from his time in the Marines. Perhaps he saw action in Vietnam. But there is no mention of serving in Vietnam. There are no flashbacks. Also, Travis lies to his par-

---

[4] Greg Johnson, "Honorable Defeatists," *In Defense of Prejudice*.

ents and then to Iris, saying he is doing secret work for the government. Maybe he was lying about the Marines too.

Today, I look at Travis and see someone on the autism spectrum who is also an incel. He does not present as a schizophrenic, like John Hinckley, Jr., who was inspired by *Taxi Driver* to shoot President Reagan, or like mass shooters Jared Loughner and James Holmes. Instead, he seems a lot like Dylann Roof, Patrick Crusius, Brenton Tarrant, and John Earnest: all ideologically motivated honorable defeatists.

Betsy isn't the only object of Travis' gallantry. He also wants to rescue Iris, a twelve-year-old prostitute from a pimp played by Harvey Keitel. Originally, the pimp was supposed to be black. There are plenty of black pimps on the streets in *Taxi Driver*. But Schrader thought it might be somehow "racist" to cast a black actor in this particular role. It is not clear why it was not "anti-Semitic" to cast Keitel though.

When his relationship with Betsy goes south, Travis buys some guns and learns to use them. He begins dieting and exercising. He is training for some sort of confrontation with evil. He is not planning on surviving. He enjoys the sense of purpose. He may even enjoy some sleep.

Is Travis a psycho or a hero? A case can be made for both.

Travis is gallant. He is a knight, a warrior. It is manly and noble to protect weaker people—especially women and children—from evil. It is also the height of nobility to be concerned solely with doing one's duty, regardless of personal consequences. Whether Travis was really in the Marines or not, he prefers death to dishonor. He will do the right thing, even if it kills him.

So how is Travis a psycho?

Travis's first target is Senator Charles Palantine. Why shoot Palantine? Travis doesn't really care about politics. He has no strong feelings about the candidate or the issues. He was ready to vote for Palantine when he was infatuated with Betsy. Now that she has dumped him, he wants to kill Palantine. Travis originally wanted to help Betsy. It is not clear how killing Palantine would do that. Maybe he is trying to hurt her. But Palantine is just a political candidate. How much emotional investment does Travis think she has in him?

Perhaps, then, Travis' purpose is not connected to Betsy. Palantine has a Secret Service detail. If Travis shoots Palantine and exchanges fire with the Secret Service, he will probably be killed. That's his real goal.

Travis can also count on the fact that by killing a political candidate, he will be famous. He won't be around for a trial, so people will speculate about his motives. Some will construct accounts of his crime that cast him in a noble light. In short, Travis is a pathological narcissist. He's another Herostratus, who burned the temple of Artemis in Ephesus so we would talk about him today. Sadly, it worked.

The problem with Travis is not that he is willing to die to do the right thing. The problem is that his primary goal is to die, for which he is willing to do anything, even wrong or stupid things.

Disaster is averted, however, when Travis is spooked by Palantine's Secret Service detail and runs away.

Travis' next mission is to rescue Iris from her pimp. This is *Taxi Driver*'s intense and unforgettable climax. The whole sequence is an orgy of violence. But it is not clean and stylized violence. People don't just die neatly after one shot. They suffer bloody wounds, scream and curse, then return fire. Travis is shot twice. He drops his first gun then empties three others to kill the pimp and a couple of goons, and he still has to pull a knife on one of them. Killing is hard, dirty, dangerous work. People just don't want to die. Then, when his enemies are dispatched, Travis puts a gun to his head and finds it empty. Another gun is empty as well. Finally, the police arrive, standing in the doorway, stunned at the carnage. Travis pantomimes blowing his brains out with his finger than passes out from blood loss.

At this point, we see the whole abattoir from above. Scorsese and Chapman actually tore the ceiling out of the apartment and hallway and built a track allowing the camera to retrace the path of the carnage from above, as if we are seeing it from the eyes of Travis' departing spirit.

The only thing that saves the scene from being a pure exercise in nihilistic aestheticism is Bernard Herrmann's music. To a funeral drum, we hear the dissonant trumpet motive associated with Travis' bad thoughts amidst swirling harp arpeggios that suggest the dissolution of the flesh. Then we hear the romantic saxophone theme associated with Travis' gallantry dissonantly played on trumpets and low brass. Darkness has finally consumed him.

The scene was so shocking that Scorsese had to desaturate the film stock, toning down the blood, to secure an R rather than an X rating.

In the epilogue, we learn that Travis survived. When he wakes up from a coma, he is hailed as a hero for saving Iris. The world didn't know that Iris' rescue was just the accidental side-effect of a failed suicide attempt.

Travis goes back to driving a cab. Does he want to live after all?

One night, Betsy gets into his cab. She has heard about Travis' heroism, and her disgust has clearly been replaced with admiration. But after Travis drops off Betsy, he is suddenly agitated by something he sees in the rear-view mirror, accompanied by a "sting" from the orchestra that sounds uncanny because it is played backwards.

It's only a matter of time before Travis Bickle goes off again.

It is interesting to read the critical responses to *Taxi Driver*. The movie is a masterpiece and deserved praise regardless of whether you think Travis is a hero or a psycho or a little bit of both. Oddly enough, though, Travis himself was regarded with a great deal of sympathy.

The seventies were the decade of the anti-hero. The organs of the culture were by then firmly in the hands of the hostile elite. Thus the instinct of the critics was to weaponize anti-heroes like Bickle against the establishment, meaning against mainstream America. There was surely some hand-rubbing on both coasts when Reagan was shot by a wannabe Travis Bickle.

Today, the hostile elite is fully in control. They *are* the establishment. They want to hold on to their power. Thus they live in terror of Travis Bickles like Brenton Tarrant and Dylann Roof. Hence the cultural organs pushed back hard against

Todd Phillips' *Joker*,⁵ which owes a great deal to both *Taxi Driver* and Scorsese's later DeNiro vehicle *The King of Comedy*.

Now that the Great Replacement is turning millions of young white men into Travis Bickles, a sympathetic portrayal of a white man turning into a murderous vigilante was deemed bad art. *Joker* was a dud, but *Taxi Driver* remains as explosive as ever. Thus it is a classic of Right-wing cinema.

The Unz Review, December 28, 2020

---

⁵ Reviewed in *Trevor Lynch: Part Four of the Trilogy*.

TENET

Christopher Nolan is one of my favorite living filmmakers. *Tenet* is Nolan's new sci-fi espionage thriller. Highly imaginative and visually striking, *Tenet* was filmed on locations in Denmark, Estonia, India, Italy, Norway, and the UK, and its cast includes Robert Pattinson, Elizabeth Debicki, Michael Caine, and Kenneth Branagh.

But *Tenet* is not Nolan's best work, for two main reasons. First, to say the plot is hard to follow would be a compliment. Second, John David Washington, who is simply known as the Protagonist, is the weakest leading man in any Nolan film.

Nolan is known for plots that are complex and intricately structured, often employing science fiction elements that strain plausibility. Just think of *Memento*, *Batman Begins*, *The Prestige*, *Inception*, and *Interstellar*. Even *Dunkirk*, which is a relatively straightforward World War II movie, has a highly complex narrative structure, with three parallel plotlines that only sync up in the last minutes of the film.

Memento, *Inception*, and *Interstellar* arguably cross the line into being simply incoherent. But there's no argument about *Tenet*. On first viewing, large chunks of the plot make no sense, and I suspect that repeated viewings won't iron out the wrinkles. What is worse, in the case of *Memento*, *Inception*, and *Interstellar*, the characters and drama are so compelling that one can forgive the occasional lapse, but not so with *Tenet*.

The central science fiction element of *Tenet* is time travel. People from the future are trying to change the past, i.e., our present. But the novel wrinkle is that certain objects can move backwards against the regular course of time. It starts out seeming fake and dumb, but as the movie progresses, there is a real payoff with brilliantly imaginative reversal sequences, in which people encounter themselves emerging from the future and interacting with them in reverse time.

The word *tenet* is a palindrome, spelled the same way forwards and backwards, which is a nice metaphor for the characters undergoing temporal inversions. These mind-blowing sequences are structured with the intricacy of Escher's most paradoxical drawings. They'll leave you simply speechless. They *might* even make sense . . . after three or four viewings.

But the most inscrutable plot elements in *Tenet* are the motives of the main characters: the good guy, played by John David Washington; the bad guy, Andrei Sator, an evil Russian oligarch played by Kenneth Branagh; the *femme fatale*, Kat, his estranged wife, played by the elegant Elizabeth Debicki; and the mysterious people from the future, who set everything in motion.

It is no spoiler to say that the movie is a conflict between people who want to destroy and save the world. Early on, there's talk of a Third World War, but that gets dropped for something much worse. This much is clear in the trailers.

But given this conflict, none of the characters behave rationally. The plan of the people from the future is staggeringly evil and utterly insane, since it would not only fail to solve their alleged problem but make their very existence impossible. Andrei Sator's behavior toward his wife, his son, and the whole planet makes no sense either. Kat's behavior is baffling, especially when she commits a pointless and unnecessary act of spite that might literally destroy the world. And given the gravity of the Protagonist's mission, his sentimentality toward Kat makes no sense either. There are half-a-dozen points when a sensible agent would have abandoned her to pursue the greater good.

The only weak link in the cast is leading man John David Washington. I confess that current events in the US have given me a powerful case of Negro fatigue, but I tried to be objective. There are fine black actors out there, and Nolan has cast two of them, Morgan Freeman and David Gyasi.

But John David Washington is not leading man material. He's shortish. He lacks charisma and physical presence. His voice is weak. He's not handsome. (He's very dark, but also oddly racially indeterminate, with a thin nose and odd beard that make him look South Asian.)

Beyond that, he didn't really sell the character or his lines. He can't do sophisticated. We are supposed to think he can glance in a bag and see that a sketch is by Goya, but it comes off as a joke. When he dresses up, he looks comical, like a pygmy oligarch. He pronounces the "x" in "expresso." He's the weakest character in any scene he's in—and he's in most of them—sucking in the rest of the movie around him like a black hole.

I wonder if Nolan felt pressure from the industry to take on a black leading man. If so, he should have resisted. John David Washington is an Affirmative Action Hero, who has risen to his level of incompetence based on race and family connections. His father is Denzel Washington, who might have done this role justice 30 years ago. (He was excellent in *Malcolm X*.)

As the movie wore on (it is two-and-a-half hours), I started mentally recasting the main role. The actor would have to be physically commanding and dynamic plus soulful to sell his strange attachment to Kat. Daniel Craig could have done it a decade ago. Tom Hardy is the right age and would have been a compelling choice. Based on his performance in *Blade Runner 2049*, Ryan Gosling also would have been excellent. But it was not to be. There is one bright side, though. This is a James Bond-style role, and if the folks at Eon Productions see this, there will never be a black James Bond.

Speaking of Bond, now that Daniel Craig is retiring, Eon needs to hire Nolan to direct Tom Hardy as the next James Bond.

If I were grading *Tenet*, I would give it a B-minus, with plenty of honorable mentions for technical details. Every Nolan fan will want to see *Tenet*, but average moviegoers will find it long, confusing, and dramatically uninvolving. Thus I doubt *Tenet* will be as successful as Nolan's recent string of blockbusters.

Indeed, *Tenet* is Nolan's worst film. *Tenet* is a far more ambitious project than his early films like *Following*, *Memento*, and *Insomnia*. It is also more ambitious than *The Prestige*, which many people find dramatically underwhelming. But in terms of plot and performances, all of these films are better realized than *Tenet*.

Christopher Nolan remains one of our most visionary filmmakers, but with *Tenet* his reach exceeded his grasp.

The Unz Review, August 26, 2020

TWIN PEAKS

I feel like I grew up in Twin Peaks, the fictional Washington logging town that gave its name to David Lynch's iconic TV series, which aired on ABC from the spring of 1990 to the spring of 1991. *Twin Peaks* has one of the best pilots in television history, which was followed by an abbreviated first season of seven episodes. A second season of twenty-two episodes was produced before the series was canceled.

Twin Peaks was a surprise smash hit and developed a fervent cult following. But few people seemed to really understand it at the time. Coastal urbanites thought Lynch was mocking wholesome hicks, when, in truth, in the character of Albert Rosenfeld—an arrogant Jewish urbanite from back East—he was mocking them.

Since its cancellation, *Twin Peaks* has receded behind a haze of nostalgia for cherry pie, damned fine coffee, cool jazz, and swaying pines, to the extent that few people seem to remember how painfully bad the series became not even halfway through its second and final season. When ABC axed the series, Lynch returned to direct the last episode, a 50-minute "fuck you" to the network, the critics, and unfortunately the fans as well.

Twin Peaks will always be David Lynch's baby—and we know from *Eraserhead* how perilous parenthood can be.[1] Although Lynch co-created *Twin Peaks* with Mark Frost and was one of fourteen directors who worked on the pilot and twenty-nine episodes, *Twin Peaks* is recognizably Lynch's vision. This becomes clear when one compares it to the movies that came immediately before and after it: *Blue Velvet*[2] (1986) and *Twin Peaks: Fire Walk with Me* (1992), projects where Lynch had complete creative control.

I read *Twin Peaks* as a sequel to *Blue Velvet*. Both are set in quaint, overwhelmingly white logging towns: Lumberton,

---

[1] Reviewed in *Return of the Son of Trevor Lynch's CENSORED Guide to the Movies*.

[2] Reviewed in *Trevor Lynch: Part Four of the Trilogy*.

North Carolina and Twin Peaks, Washington. Both towns are brimming with quirky Americana, much of it with an anachronistic 1950s flavor. The lead characters in both movies are played by Kyle MacLaughlin: *Blue Velvet*'s callow college-boy Jeffrey Beaumont and *Twin Peaks*' FBI Special Agent Dale Cooper.

Both stories are set in motion by a shocking crime that reveals evil forces beneath the idyllic surface of small-town life. Both movies involve (metaphorical and real) descents into the underworld, in which the hero encounters evil and vanquishes it — although not completely in *Twin Peaks*.

Both stories give prominent and positive roles to law enforcement in fighting evil: in *Blue Velvet*, the Lumberton police; in *Twin Peaks*, the local sheriff's office, plus the FBI, the US Airforce, and a secret society called the Book House Boys, who go outside the law when justice requires.

Both stories also involve young amateur sleuths: Jeffrey and Sandy in *Blue Velvet*, Donna Hayward, James Hurley, Madeleine Ferguson, and Audrey Horne in *Twin Peaks*.

In *Blue Velvet*, Jeffrey is mentored by Detective Williams, and after his successes as an amateur detective, it would be quite logical for him to go into law enforcement once he learned of the dark side of life and what is necessary to preserve order and goodness. Thus it is tempting to view FBI Special Agent Dale Cooper as what Jeffrey Beaumont might have become just a few years later.

Both *Blue Velvet* and *Twin Peaks* have elements of the supernatural. In *Blue Velvet*, this is merely hinted at with the surging electricity that accompanies Frank Booth's death. In *Twin Peaks*, it is quite explicit: killer Bob is a possessing demon. In both stories, evil is strongly connected to sexual desire and drugs, both highly addictive pleasures. (Caffeine and sugar are the addictions of the wholesome characters, while smoking straddles the line. It's only a bit naughty.) In both stories, dreams are also prophetic, very much so in *Twin Peaks*. Finally, both stories make a great deal of mysteries and secrets: mostly criminal and sexual, but also supernatural.

Kyle MacLaughlin was not the only *Blue Velvet* cast member to appear in *Twin Peaks*. Jack Nance and Frances Bay also had roles, although in all fairness, Lynch liked working with them. (Nance also had roles in *Eraserhead*, *Dune*,[3] *Wild at Heart*,[4] and *Fire Walk with Me*; Bay was in *Wild at Heart* and *Fire Walk with Me*.) More significantly, Isabella Rossellini was originally going to play Joan Chen's role of Josie Packard. (Her name was originally to be Giovanna Packard.)

Composer Angelo Badalamenti and singer Julee Cruise first worked with Lynch on *Blue Velvet* and then went on to define the sound of *Twin Peaks*. It was their best work.

Many of *Blue Velvet*'s crew also worked on *Twin Peaks*, but the only one who had a creative impact on *Twin Peaks* was video editor Duwayne Dunham, who also directed three episodes.

Lynch remains bitter to this day about his lack of final cut control on *Dune*. So why was he willing to take his ideas to network television? He had creative control of the pilot, but if the series were picked up, he could hardly have expected to control its subsequent development.

I think the connection with *Blue Velvet* throws some light on this. Lynch made *Blue Velvet* exactly as he wanted it. He made the *Twin Peaks* pilot exactly as he wanted it. Thus he could risk letting others make their mark, knowing that any subsequent developments could not change the originals.

What's so great about *Twin Peaks*?

First, there is a compelling story that arcs through the pilot and the first sixteen episodes: discovering who killed Laura Palmer.

Second, this serious story is counter-balanced by warm-hearted Americana, quirky side characters, and some genuine hilarity: Audrey Horne's cherry stem stunt, Mr. Tojamura, Leland Palmer calling out "Begin the Beguine," any scene with David Patrick Kelly as Jerry Horne or Russ Tamblyn as Dr. Jacoby, and the fact that practically everyone smokes, even in the hospital.

Third, there are a lot of interesting, well-drawn characters,

---

[3] Reviewed in *Return of the Son of Trevor Lynch's CENSORED Guide to the Movies*.

[4] Reviewed in *Return of the Son of Trevor Lynch's CENSORED Guide to the Movies*.

some of them horrible, some of them quite likeable. My favorites are Kyle MacLaughlin as Dale Cooper, Michael Ontkean as Sheriff Truman, Ray Wise as Leland Palmer, Grace Zabriskie as Sarah Palmer, Peggy Lipton as Norma Jennings, Jack Nance as Pete Martell, Piper Laurie as Catherine Martell, Dana Ashbrook as Bobby Briggs, Don Davis as Major Garland Briggs, Warren Frost (father of Mark Frost) as Doc Hayward, and Catherine Coulson as the Log Lady.

Fourth, there is a great-looking cast, including Lara Flynn Boyle, Mädchen Amick, Sherilynn Fenn, Sheryl Lee, Heather Graham, Peggy Lipton, James Marshall, Dana Ashbrook, Gary Hershberger, Kyle MacLaughlin, Michael Ontkean, and Billy Zane.

Fifth, there is some excellent acting, especially by Ray Wise (Leland Palmer) and Grace Zabriskie (Sarah Palmer). Dana Ashbrook as Bobby Briggs is also surprisingly good, something I appreciated only on a recent viewing.

Finally, there is the series' metaphysical depth. For Lynch, good and evil are not merely social or merely human. They are metaphysical forces. This is what the urbanites and Leftists cannot understand about Lynch: he is a fundamentally religious and conservative filmmaker with a strong populist bent.

What went wrong?

The serious and comic elements of *Twin Peaks* existed in a delicate balance through the end of episode sixteen (episode nine of season two), when the murder of Laura Palmer was solved. At that point, there was no reason for agent Dale Cooper to stay in Twin Peaks and nothing to counter-balance the goofier elements, which rapidly became tiresome. Remember super-strong Nadine Hurley, with amnesia, going back to high school and joining the wrestling team? Ben Horne reenacting the Civil War? David Duchovny in drag? Dick Tremaine and little Nicky? The little pine weasel? Dougie, Dwayne, and the seductive Lana? The Miss Twin Peaks pageant?

(Even at its worst, though, *Twin Peaks* was un-PC: for instance portraying the South winning the Civil War as therapeutic and showing how sociopathic businessmen use environmentalism as a weapon against their rivals.)

The writers contrived ways to keep Cooper in Twin Peaks: first a DEA/FBI investigation then the return of Cooper's old nemesis Windom Earle. There were lame attempts to add some drama and romance to the silliness, usually in the form of useless new characters. Remember James Hurley and Evelyn Marsh? The return and death of Josie Packard? Sheriff Truman's bender? The return of Andrew Packard? Thomas Eckhardt and his assistant Jones? Donna Hayward wondering if Ben Horne is her father? Billy Zane and his screamingly gay jumpsuit?

Some blamed the death of *Twin Peaks* on schedule changes and the Gulf War, which preempted a lot of programming. But these explanations don't wash. People would have followed the show to new days and times if it had remained compelling, and pretty much all shows got preempted by the war, but not all of them failed.

How should you approach *Twin Peaks* if you've never seen it, or want to see it again? My recommendation is simply to watch the pilot and the first sixteen episodes (all of season one and the first nine of season two). Then stop. You'll enjoy everything quintessentially *Twin Peaks*. The Laura Palmer story arc will be resolved. And you'll miss almost all of the bad and boring stuff, including the absolute nadir of the series: episode twenty-two, directed by Diane Keaton with such pretentious Bergmanisms and poisonous contempt for the bumpkins that it might as well have been shot by Woody Allen.

Here are some highlights to look for. The best part of the pilot is everything up to the introduction of Dale Cooper: the discovery of the body of Laura Palmer; the exquisite tension and pathos of the scene in which she is rolled over, unwrapped, and recognized; cut to Laura's mother Sarah calling her to get ready for school, discovering she is missing, and with mounting anxiety calling around to track Laura down; Sarah talking to her husband Leland as the sheriff's truck pulls up at the Great Northern Hotel to tell him the terrible news; Leland realizing something is wrong as the sheriff approaches, while his wife melts down on the other end of the phone. Another brilliant sequence is the word of Laura's death spreading at the High School. It is exquisitely heartbreaking. Aside from *Blue Velvet*, the *Twin Peaks* pilot is Lynch's best work and blows away anything on television before or since.

Other highlights include episodes seven through nine, beginning with the brilliantly constructed cliffhanger at the end of season one and continuing into the first two episodes of season two. Episode seven is directed by Mark Frost, episodes eight and nine by David Lynch. They are wonderfully bizarre and imaginative.

Also outstanding are episodes fourteen through sixteen, directed by David Lynch, Caleb Deschanel, and Tim Hunter respectively. In this sequence we learn who the killer of Laura Palmer is and see him brought to justice.

The Lynch-directed episode fourteen is one of the best in the series, and one of the most difficult to watch as it ends with the murder of Maddie Ferguson.

Episode fifteen is an utterly creepy game of cat and mouse as the killer covers up his crime and disposes of the body. It brilliantly portrays a combination of madness and cunning. It ends with the discovery of Maddie's body.

Episode sixteen begins the morning after Maddie's discovery. Dale Cooper, Sheriff Truman, Deputy Hawk, and agent Rosenfeld are walking after a sleepless night at the crime scene. Once the killer is caught, the episode ends with Cooper, Rosenfeld, and Truman meeting Airforce Major Briggs on a path and discussing their common commitment to the fight against evil. It is a fitting end to the whole series.

Don't be tempted to watch further thinking that certain plot lines might be resolved, because they won't. You'll just be strung along a bit more, as television is wont to do. You'll sit through hours of crap and then be left hanging anyway because the series was canceled. So you might as well just accept that you'll be left hanging and avoid the bad stuff.

Or, if you can't resist looking at the later episodes, give yourself a week's break, then go back to it with the idea that you are just watching outtakes and deleted scenes. It will make it easier.

Twin Peaks is not free from the farcical and manipulative elements of television. Certain conceits are repeated to the point of absurdity. For instance, in a total of thirty episodes, there are eleven murders and at least ten attempted murders—in town of 51,201 people. (By the way, that number seems high for the area. Apparently, it was originally 5,120, but ABC thought that shows set in small towns would not attract viewers, so they added a digit. I'd prefer to think they were inspired by the Hindu idea that when a town has more than 50,000 people, decadence is inevitable. Sadly, even much smaller logging towns are now rotted by drugs and deindustrialization.)

There are a lot of stupid plot elements and lapses of continuity. The business intrigues of Ben Horne, Catherine Martell, and Josie Packard don't really make sense. Agent Cooper asks a lawyer to represent the man he is arresting for killing the lawyer's own daughter—and the lawyer agrees. Court hearings and other important community events are held in a dive bar. Ben Horne is allowed to wear a tie in his jail cell, where he is being held on suspicion of murder. Then he is magically released even though he is known to have been involved in racketeering, arson, and attempted murder. The show is set in February and March—April at the latest—but people go deer hunting and autumn leaves litter the ground in several scenes.

At its worst, *Twin Peaks* is just a prime-time soap opera. It keeps you watching by stringing you along with various unresolved subplots, especially romances. Because soaps lack finite stories with dramatic closure, the whole medium is empty and unrewarding. But at its best, *Twin Peaks* is better than anything on TV.

The Unz Review, October 29, 2020

TWIN PEAKS: FIRE WALK WITH ME

David Lynch's 1992 movie *Twin Peaks: Fire Walk with Me* is his prequel to the *Twin Peaks* series, which ran on ABC from 1990 to 1991. *Fire Walk with Me* was a flop with critics and moviegoers, except in Japan.

This is unjust, because *Fire Walk with Me* is a very fine movie. I won't say it is Lynch's best work. That praise belongs to *Blue Velvet* alone. But the music to *Fire Walk with Me* is composer Angelo Badalamenti's best work ever.

Like many Lynch fans, I was slow to warm to *Fire Walk with Me*. I never thought it was a bad movie, just an unpleasant one. I missed it in theaters when it was released in 1992 and saw it only on VHS. I bought the DVD, but I don't think I ever watched it. Then I bought the Blu-ray, which I never watched until after I finally saw the film on the big screen in a film festival in Budapest. Then it hit me: *Fire Walk with Me* belongs in a special category of films like *Vertigo* and *Grave of the Fireflies*: dark films that are so well-done that it is hard to *enjoy* them.

I have trouble ranking David Lynch's work. *Blue Velvet* is easy to place at the top,[1] *Inland Empire* at the bottom. But between them, there are only two categories: the mixed, including *Dune*,[2] Lynch's *Twin Peaks* episodes, and *Twin Peaks: The Return*—and the excellent, which includes everything else Lynch did, including the *Twin Peaks* pilot and *Fire Walk with Me*.

There are several reasons why *Fire Walk with Me* flopped.

First, it wasn't as light as *Twin Peaks*. It lacked the quirky characters and offbeat humor of the series. Kyle MacLaughlin and Peggy Lipton both felt this way about the film. So did the critics. So did the viewers. There are two reasons for this effect, one deliberate, one accidental.

The first thirty-three minutes of *Fire Walk with Me* are set one

---

[1] Reviewed in *Trevor Lynch: Part Four of the Trilogy*.
[2] Reviewed in *Return of the Son of Trevor Lynch*'s CENSORED *Guide to the Movies*.

year before the *Twin Peaks* pilot in the town of Deer Meadow. Then the movie jumps ahead one year to the last seven days of Laura Palmer's life.

Lynch conceived Deer Meadow as the anti-Twin Peaks: the people are ugly and unfriendly, the town is cheap and seedy, and the coffee sucks. Hap's Diner is no RR: the manager is old and unpleasant, the waitress is old and unsavory, and there aren't any specials. The sheriff, his deputy, and his receptionist are polar opposites of their lovable equivalents in Twin Peaks.

FBI agent Chet Desmond is dispatched to Deer Meadow to investigate the murder of Teresa Banks. Chris Isaak is excellent as Desmond. He is a wholesome-looking, all-American type like MacLaughlin's Dale Cooper. But Desmond is smug and condescending to his assistant, Sam Stanley (Kiefer Sutherland) and metes out brutal but well-deserved violence to the sheriff (in a deleted scene) and his deputy. (Stanley, however, is a nice guy, which is a pleasant inversion of Cooper's assistant, Albert Rosenfeld.)

I found the whole sequence extremely droll, especially Harry Dean Stanton as Carl Rodd and Sandra Kinder as Irene the waitress (best line: "It's what you call a freak accident."). But apparently others found it off-putting.

Once the setting switched to Twin Peaks, Lynch filmed a number of scenes with favorite characters from the series: Ed and Norma, Lucy and Andy, Truman and Hawk, Pete Martell and Josie, etc. But he had to drop them due to the running time. (The extended and deleted scenes are available on the Blu-ray releases.)

This brings us to the second reason *Fire Walk with Me* failed. Once Lynch dropped the light moments from the final cut, naturally what remained was quite dark. The series worked because the darkness cast by the murder of Laura Palmer was offset by the lighter characters and subplots. When the Palmer murder was solved, the series became silly and flopped. *Fire Walk with Me* suffers from the opposite malady: unremitting darkness.

Not only did Lynch drop the lighter elements of the series, he also put on screen what existed only in the backstory of the series: incest, rape, and finally the murder of Laura Palmer. *Fire Walk with Me* really belongs in the genre of horror, both supernatural and psychological horror, undiluted with the camp elements of slasher flicks. It was just hard for a lot of people to take. This is the view of Al Stroebel, who played the One-Armed Man. People were not prepared for the darkness.

Another reason for the poor reception of *Fire Walk with Me* is the Christian religiosity of the film. Laura Palmer speaks of being abandoned by a guardian angel, falling through endless space, and bursting into fire. In her bedroom, there is an illustration of children with a guardian angel. Laura looks on in horror as the angel disappears from the picture.

In the terrifying scene in the train car where Laura is murdered, Ronette Pulaski prays: "Father, if I die now, please see me. Don't look at me. I'm so dirty. I'm not ready. I'm sorry. I'm sorry." Then Ronette has a vision of an angel. Then her bonds become severed. The One-Armed Man bangs on the door of the train car to get in. Ronette tries to escape, is knocked unconscious, and falls from the train. But she survives.

When Laura is murdered we hear Cherubini's *Requiem*. At the very end, Laura and Dale Cooper are in the red room/ Black Lodge. Laura is seated. Cooper stands near her protectively, with a benign expression. Then Laura has a vision of an angel, a different angel than the one seen by Ronette. Laura cries but then through her tears begins to smile and laugh. It is a moment of catharsis, of redemption. Laura has died, but her soul was saved from the possession that turned her father into a monster. Again we hear Cherubini's sublime music. The End.

Most movie critics are allergic to this sort of stuff. It may explain the boos and hisses when the film was screened in Cannes. (The co-author of the script, Robert Engel—a bit of an omen there—denies it happened.)

A fourth element that some found off-putting is the relentless hermeticism of the movie: the blue rose, the mysterious ring, the room above the convenience store, the Red Room, the One-Armed Man, the Little Man from Far Away, Mrs. Tremond/Chalfont and her grandson, the Formica table, Judy, the monkey face, the disappearance of Chet Desmond and brief reappearance of Philip Jeffries (David Bowie), and, of course, the creamed corn. I find it fascinating and plan one day to tie it all together in a commentary, but for a lot of moviegoers, it was a bit much.

Finally, anyone who watched the series knew what was coming in the movie. People who don't like spoilers couldn't really look beyond that fact.

But now that you know what you are getting into, I urge you to give *Fire Walk with Me* a chance. In addition to the fantastic music and imaginative storytelling, Ray Wise, Grace Zabriskie, and Sheryl Lee give outstanding performances.

Three sequences are especially riveting.

First, there is Laura Palmer's dream induced by the mysterious picture given to her by Mrs. Tremond/Chalfont. Lynch is one of cinema's supreme masters of the dream sequence: more than half of *Mulholland Drive* is a dying woman's dream.[3] In *Mulholland Drive*, Lynch brilliantly constructs a wish-fulfillment dream that collapses in on itself, ultimately because reality is very different. In *Fire Walk with Me*, the dream's logic is less psychological than metaphysical. It is revelatory. Laura is remembering and collating experiences, but there is something more: a message from outside her consciousness entirely. The false waking (Laura dreams she has awakened) is particularly effective.

Second, when Leland and Laura Palmer are driving, they are menaced by the One-Armed Man who screams to Laura "It's your father!" (He also screams to Leland "You stole the corn!") The revving engines, squealing brakes and tires, and Badalamenti's keening electronic music will have you on the edge of panic.

Third, there is the terrifying murder, which in terms of technique and effect should be ranked with Hitchcock's shower scene in *Psycho*. Again, the music and sound design will take you from hell to heaven and back instantly.

Lynch made *Fire Walk with Me* because he wanted to go back to the world of *Twin Peaks*. So did his audience. But instead of

---

[3] My first published review is of *Mulholland Drive*. It is reprinted in *Son of Trevor Lynch's White Nationalist Guide to the Movies*.

delivering damn fine coffee and cherry pie with a scoop of nostalgia on top, the logic of the story led him into a Stygian darkness where the critics and audiences did not want to follow. That's a shame, because once you walk through the fire, the angels win out in the end.

The Unz Review, November 8, 2020

WITHNAIL & I

Withnail & I (1987) is a masterpiece of British dark-comic satire written and directed by actor, novelist, and screenwriter Bruce Robinson, who went on to write and direct *How to Get Ahead in Advertising* (1989), another strong film in a similar vein. His career seems to have petered out, though, after a couple of flops, *Jennifer 8* (1992) and *The Rum Diary* (2011).

Richard E. Grant made his film debut playing Withnail. (He was also the lead in *How to Get Ahead in Advertising*.) Paul McGann played Marwood, the "I" in the title. Richard Griffiths played Withnail's uncle Monty. Ralph Brown played the drug-dealer/stoner Danny. The film also has lovely original music by David Dundas and Rick Wentworth and makes memorable use of a couple of songs by Jimi Hendrix.

Withnail & I was tastefully produced on a modest budget and became a commercial and critical success, routinely included in various critics' "best of" lists, launching both Robinson's and Grant's careers, and influencing many other writers and directors. But don't let that discourage you: *Withnail & I* is genuinely good.

Withnail & I takes place in London and the Lake Country of northern England in September of 1969. Withnail and Marwood are two drunken, drug-addicted, unemployed actors living in a filthy and freezing apartment in London's Camden Town.

The movie opens as they are coming down from a sixty-hour speed trip. Marwood puts a kettle on the stove, then forgets about it, wandering off to a greasy spoon for some breakfast. But he is too paranoid and frazzled to function, so he retreats home, where he bickers with Withnail, then ends up spooning coffee from a bowl as Withnail rants about the cold, his career, and his need for a drink. In desperation, Withnail downs lighter fluid then vomits on Marwood's shoes. Then they go out to a pub, where they order gin and ciders. This is still morning, mind you. Yes, alcoholism and drug addiction "aren't funny," but Withnail and Marwood are totally hilarious.

Marwood really needs a break, a reset. Like many city people, he has a romantic image of the countryside but little experience of it. He persuades Withnail to ask his rich uncle Monty for the key to his cottage in the Lake Country. So Withnail and Marwood go off to Monty's luxurious house in Chelsea for drinks.

Monty, brilliantly played by Richard Griffiths, is a fat, middle-aged eccentric. (He decorates with potted vegetables rather than flowers, flowers being "essentially tarts, prostitutes for the bees.") Educated at Harrow and Oxford, he is an upper-middle-class aesthete, gourmand, and homosexual. After an enormous amount of alcohol and a couple of whispered confidences, Withnail extracts the key from Monty.

When Withnail and Marwood arrive at Monty's cottage, it is not what they expected: no electricity, no running water, no fridge full of food. Withnail is perpetually drunk and helpless, always whining and complaining. But Marwood rises to the occasion. He proves to be down-to-earth, capable, and responsible, securing food and firewood.

As they wander the green hills to lovely pastoral music and encounter a gallery of colorful rural types—a farmer, a poacher, an old drunk—you sense something awakening in Marwood. Withnail, however, remains entirely self-absorbed, wrapped up in his insecurities, ambitions, and the quest for his next drink. "We want the finest wines available to humanity," he shouts in the Penrith Tearoom. "We want them here, and we want them now!"

After a couple days, uncle Monty shows up in his majestic Rolls Royce, heaped with hampers full of gourmet food and wine. Withnail rejoices at the food and especially the wine. But Marwood finds it an extremely uncomfortable experience, for Monty has somehow gotten the idea that Marwood is sexually interested in him. (It is never made clear if Marwood and Withnail are homosexuals or not.)

After an excruciatingly embarrassing attempt at seduction, the truth comes out. Withnail told Monty that Marwood was a closeted homosexual, a "toilet trader" no less. He also apparently led Monty to believe that there was mutual interest. Why? Simply to secure the cottage for a week. It is a cruel, irresponsible trick on both Marwood and Monty. Monty, however, is not a bad man. He has a sense of shame, which is deeply stirred.

Monty is an unmarried man past middle age at a crossroads faced by straight and gay alike: Does he pursue people young enough to be his children, inevitably playing and looking the fool, or does he magnanimously retire from the scene and instead devote himself to fostering the happiness of the next generation? He chooses the latter.

The next morning, Monty is gone, leaving an exquisitely sensitive note of apology. Withnail, being a sociopath, is unmoved by Monty's plight but delighted that he left his supply of food and drink. Marwood, however, is outraged, both for Monty and for himself.

Marwood insists on rushing back to London. He has been offered a part in a play in Manchester. He ends up with the lead. When they return home, they find their drug dealer, Danny, and a "huge spade" named Presuming Ed squatting in their apartment. The contrast to the countryside could not be more striking. It is a revolting situation.

As Danny rolls a huge joint and passes it around, he discourses hilariously about the historical moment:

> If you are holding onto a rising balloon you are presented with a difficult political decision—let go while you've still got the chance or hold onto the rope and continue getting higher. That's politics man. We are at the end of an age. The greatest decade in the history of mankind is nearly over. They're selling hippy wigs in Woolworth's. It is ninety-one days to the end of the decade, and as Presuming Ed here has so consistently pointed out, we have failed to paint it black.

When they find an eviction notice, Marwood freaks out while Withnail can't stop laughing. Clearly this living arrangement has no future.

The next morning, Marwood is packing up his stuff. His hippy shag has been replaced with a short haircut. He looks handsome, healthy, and purposeful. Withnail is his typical shambling wreck of a self. It's morning, so naturally, he wants to get drunk. Given a choice between a drink and catching his train — a drink or his future — Marwood chooses life.

Withnail walks with him to the station through Regent's Park in the rain, drinking, until Marwood tells him that he will miss him but not to follow him to the station. This is where their ways must part. Withnail then drunkenly launches into Hamlet's soliloquy on "What a piece of work is man" to an audience of wolves in the zoo. The end.

Withnail & I comes off as a somewhat random sequence of amusing events. I have left out quite a few of them, so if you haven't seen it, there will be plenty of surprises. However, the movie hangs together as a story because the events reveal the characters of Withnail and Marwood (as well as Monty), and their characters ultimately determine their destinies.

Both Withnail and Marwood are drunkards, addicts, and actors. But even though you do not see their fates, you know that they will be very different.

Withnail is from the upper-middle class. His suits are from Saville Row. His father is rich like his uncle. Like Monty, he went to Harrow. Withnail's chief character traits are vanity, cowardice, and dishonesty. He lies constantly. He tells a bully in a bar that he has a heart condition and a pregnant wife. He tells Monty that Marwood went to Eton and lies about his sex life. He tells a bartender that he was in the military to get free drinks. He tells the customers of the Penrith Tearoom that he is scouting a location for a movie. Withnail doesn't seem to have any practical skills at all, beyond knowing how to mix drinks and choose a tie. He is extremely far gone into addiction, and he probably won't pull out. But the safety net of his family is good for a few bounces before he ends up in the gutter.

Marwood is from a lower social rung. There is no mention of family money or a safety net. Marwood is cowardly and dishonest too, but he has a sense of shame. Marwood is also much more serious and capable than Withnail. He makes a go of things at the cottage, manages to get the lead in a play, cuts his hair, and heads to Manchester.

Danny's discourse on the historical moment is also about Withnail and Marwood. Addiction is the balloon. Marwood has let go, but he will survive his fall back to earth. Withnail will keep holding on as the balloon goes up. His long-term prospects are bleak.

The title of the film is significant. Marwood is "I," not "me." He is an agent, about to embark on the next chapter of his life, leaving Withnail behind. If Withnail were to tell the story, it would be called *Marwood & Me*, because as an addict, Withnail is not an agent but someone to whom things happen, someone for whom people like Marwood have to do things. Marwood is an enabler, Withnail the enabled. But it is time for Marwood to enable himself.

Withnail & I is a hilarious film about serious things. It is a coming-of-age film, a parting-of-ways film, with a wonderful script, superb acting, and tasteful music. Richard Grant is utterly hilarious playing a narcissist and drunk. Richard Griffiths is brilliant as uncle Monty, playing him as a buffoon, then a pest, then a sensitive and gracious gentleman. He's a genuinely tragic figure. (If Monty had gotten his chance to "play the Dane," he would have done him justice.) Paul McGann is also outstanding as Marwood. He's flawed but starts showing real character and maturity. You will be rooting for him.

Perhaps the soberest thing about *Withnail & I* is its treatment of addiction. Yes, Richard E. Grant is a hilarious drunk, but it's no laughing matter. Perhaps the worst reaction to *Withnail & I* is that it has spawned a drinking game, in which people try to keep up with Withnail, who in the course of the film downs "9 ½ glasses of red wine, one-half imperial pint (280 ml) of cider, one shot of lighter fluid (vinegar or overproof rum are common substitutes), 2 ½ measures of gin, six glasses of sherry, thirteen drams of Scotch whisky, and ½ pint of ale" according to a DVD featurette "The *Withnail & I* Drinking Game." It's rather like taking up heroin after watching *Requiem for a Dream*. The only way you can win is not to play.

I don't know what Bruce Robinson's politics are, but objectively *Withnail & I* is a conservative film. (I highly recommend Millennial Woes' 2017 speech on this subject, "*Withnail & I* Viewed from the Right,"[1] which was my introduction to the film.) *Withnail & I* is not just about growing up, but about growing out of the 1960s, including its culture of expressive individualism and addictive self-indulgence.

Even uncle Monty is a conservative of sort. Like many pre-Stonewall homosexuals of his class, he is educated, cultivated, and sees himself as a repository and guardian of history and culture. He knows Shakespeare and Baudelaire by heart, speaks French and Latin, listens to classical music, cooks well, and keeps an excellent cellar. He acted in his youth but couldn't make a career of it, so he made a good living doing something else. (It is never clear what Monty actually does, but then a gentleman wouldn't talk about such things.)

Monty asks Marwood: "Are you a sponge or a stone?" A sponge absorbs new experiences; a stone is closed off to them. Monty is a sponge. He is a refined materialist rueful of England's decline into vulgar materialism. He's a fat man, so he's clearly self-indulgent, but unlike his nephew, he doesn't seem to be a drunkard. Nor is Monty a sponge in the sense of a parasite on others. He's self-sufficient, practical, and accomplished: he has an income, he can cook, he can plan excursions, etc. He knows how to live. Withnail is a sponge of a lower order. He's undiscriminating enough to drink lighter fluid. He's also a parasite on the money, expertise, pity, and opinions of others.

The first morning at the cottage, Monty launches into a hilarious little speech over breakfast:

> The older order changeth, giving way to the new, and God fulfills himself in many ways, and soon, I suppose, I shall be swept away by some vulgar little tumor. My boys, we are at the end of an age. We live in a land of weather forecasts and breakfasts that set in. Shat on by Tories, shoveled up by Labour. Now which of you is go-

---

[1] Millennial Woes, "*Withnail & I* Viewed from the Right," May 28, 2021.

ing to be a splendid fellow and go down to the Rolls for the rest of the wine?

Monty senses that the age of British high culture is ending with "the sixties." But Danny laments that the sixties are almost over. Sadly, we still haven't come down from that trip. Is it too much to hope that the end of Danny's age will be the return of something like Monty's? Perhaps that's Marwood's future. It's up to all of us to write the sequel. But to do so, we've all got to say goodbye to our Withnails.

The Unz Review, November 15, 2020

Louis Theroux Meets Nick Fuentes

Louis Theroux has made a career as a documentarian by going out into the "bush"—basically, anywhere outside the urban and online bubbles where his kind dwell. There he meets weird and marginal people. He is nice to them in order to get them on film. Then he displays them—like so many Hottentot Venuses—for the amusement of condescending liberal urbanites like himself. This allows Theroux's audience to feel doubly superior. They can look down on "those people," but they can also pretend that they are being classy, respectful, open-minded, and even willing to be "challenged."

The first episode of Theroux's new BBC documentary series *Forbidden America* is called *Extreme and Online*. It focuses on Nick Fuentes and three associates: Baked Alaska, Beardson Beardly, and Brittany Venti.

If this was supposed to be a hit piece, it is extremely inept. Fuentes comes off looking great: intelligent, articulate, and self-confident. Baked Alaska looks pretty good too: buffoonish and insincere, but also self-confident and on message. Before watching this, I knew Beardly only by his reputation, which is terrible, but I can't really criticize how he handles Theroux. He patiently endures Theroux until it becomes obvious he's just a jerk, then throws him out. Humiliated, Theroux gets revenge by playing a clip of Beardly threatening to anally rape Brittany Venti. Beardly is hardly good optics, but Fuentes has stuck by him, and—amazingly—serious people are sharing a platform with him at Fuentes' 2022 AFPAC conference. Venti scores some sympathy points, but she's neither interesting nor impressive. Theroux only includes her because she is a woman with visible non-white ancestry.

The big loser, however, is Louis Theroux himself. This time, it is no more Mr. Nice Guy. Theroux hectors and badgers his interviewees. The mask of respect is discarded. The arrogant liberal jerk is fully on display. It isn't pretty. Nor is it formidable.

Fuentes and company easily parry Theroux's challenges, making him look inept. But Theroux is not the only one being humiliated. With his dorky persona, wretched posture, slovenly clothes, and middlebrow smugness, Louis Theroux is the embodiment of the international bugman. His humiliation is their humiliation. He really let down the team.

The net result is that Fuentes and Co. come off as smart, funny, and relatable even while saying outrageously politically incorrect things, whereas Theroux seems like a sanctimonious scold accusing his interviewees of the sins of racism, sexism, and homophobia. Like the priest of a dying god, he is often visibly frustrated when these magic words fail to induce stammering disavowals and apologies.

Leftists should be livid. Theroux has given Fuentes and company a mainstream platform where they shine. Theroux could have included footage of Fuentes and Baked Alaska that is every bit as obnoxious and embarrassing as Beardly's anal rape rant. But he chose not to. This is tantamount to whitewashing Fuentes. One wonders why. Is Theroux a secret sympathizer? Is his ineffectual badgering an attempt to provide cover for himself? I am sure Theroux's superiors will get to the bottom of this.

Theroux repeatedly accuses Fuentes and Co. of being "Alt Right" and "White Nationalists." They deny these charges, and correctly so. They really aren't White Nationalists, because White Nationalists want to create or restore homogeneously white ethnostates. But Fuentes and Co. are not just color-blind civic nationalists like the so-called "Alt Lite." Civic nationalists believe that race doesn't matter as long as we all think American thoughts.

Instead, Fuentes and Co. are what I call "uppity white folks": white people who take race and demographics seriously, who defend the essential whiteness of America, and who wish to take their own side in a fight. As Fuentes says in one of Theroux's clips: "White people founded this country. This country wouldn't exist without white people. And white people are done being bullied." Fuentes also openly talks about white genocide, the Great Replacement, and Jewish power.

Even though Fuentes and Co. don't want to live in a white

ethnostate, they insist that they want to live in a normatively white America, with a white supermajority. This means a return to the immigration and naturalization policies that were in place during most of American history, from 1790 to 1965. They would probably uphold freedom of disassociation among the races as well.

Although it is not White Nationalism, this could be justly called "white privilege," even "white supremacism." But if America is the homeland of Americans, who are a white people, why is it problematic for a people to be "privileged" and "supreme" in its own homeland? Is it problematic for the Japanese to be "privileged" and "supreme" in Japan?

A place where one enjoys power and privilege as a birthright—a place where you speak the language, understand the customs, and feel comfortable—a place where nothing is alien to you—is pretty much the definition of a homeland. There is nothing unfair about the privileges that come with a homeland, as long as you don't deny other peoples the privileges of having homelands as well.

Fuentes and Co. are perfectly positioned where American nationalism and populism are growing: the space between White Nationalism and the Republican Party. There are millions of white Americans who have positive racial identities, reject white guilt, see that whites are under attack, and want to organize to fight back. They are, in short, uppity white folks, ready for white identity politics but not (yet) ready for White Nationalism because they don't envision the ethnostate as a solution.

Uppity white folks are a constituency looking for political representation. But most Republican politicians will not represent them (yet) because Republicans hold the absurd view that there's nothing worse than identity politics, but only when white people practice it. That would be "racism," and there's nothing worse than racism, but only when it benefits white people.

This morally repugnant double standard is, however, crumbling, and when it finally gives way, the dammed-up floodwaters of white identity politics will completely remake America's political landscape. Fuentes' America First movement is one of the places where this dogma is breaking down, hence his association with former Representative Steve King and sitting Representative Paul Gosar.

I find it annoying when Theroux repeatedly trots out "White Nationalist" as an accusation. I am not annoyed that Fuentes and Co. deny the charge, since it really is untrue. White Nationalists need to work harder to destroy the stigmas attached to our ideas. We can't expect anyone else to do that for us. To their credit, however, Fuentes and Co. do dismiss such stigmatizing words as "racism," "sexism," and "homophobia." They also treat Theroux and the rest of the mainstream media with well-earned contempt.

Theroux doesn't just show Fuentes' strengths. He also shows his limits. Fuentes is what I call a "Right-wing sectarian." He wishes to link white identity politics with Right-wing add-ons such as Christianity, which split white identitarians. This strengthens Fuentes as a leader of his sect while making the movement as a whole weaker and less capable of cooperation. Fuentes, moreover, has made his bones attacking other individuals and groups on the Right. This has created a great deal of bitterness and a large number of people who want him to fail.

But wishing won't make it so. One reason I advocate "big tent" nationalism is that you really can't purge people from a decentralized movement anyway, so it is best to try to live with them. Fuentes is extremely effective at arguing that America is a white nation, that white people are under attack, and that white people should fight back. He is humiliating our common enemies and mainstreaming our issues and talking points. He's an agent of radicalization. White Nationalists can build on that. We need to provide humane and workable proposals to halt and reverse the Great Replacement and restore white homelands. More people than ever are receptive to our message. If we can't persuade them of our vision, the fault is ours alone.

It is always a gamble for white advocates to talk to the press. I don't recommend it. But in this case, Fuentes lucked out. Thus I recommend *Extreme and Online*. I think it is a net positive for the cause of white identity politics.

Counter-Currents, February 15, 2022

INDEX

Numbers in bold refer to a whole chapter or section devoted to a particular topic.

A
Abrams, J. J., 129
adventure, 15, 112, 147, 160
aestheticism, 13, 39, 98
affirmative action, 6, 44, 181
Africa, **1–4**
Africa Addio, **1–4**
Ahab, Captain, 150, 167
Akuta, Masahiko, 137–38
Alford, Kenneth, 105
Allen, Woody, 186
Alt Lite, 202
Alt Right, 172, 202
altruism, 23
American History X, **5–11**
American Sniper, 37
Anderson, Kevin J., 54
Annis, Francesca, 58, 65
anti-colonialism, 14, 25, 63, 106
anti-communism, 47, 53, 93, 119, 136
anti-imperialism, 14, 25–26, 63
anti-Semitism, 175
Apocalypse Now, 65
Armas, Ana de, 146
Arnold, Malcolm, 26, 105
Arterton, Gemma, 15
Ashbrook, Dana, 185
Atterton, Edward, 57
Arrival, 55, 67–68
artificial intelligence, 56, 62, 126
Austen, Jane, 161
authenticity, 119, 138
autism, 7, 52, 87, 101–102, 172, 175

B
Badalamenti, Angelo, 184, 189, 192
Baked Alaska, 201, 202
Bancroft, Anne, 69, 73
Barber, Samuel, 75
Bardem, Javier, 59, 65
Barry, John, 92
Batman Begins, 179
Bautista, Dave, 58, 64
Bay, Frances, 183–84
BBC, 15, 201
Beardsley, Beardson, 201, 202
Being and Nothingness (Sartre), 137
Ben Hur (film), 35
Bergman, Ingmar, 78, 80, 81, 85, 186
Berkoff, Steven, 59, 65
Bertolucci, Bernardo, 93, 98
Bird, Brad, **88–92**
Black Narcissus; Michael Powell movie, **12–15**; television miniseries, 15
Blade Runner, 66, 67
Blade Runner 2049, 55, 67, 181
blacks, **1–4**, **5–11**, 15, 17, 32, 35, 38, 39, 43, 45, 59–60, 63–64, 88, 134, 141–44, 146, 167–68, 175, 180–81
Blake, William, 73
Blue Velvet, 71, 73, 182–84, 187, 189
bohemians, 80, 84; *see also* hippies
Bolsheviks, 51
Bolt, Robert, 47–48, 52–53, 67, 99
Bond, James, 1, 88, 92, **140–44**, **145–46**, 181
The Bostonians, **16–21**
Boulle, Pierre, 22–23, 25, 26
bourgeois ethos, 23, 25, 51, 138, 160–61
Bowie, David, 192
Boyle, Danny, 140
Branagh, Kenneth, 179, 180

Brando, Marlin, 65
Brandon, Henry, 169
The Bridge on the River Kwai, **22–26**, 99, 105
British Empire, the, 1–2, 14, 22–26, 100, 102, 106–107, 109
Broccoli, Barbara, 141
Brolin, Josh, 58
Brooks, Avery, 6
Brooks, Mel, 69
Brosnan, Pierce, 141
Browning, Todd, 74
Buddhism, 75, 137
Burgess, Anthony, 27, 29–30
Byron, Kathleen, 14

C
Caine, Michael, 179
camp, 32, 33, 35
Carey, Harry, Jr., 165
Carlino, John Lewis, 162
Casablanca, 99, 111
Casino, 87
Casino Royale, 143, 145, 146
Chalamet, Timothée, 57–58, 65
Chaplin, Geraldine, 50
Chen, Joan, 93, 184
Children of Dune, 54, 57, 58, 59, 61, 62, 65, 67
Christianity, 13–14, 24, 27, 62, 73, 75, 78–81, 83, 85, 133–34, 191, 204
Christie, Julie, 50
CIA, the, 47
Citizen Kane, 99, 111
Civil War, American, 150, 185; Russian, 50, 51
class, 73, 117, 162, 195, 197, 199; *see also* elites
Clift, Montgomery, 147, 149
A Clockwork Orange, **27–30**
colonialism, 1–2, 14, 25–26, 63, 106, 116
coming-of-age stories, 151, 170, 198
communism, 3, 25, **47–53**, 93, 97–98, 119, **136–38**

compassion, 72, 76, 77; *see also* empathy
Conan the Barbarian, **31–35**
Confederacy, the, 10, 185
conformity, 49, 92
consciousness, 75, 192
conservatism, 8, 17, 25, 185, 198–99
Courtenay, Tom, 50
COVID-19, 54, 60, 140, 142
Craig, Daniel, 140, 143, 145, 181
crime, 27, 29, 36, 39, 41, 88, 166, 173, 176, 183, 187
Crowley, Aleister, 100
Cruise, Julee, 184
Crumb, R., 30
culture, 13, 81, 117, 136, 139, 159, 177, 199–200
Cyrus the Great, 104

D
Dalton, Timothy, 145
Daly, Tyne, 44
Dark Triad traits, 20, **27–30**, 145, 161–62, 167, 175–77, 185, 196, 198
Dastmalchian, David, 59
The Dead Pool, 41, **45–46**
death, 3, 20, 23–25, 34, 37, 48, 52, 75–76, 79, 122–24, 140, 152, 158, 165, 167, 168, 175
Debicki, Elizabeth, 179
degeneracy, 33, 36, 40, 42
democracy, 61–62, 92, 148, 159
Dench, Judy, 141
De Niro, Robert, 172, 178
Deschanel, Caleb, 187
Descartes, René, 126
Devine, Andy, 118
Diaghilev, Sergei, 154
Die Meistersinger, 152
Dirty Harry, 31, **36–40**, **41–46**
diversity, 16, 35, 45, 64, 87, 92, 134, 146
Disney, 60, 92, 141
Doctor Zhivago, 21, **47–53**, 93, 99
Dostoevsky, Fyodor, 38

Index

Dourif, Brad, 59
dreams, 66, 74, 183, 192
Driver, Adam, 86
dualism, 30
Dudley, Anne, 11
Duncan-Brewster, Sharon, 59
Dundas, David, 194
Dune, Frank Herbert's novel, 54–56, 59, 61–64, 66, 67; Alejandro Jodorowski's movie, 54, 61, 67; David Lynch's movie, 54, 55, 61, 66, 67, 69, 71, 75, 184, 189; Sci-Fi miniseries, 54, 61; Denis Villeneuve's *Dune*, Part 1, **61–68**; Denis Villeneuve's trailers, **54–60**
Dunham, Duwayne, 184
Dunkirk, 179
dystopias, 126, 174

E

Easdale, Brian, 14
Eastwood, Clint, 36–37, 39, 41–42, 44, 46
Eilish, Billie, 140
El Cid, 35
The Elephant Man, **69–77**
elites, 2, 20, 37, 138, 177; *see also* class
empathy, 29–30; *see also* compassion
empire, 62, 100, 104, 106, 149
enemy, 3, 20, 23, 103–104, 137
The Enforcer, 41, 43–44, 46
Engel, Robert, 191
Eno, Brian, 67
equality (egalitarianism), 62, 90–91, 119, 147
Eraserhead, 69–70, 72–73, 182, 184
Erikson, Erik, 152
escapism, 8, 21
ethnostate, 202, 203
eugenics, 56, 62
evil, 29, 60, 81, 82, 89, 92, 113, 175, 180, 183, 185, 187
existentialism, 137

Extreme and Online, **201–204**

F

family, 51, 53, 78–80, 86–89, 92, 103, 145, 156, 161, 164, 166–67, 169, 173
Fanny & Alexander, **78–85**
Fargo, James, 44
Farrar, David, 14
fascism, 36, 41
fatherhood, 151–52, 154, 160–61
femininity, 88–89, 112, 121, 160–61
feminism, **16–21**, 36, 44, 80, 90, 142
Ferguson, Rebecca, 58, 65
Ferrer, José, 99
feudalism, 56, 62
Fielding, Jerry, 44
Fight Club, 5, 173
Finney, Albert, 145
First World War, the, 49, 99–100, 114, 116
Floyd, George, 64, 131, 144
Forbidden America, 201
Foreman, Carl, 26
Foster, Jodie, 168, 172
Ford, John, 107; *The Man Who Shot Liberty Valance*, **118–25**; *The Searchers*, 107, 147, **164–71**
Franciosi, Aisling, 15
Francis, Freddie, 69
Franco, James, 133
Freaks, 74
freedom, 29–30, 32, 50–51, 62, 147
Freeman, Morgan, 34, 180
Frost, Mark, 185, 187
Frost, Warren, 185
Fuentes, Nick, **200–204**
Frazetta, Frank, 31, 35
Fukunaga, Cary Joji, 140, 146
Furlong, Edward, 9

G

Gandhi, Mohandas, 25–26
Gangs of New York, 172
Geislerová, Zuzana, 57
generativity, 152, 196
genocide, 3; white genocide, 59,

131, 202
Ghostbusters (2016), 142
Giacchino, Michael, 92
Gielgud, John, 69
Gnosticism, 72, 73
Goad, Jim, 167
God, 8, 19, 76, 81, 83, 85, 91, 102, 105, 173, 199
Goebbels, Joseph, 113
Goodfellas, 172
Goring, Marius, 154
Gosar, Paul, 204
Gosling, Ryan, 181
Gould, Elliot, 5
Grant, Richard E., 194, 198
Grave of the Fireflies, 189
Great Britain, 27, 30
Great Replacement, the, 5, 60, 131, 141–43, 178, 202, 204
Griffiths, Richard, 194, 195, 198
Guinness, Alec, 24, 26, 50, 99, 101
guy movies, 42
Gyasi, David, 180

H
Hardy, Tom, 145, 181
Hawkins, Jack, 26, 99, 105
Hawks, Howard, 147
Head, Edith, 91
Hegel, G. W. F., 23–24
Heidegger, Martin, 138
Henderson, Stephen McKinley, 58
Herbert, Brian, 54
Herbert, Frank, 54–55, 58–59, 61–63, 67
hereditarianism, 53, 91
heroism, 23, 31, 35, 37, 43, 91, 151, 160–61, 175, 177, 183; *see also* superheroes
Herrmann, Bernard, 172–73, 177
high culture, 159, 200
High and Low, 161
Hiller, Wendy, 69
Hinduism, 12, 69, 75, 188
hippies, 34–35, 36, 39, 43, 84, 133, 137, 196–97; *see also* bohemians

Hirano, Keiichiro, 137
history, 23, 51–52, 94, 97, 100, 115, 152, 196, 199; of film and television, 12, 78, 109, 182
Hitchcock, Alfred, 111, 161, 192
Holbrook, Hal, 43
Holden, William, 25–26
Hollywood, 34–35, 36, 39, 43, 133, 137, 196–97
Holocaust, 85
homelands, 203–204
homophobia, 202, 204
homosexuality, 16, 41, 66, 76, 85, 101, 108, 131–35, 141, 195–96, 199
honor, 17, 23–25, 63, 113, 114, 122, 136, 138, 147, 152, 175
Hopkins, Anthony, 69, 71
horror, 14, 20, 76, 112, 149, 162, 170, 191; of communism, 50, 52
House of Gucci, **86–87**
How to Get Ahead in Advertising, 194
Howard, Robert E., **31–35**
Hunt, Linda, 17, 18
Hunter, Jeffrey, 165, 169, 170
Hunter, Tim, 187
hunting and hunters, 4, 114, 188
Hurt, John, 69, 72
Hurt, William, 58, 65

I
identity, 87, 131, 138
identity politics, 62, 135, 203–204
immigration, 5, 131; *see also* Great Replacement, the
incels, 172, 175
individualism, 8, 147, 199
Inception, 179
The Incredibles & The Incredibles, **88–92**
Inland Empire, 189
ironism, 33, 129
Irons, Jeremy, 86
Isaac, Oscar, 58, 65
Isaak, Chris, 190

Ivory, James, 16

J
Jackson, Peter, 35, 61
Jacopetti, Gualtiero, 1
James, Henry, **16–21**
Japan, 22, 24–25, 93, **136–39**, 161–62, 189
Jarre, Maurice, 47, 50, 99
Jews, 5, 11, 12, 16, 20, 31, 39, 47, 58, 79–80, 83, 85, 112, 119, 128, 131–32, 168, 182, 202
Jhabvala, Ruth Prawer, 16
Jodorowsky, Alejandro, 54, 55, 61, 67
Joker, 178
Jones, Freddie, 71
Jones, Grace, 143, 144, 146
Jones, James Earl, 32, 35
Jones, Jim, 132
Jones, Leslie, 142
Jordan, Richard, 57
journalists; *see* the press

K
Kael, Pauline, 36
Kant, Immanuel, 85
Kaye, Tony, 5–11
Keach, Stacy, 5
Keaton, Diane, 186
Keitel, Harvey, 168, 175
Kerr, Deborah, 14, 114
Kinder, Sandra, 190
King, Steve, 204
Kinski, Klaus, 50
The King of Comedy, 178
Krige, Alice, 58, 65
Kristofferson, Kris, 162
Kubrick, Stanley, 5, 27, 30
Kurosawa, Akira, 161

L
Lady Gaga, 86
The Last Emperor, **93–98**
laughter, 76–77
law, 36–37, 40, 41, 82, 83, 94–95, 101, 119–25, 172, 183

Lawrence, D. H., 162
Lawrence, T. E., 25, 52, 67, **99–110**
Lawrence of Arabia, 66–67, **99–110**
League of Nations, 112
Lean, David, 66–67, 111; *The Bridge on the River Kwai*, **22–26**; *Doctor Zhivago*, **47–53**; *Lawrence of Arabia*, **99–110**
Lee, Sheryl, 192
Le May, Alan, 168
Leto, Jared, 86
liberalism, 11, 16–17, 20, 21, 26, 31, 35, 36, 39–40, 41, 46, 48, 55, 61–62, 98, 118, 119, 124–25, 147–48, 164, 167, 172
liberty, 120
License to Kill, 145
lies, 49–50, 114, 124, 174, 197
The Life & Death of Colonel Blimp, **111–17**
Lincoln, Abraham, 10
Lipton, Peggy, 185, 189
Livesey, Roger, 113
Lockeanism, 149
Locke, Sondra, 44, 49
Lohengrin, 18
Lone, John, 93
The Lord of the Flies, 161
The Lord of the Rings, 35, 61, 62
Lost Highway, 70
Low, David, 112
Lucas, George, 109, 141, 170
Ludovici, Anthony M., 76
Lynch, David; *Dune*, 54–55, 57–59, 61, 65–68; *The Elephant Man*, **69–77**; *Twin Peaks*, **182–88**; *Twin Peaks: Fire Walk with Me*, **189–93**
Lynch, Lashana, 141–44, 146

M
MacLaughlin, Kyle, 57, 183, 185, 189, 190
MacMillan, Kenneth, 65–66
Magma (rock band), 67
Magnum Force, 31, 41–43, 45
Malek, Rami, 140, 145

Mancini, Henry, 92
A Man for All Seasons, 48, 99
The Man Who Shot Liberty Valance, **118–25**, 149, 167
Mao Zedong, 97
Marxism and Marxists, 98, 126, 136, 138
Marvin, Lee, 120
masculinity, 31, 35, 38, 88–89, 152, 160–61
master-slave dialectic, 24–25
Masterpiece Theatre, 163
materialism, 51, 63, 199
Matheson, Tim, 42
The Matrix Reloaded, 127
The Matrix Resurrections, **126–30**
The Matrix Revolutions, 127
McDowell, Malcolm, 27
McGann, Paul, 194, 198
McKenna, David, 6
McKenna, Siobán, 50
McNeice, Ian, 66
Meditations (Descartes), 136
The Matrix, **126–30**
Merchant, Ismail, 16
Merchant-Ivory Productions, 16
Merrick, Joseph, **70–76**
metaphysics, 84–85, 91, 185, 192
Metzger, Tom, 5
Miles, Sarah, 162
Miles, Vera, 120, 170
Milk, **131–35**
Milk, Harvey, **131–35**
Milius, John, **31–35**, 42–43
Millennial Woes, iii, 199
Mishima, 172
Mishima: The Last Debate, **136–39**
Mishima, Yukio, **136–39**, **160–62**
modernity, 35, 39, 55, 160–61
Momoa, Jason, 57, 58, 63, 65
monarchy, 62, 65, 94–96
moral sentiments, 30; *see also* virtue
More, Thomas, 52
Morricone, Ennio, 1
Moss, Carrie-Anne, 127
Mulholland Drive, 192

mystery, 89, 115, 180, 183, 191–92

N
Nance, Jack, 183–84
nationalism, 14, 63, 100, 106, 135, 136, 204
nations, 101; *see also* tribes
National Socialism, 85, 112, 115, 158
Neeson, Liam, 46
neo-Nazism, 5–7, 11
neo-*noir*, 38, 41
Network, 99
Newman, Alec, 57, 65
Newman, Paul, 36
Nietzsche, Friedrich, 91, 100, 160–61
Niven, Kip, 42
Nivola, Alessandro, 15
No Time to Die, **140–44**, **145–46**
Nolan, Christopher, 68, 145, **179–81**
Norton, Edward, 5, 11
nostalgia, 16, 21, 86, 129, 159, 182

O
Obama, Barack, 121
Odysseus, 167
On Her Majesty's Secret Service, 145
Once Upon a Time in the West, 147
One of Our Aircraft Is Missing, 111–12
Ortolani, Riz, 1
Oscars (award), 47, 94
O'Toole, Peter, 49, 94, 101

P
Pacino, Al, 86
paganism, 75, 80–81, 84–85, 166
Paglia, Camille, 152
A Passage to India, 22, 26
Pasternak, Boris, 47–49
Pattinson, Robert, 179
Pearson, Durk, 46
pedophilia, 65, 85
Penn, Sean, 132
Peploe, Mark, 93
phenomenology, 136–37

Index

Phillips, Siân, 57, 65
Phillips, Todd, 178
philosophy, 18, 21, 50, 91, 100, 101, 137, 138, 147
Pink Floyd, 67
Pitt, Brad, 5
Plato (Allegory of the Cave), 107, 126
Poledouris, Basil, 35
Polignano, Michael, 128
political correctness, 6, 15, 19, 31, 38, 59, 87, 92, 141
populism, 37, 185, 203
Popwell, Albert, 45
Post, Ted, 43, 44
Powell, Michael, **12–15**, 50, 111–12, 154, 159, 161
press, the, 46, 204
Pressburger, Emeric, 12, 14–15, 112–17, 157
private life, 19, 51–52
Prochnow, Jürgen, 58, 65
progress, 19, 119–20, 124
propaganda, 1, 5, 12, 14, 16, 35, 63, 97, 112–15, 128, 141
Prosperi, Franco, 1
psycho or psychopath, 167, 175, 177,
Psycho, 192
psychology, 19, 29, 191–92
pulps, 35, 67

Q
Quantum of Solace, 145
Quinn, Anthony, 99, 105
Quo Vadis (film), 35

R
race, **1–4**, 5–7, 9–11, 14–15, 16, 36, 58–60, 63, 108, 118–19, 128–29, 131, 141, 146, 168–69, 181; *see also* blacks
racism, 1, 6, 38, 41–43, 45, 142, 164, 167–70, 175, 202, 203, 204
Raging Bull, 113, 172
Rains, Claude, 99
Rampling, Charlotte, 57

Rand, Ayn, 90–91
Red Guards, 97, 98
red pill, **127–30**
Red River, **147–53**
The Red Shoes, 12, 14, 50, 154–59
Redgrave, Vanessa, 17
Reeve, Christopher, 17, 20
Reeves, Keanu, 127
Reeves, Saskia, 58
reincarnation, 75
religion, 56, 80, 83, 154, 185, 191; *see also* Christianity, God, Hinduism, paganism
Republic, The (Plato), 126
Republican party, 203
revolutions: Chinese, 93; Communist, 3, 93; cultural, 132; Russian, 49–51, 93; sexual, 92
Richardson, Ralph, 50
Rigg, Diana, 15
Rockwell, George Lincoln, 139
Robinson, Andy, 36, 38
Robinson, Bruce, 194, 199
romance, 13, 18, 25, 42, 112–14, 122, 125, 152, 154, 156–57, 186, 188
Rope, 161
Rossellini, Isabella, 184
Rózsa, Miklós, 35
Roof, Dylann, 172, 175, 177
Russia, 24, 47–49, 51, 93

S
The Sailor Who Fell from Grace with the Sea, **164–67**
Sakamoto, Ryuichi, 94
Sartre, Jean-Paul, 137
scapegoat or scapegoating, 49, 103
Schifrin, Lalo, 36, 41–43, 46
Schmitt, Carl, 39, 103, 119, 148n1
Schrader, Paul, 168, 172, 175
Sci-Fi Channel, 54–55, 57–58, 61, 65, 67
science fiction, 54–55, 51, 67, 126, 179; *see also Dune, The Matrix, Tenet*

Scorsese, Martin, 86, 87, 111, 113, 168; *Taxi Driver*, 168, **172–78**
Scott, Ridley, 67; *House of Gucci*, **86–87**
Schwarzenegger, Arnold, 31, 32, 34
The Searchers, 107, 147, **164–71**
Second World War, the, 12, 22, 52, 85, 112, 115–16, 179
sectarianism, 133, 204
self-defense, 29, 123, 165
Semple, Jr., Lorenzo, 33
Setouchi, Jakucho, 137
Seven Pillars of Wisdom, 99, 100, 109
sex, 7, 14, 28, 30, 42–44, 56, 157, 162–63, 183, 197
sexism, 202, 204
Seydoux, Léa, 140, 145
Shakespeare, William, 125, 199
Sharif, Omar, 49–50, 99, 101
Shaw, Sandy, 46
Shearer, Moira, 154
Sicario, 55, 67–68
Siegel, Don, **36–40**, **41–46**
Siegfried, 151
sin, 156–57, 167
Skarsgård, Stellan, 58, 65
Skyfall, 141, 143, 145, 146
Snyder, Zack, 68
soap operas, 160, 188
sociopaths, sociopathy, **27–30**, 145, 161, 162, 185, 196
Sophocles, 23
Soul, David, 42
The Sound of Music, 47
South, the (American), 10, 17, 150, 185; versus the North, 10
spy movies, 88
Stanton, Harry Dean, 190
Star Wars, 55, 60, 61, 66, 128–29, 141, 170
state of nature, 120, 124, 149, 165–66
Steiger, Rod, 50
Stewart, Jimmy, 118, 121
Stewart, Patrick, 58

Stone, Oliver, 31
Strindberg, August, 80, 84–85
Stroebel, Al, 191
Sudden Impact, 41, 44–46
suicide, 24, 28, 75, 136, 138, 158, 177
superheroes, 40, **88–92**
supernatural, the, 82–83, 183
Sutherland, Kiefer, 190
Swedenborg, Emanuel, 85
Sydow, Max von, 33, 35, 59, 63

T

Tandy, Jessica, 17
Taxi Driver, 168, **172–78**
Tarrant, Brenton, 175, 177
technology, 55, 62, 66, 67, 69, 89, 91
television, 31, 33, 43, 45, 182, 184, 187 ~~188~~
Tenet, **179–81**
Tennyson, Alfred Lord, 75
Theroux, Louis, **201–204**
thumos, 151
The Thunderbirds, 1
time, 79, 84–85, 125, 179
Tiomkin, Dimitri, 147
Tolkien, J. R. R., 35
Toto, 67
Toyoshima, Keisuke, 136, 139
tragedy, 2, 86, 152
tribes, 101, 103–104, 106, 108; *see also* nations
truth, 26, 51–52, 124, 127, 147
Twilight Saga, 62
Twin Peaks, 73, 74, **182–88**, 189–90, 192
Twin Peaks: Fire Walk with Me, 182, **189–93**
Twin Peaks: The Return, 74
Tyler, Brian, 67

U

Unz, Ron, iii
uppity white folks, 202–203
Urich, Robert, 42

V

Van Cleef, Lee, 120
Van Horn, Buddy, 46
Van Sant, Gus, 132
Venti, Brittany, 201
Vertigo, 99, 189
vigilantism, 36, 40, 41–43, 45, 88, 172, 178, 183
Villeneuve, Denis, 54, 55, 58–60, 61–68
violence, 5–6, 11, 13, 27–30, 41–44, 51, 103, 119, 125, 137, 167, 176, 190
virtue, 17, 23, 30, 107, 138; *see also* moral sentiments

W

Wachowski, Andy and Larry, **124–31**
Wagner, Richard, 18, 151–52
Walbrook, Anton, 111, 113, 154
Wallace, Stewart, 132
Wållgren, Gunn, 80
war crimes, 115–17
Warner Brothers, 128, 130
Washington, Denzel, 181
Washington, John David, **179–81**
WASPs, 20, 119
Watchmen, 89
Watson, James, 57
Wayne, John, 39, 118, 120–21, 147, 148, 151, 165
Wentworth, Rick, 194
Westerns, 147; see also *The Man Who Shot Liberty Valance, Red River, The Searchers*
Whedon, Joss, 68
white nationalism and white nationalists, 172, 202–204
Wild at Heart, 71, 184
Wilson, Michael (producer), 141
Wilson, Michael (writer), 26, 99
Withnail & I, **194–200**
Wise, Ray, 185, 192
women, 13, 17–19, 25, 30, 34, 62–63, 116, 122–23, 141, 148–52, 167, 175
Wotan, 151

X

Xenophon, 104

Y

Yiannopoulos, Milo, 142

Z

Zabriskie, Grace, 185, 192
Zendaya, 59, 63
Zimmer, Hans, 67, 140, 146

About the Author

Trevor Lynch is a pen name of Greg Johnson, Ph.D., Editor-in-Chief of Counter-Currents Publishing Ltd. and the *Counter-Currents* webzine (http://www.counter-currents.com/).

He is the author of the following books (all published by Counter-Currents, unless otherwise noted): *Confessions of a Reluctant Hater* (2010; 2016), *Trevor Lynch's White Nationalist Guide to the Movies* (2012), *New Right vs. Old Right* (2013), *Son of Trevor Lynch's White Nationalist Guide to the Movies* (2015), *Truth, Justice, & a Nice White Country* (2015), *In Defense of Prejudice* (2017), *You Asked for It: Selected Interviews*, vol. 1 (2017), *The White Nationalist Manifesto* (2018), *Toward a New Nationalism* (2019), *Return of the Son of Trevor Lynch's CENSORED Guide to the Movies* (2019), *From Plato to Postmodernism* (2019), *It's Okay to Be White: The Best of Greg Johnson* (Ministry of Truth, 2020), *Graduate School with Heidegger* (2020), *Here's the Thing: Selected Interviews*, vol. 2 (2020), *Trevor Lynch: Part Four of the Trilogy* (2020), *White Identity Politics* (2020), and *The Year America Died* (2021).

He is editor of *North American New Right*, vol. 1 (2012); *North American New Right*, vol. 2 (2017); *The Alternative Right* (2018); Julius Evola, *East & West: Comparative Studies in Pursuit of Tradition* (with Collin Cleary, 2018); Collin Cleary, *Summoning the Gods: Essays on Paganism in a God-Forsaken World* (2011); Collin Cleary, *What Is a Rune? & Other Essays* (2015); and many other books.

His writings have been translated into Arabic, Czech, Danish, Dutch, Estonian, Finnish, French, German, Greek, Hungarian, Norwegian, Polish, Portuguese, Russian, Slovak, Spanish, Swedish, and Ukrainian.

www.ingramcontent.com/pod-product-compliance
Lightning Source LLC
Chambersburg PA
CBHW021327190426
43193CB00039B/222